# VISIONS

# FOR A NEW AMERICAN DREAM

PROCESS, PRINCIPLES, AND AN ORDINANCE TO PLAN AND DESIGN SMALL COMMUNITIES

## Anton Clarence Nelessen

**Planners Press**
American Planning Association
Chicago, Illinois   Washington, D.C.

Second edition copyright 1994 by the American Planning Association
122 S. Michigan Ave.
Suite 1600
Chicago, IL 60603

Paperback copies ISBN 1-884829-00-7
Hardbound copies ISBN 1-884829-01-5

Library of Congress Catalog Card Number 94-71145

Printed in the United States of America

The first edition of this book was copyrighted in 1993 by Anton C. Nelessen and printed in January 1994.

All photographs and illustrations contained in this book have been generated by A. Nelessen or A. Nelessen Associates unless noted otherwise.

The Visual Preference Survey is a registered trademark of A. Nelessen Associates, Inc., and is indicated as Visual Preference Survey ™ (VPS ™).

Printed on recycled paper.

This volume provides guidelines to plan and design small communities including hamlets, villages, and neighborhoods in the urban fringe whether they are new or to be retrofitted.

The recommendations are generic. Adaptation and variation will be required in the specific site application.

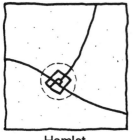
Hamlet

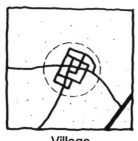
Village

Neighborhood

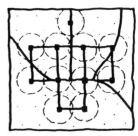
The Neighborhood within the Town

Anyone who wants to plan and build a community must be able to visualize two- and three-dimensional space and the four-dimensional impact on the user. One must understand these relationships at the smallest scale first, in order to apply them to a larger scale.

# ACKNOWLEDGMENTS

The production of this book was made possible by a grant from the Victoria Foundation. The grant allowed me to summarize years of research, lecturing, and practice, to hire editing and graphics help, and to have the first edition of this book printed. Special thanks to Catherine McFarland, Executive Director of the Victoria Foundation.

This book offers recommendations for the planning and design of the smallest size of communities: Hamlets, Villages, and Neighborhoods within Towns. It is intended as a response to the centers concept of the *State Development and Redevelopment Plan for the State of New Jersey.* Consequently it focuses upon New Jersey. However, this should not lead the reader to feel that this process and these principles are not applicable elsewhere. They are.

The planning process and design principles in this book are a response to over 25 years of planning and urban-design practice, research, and teaching. These ideas are, in part, a product of the biography of my past, my mentors, the partners and associates in my offices, the many studios, workshops, and seminars that I have taught, and the many lay planners I have interacted with. It is a product of uncounted hours of discussions and research with planning graduate students and with participants in the Visual Preference Surveys™ (VPS)™ and Hands-On Model Workshops around the country. Most of the ideas have been tested in my professional practice at Community Alternatives Inc., Nelessen-Helb, Hintz-Nelessen Associates, Inc., and now at A. Nelessen Associates, Inc. The handbook reflects the application of these concepts in the real world in master plans, vision plans, and developments plans prepared for local municipalities in New Jersey and throughout the country.

The motivation to create communities was infused by a close working relationship first with Victor Gruen in Los Angeles and Europe, then with Jose Louis Sert as a research assistant at Harvard during the design of the HUD New Community Project, and with David Crane Associates. All were critics of sprawl, and advocates of multiple-use, human-scaled communities.

The specific ideas for smaller communities first crystallized in 1972, during the first studio I taught in the Graduate Department of Urban Planning and Policy Development at Rutgers, the State University of New Jersey. The Sussex County Planning Department sponsored the studio and charged us with creating a master plan for this rural, emerging suburban county in the most densely populated state in our country. This Master Plan was based on a county-wide natural resource and infrastructure capacity analysis. It directed future growth into new communities of villages, hamlets, and one larger new town. It recommended that environmentally sensitive and agricultural land be retained at low densities through Transfer of Development Rights (TDR). It recommended a balance of roads and transit. It was a vision that was thirty years ahead of its time.

The vision of small communities has been in continuous evolution. Twenty years after the first studio, we were testing the ramifications of applying the concept of multiple communities of place to a regional area in central New Jersey. I am deeply grateful for the opportunity to direct the Urban Design Studio at Rutgers, an opportunity that allows for academic research and the application of the planning process to conceptual designs of place.

I want to thank those students who over the years have taken my design courses. They are sincerely interested in and understand the importance of the built environment. These students tested and refined many of the principles that are found in this book. It has been an exciting and optimistic time of discovery and failure, of frustration and hope. While I am thankful for these students, I am also saddened that so many more are scared of design. Design is not a required course in most planning schools today, whereas social policy, economics and law are. Design is an elective. Most planning students have no design training and never have been asked to do visual thinking. I hope this book helps remove some of these fears. I believe that when non-designers become more involved in the design process, the quality of our living environment will improve. I have provided some practical techniques, processes, and principles to stir the imagination and the imaginative process, the keys to good design. The VPS ™ and the Hands-On Models are two very practical tools.

Every time the VPS ™ technique is used, it proves that people throughout this country want a specific vision of community. In 1979 the first VPS ™ was tested in the redevelopment process for downtown Metuchen, New Jersey. Former Mayor John Wiley Jr. and attorney Harry Pozycki were instrumental in providing the challenge for generating a vision of a community-based redevelopment process and plan.

Numerous individuals and organizations have contributed to this work over the years and I owe them many thanks: Bob Schneider, whose early death we all mourn, my first teaching assistant and partner in Community Alternatives; The Association of New Jersey Environmental Commissions (ANJEC), who gave me a grant to build the first Hands-On Models and to conduct the first set of statewide workshops; Jim Gilbert, chairman of the New Jersey State Planning Commission, and Bill Purdie and Joe Kocy from the staff of the State Planning Commission for their initial encouragement;

the New Jersey Chapter of the American Planning Association, who asked me to present my research on Hamlets and Villages at their state conference; the National Capital Chapter of the American Planning Association, and the American Institute of Certified Planners, which sponsored the National workshops on neo-traditional communities, which introduced the Visual Preference Survey ™ (VPS) ™ and the Hands-On Model Workshops nationally; Andres Duany and Peter Calthorpe, who got the first new small communities built; numerous graduate students including Steve Yeager and especially Melissa Saunders; Randall Arendt, Tom Dalessio, Joe Kocy, Professor Mike McCoy, and Dean Mark Lapping for reading the first draft of the manuscript. My thanks to Sarah Barrows for her graphic translation of my rough sketches into printable illustrations, and to Juan Ayala for assistance with the final layout. Special thanks to the staff at A. Nelessen Associates, who supported this effort with facilities and supplies. To my wife and children for their patience and understanding of the time I had to be away. To my parents, who raised me in a village. And finally, to the tens of thousands of people all across the country who have participated in Visual Preference Surveys ™ and the Hands-On Model Workshops. They have clearly expressed a rejection of sprawl in favor of a desire for small communities.

In closing I would like to thank you, reader/viewer. My forte is not that of a writer, but a lecturer and a producer of multimedia productions. The photographs and illustrations are meant to create a vision in which text and image reinforce one another. These images complete what I have not been able to adequately describe in the text. Many of the images have been used in Visual Preference Surveys ™ around the country. I hope these photographs and illustrations fill in the gaps that I have missed.

Table of Contents

## STEP I AND II

UNDERSTANDING THE BIOGRAPHY OF THE PAST --ANALYZING AND UNDERSTANDING THE PROBLEMS

## STEP VI

WRITING AND ILLUSTRATING CODES

## STEP VII

THE SUBMISSION AND APPROVAL PROCESS

# P R E F A C E

The American Dream has always been that of a good neighborhood and community, one's own house with a private yard. I consider myself enormously fortunate to have grown up in a house that my parents owned, which had a yard and a vegetable garden, and was located in a village. Life in a village offered many advantages. I experienced what it was like to be able to walk to school, church, the park, the post office, Hazsacker's woods, a viable downtown, and my summer and after-school jobs. I was part of a neighborhood and a community. Most of the people in the village knew my parents and knew my name. I experienced tree-lined streets and the joy of riding my bicycle. I could pedal across the village in about 15 minutes. The village was surrounded by farms and woods with a canal and river on one side. The village was important in the biography of my past; it was a small community.

Over the last forty years that village has been transformed, eroded by the thoughtless and insensitive application of modern standards of highway design and land use. The widening of the state highway through the village removed sidewalks, street trees, and the planted boulevard down Grand Avenue. The streetcar tracks were removed. Main Street became a highway. Soon new retail and commercial buildings were built. They located along the highway outside the village, not in the traditional downtown core. Industrial parks, garden apartments and residential subdivision tracts replaced the small farms which once formed a greenbelt surrounding the village. The downtown was not within walking distance of this new development. This was all done in the name of progress. We all thought that it was good and modern. No one knew better or realized what would be lost. When the commercial strip began competing with the downtown stores, the village department store closed; the grocery store closed and moved to the strip; the movie theater closed; the post office moved; several of the local gas stations closed; the local high school moved out of the downtown; the railroad station was torn down; and the grain elevator and lumberyard disappeared.

In an attempt to compete with the strip malls, the buildings that remained downtown were rehabilitated and new buildings were constructed in the strip mall style with their requisite parking lots. These were built to a scale and character that was completely unsympathetic to the traditional downtown. The vision of the American Dream that dominated from the 1930s to the 1970s faded in an attempt to accommodate sprawl, and the positive quality of the traditional small community deteriorated. No one realized then that the same amount of new construction could have been formed into one or more new hamlets, villages, or traditionally designed neighborhoods. This story of sprawl or variations of it can readily be found in municipalities across the country.

Sprawl is a pattern of physical development characterized by the decentralization of land uses. The sprawl pattern is Euclidean--formed by separate zones of single-use buildings--based on the 1927 U.S. Supreme Court case, Euclid vs. Ambler. Fundamentally, this case upheld the municipality's right to designate areas as single-use zones. The need for single use zones was primarily a response to the awful conditions created by the mix of polluting and unhealthy industrial uses and residential areas. Modern zoning since the late 1920s has primarily involved such a separation of uses.

Sprawl is the physical/financial image of the American Dream as envisioned in the 1939 New York World's Fair. Sprawl requires the use of a private vehicle to move from one single-use zone to another. It augmented the auto, oil, rubber, concrete, and road construction industries. Its success destroyed the walking suburb and the streetcar. Jobs, grocery stores, community centers, even schools are separated from housing, thereby requiring new roads and vehicles that fuel the consumer economy. The sprawl pattern discourages a sense of community. It encourages land speculation. It requires high infrastructure investments. It requires high energy consumption and is a major source of air and water pollution. Sprawl is the ultimate pattern of secular consumerism.

It is ironic that the separation of uses, the basis of the Euclid case, is today causing so much pollution and the destruction of natural resources. The many cars traveling to and from the separated uses now cause the same kind of pollution that single-use zones were created to eliminate. What was validated for health, safety, and welfare in 1927, has destroyed communities and created negative visions which today are the catalyst for the reformulation of small communities.

There are other unfortunate psychological and economic effects of sprawl development. Sprawl is privately expensive to maintain. The financing of home and car ownership is getting more difficult for most wage earners. Both members of a couple must work in order to cover the high suburban costs, including the house mortgage, credit payments, insurance, taxes, and two or more cars. On average, a two- year-old car costs $5,000 per year to own and maintain, according to the American Automobile Association. Commuters moving along at stop-and-go speeds, spending one hour, or more, per day--totaling five weeks per year--in their cars traveling between their subdivision house and the office park or the mall. The visual impact of constantly looking at the negative road edge causes cognitive pain.

The public costs to maintain suburban mobility are high, approximately $4,000 to $9,400 per car per year depending on how many miles are driven. Six to seven parking spaces are required for each new car. Municipal and state taxes for continued road improvements, drainage, and police protection are high. User fees are growing. We seem to get less and less mobility for our tax dollar.

Considerable amounts of time are required to use the current pattern of sprawl. Time is at a premium. Time spent with children, the family, with neighbors, and with the community is limited. Sometimes parents have little time for themselves. Often both parents, in the shrinking number of nuclear families, must work long hours to make all of the payments to maintain the programmed consumer status; some even hold two jobs to support their large house and two cars. Imagine the new sprawled developments with 3 people living in 3,500 square feet, an attached two- or three-car garage, and several rooms with no furniture. You bought it so your friends and associates will think "you've made it." Have you? Congratulations, you're now a major contributor to sprawl, the ultimate consumer. "But," you say, "there are no alternatives that I can afford half way between where we work."

Who suffers most in this? I think it is the children first and the community next. We have less time for children. Too many children don't get the opportunity to have a daily meal with their parents. They learn the values of consumerism from their parents, or on TV, or from their peers, who come from similar backgrounds. On the bottom of the social economic ladder, many cannot afford a house, or health care, or good schools, in addition to all of the consumer items that the media tells us we must have. Is something wrong? You bet there is.

The family as we knew it in the 1950s is disappearing. We have a smaller number of nuclear families. According to the Census Bureau in 1990:
- 1/2 of marriages end in divorce
- Births to single mothers make up 1/2 of all births
- 1 in 4 Americans over 18 have never married
- Only 25.4 % of U.S. households consist of a married couple with children and there has been a steady decline since 1970 when the number was 43.3%
- 25% of households consist of people who live alone
- 29.4% of the population are married without children
- 4.7% of households consist of unrelated people living together

A new era is beginning. The evolution of the built form spiral will return to a more mixed and multiple-use pattern of development in a positive response to the new conditions. We must plan for a new sense of community, of extended families which will fulfill our fundamental social need for kinship and a sense of social well-being.

If we can design small communities which allow people home ownership and a private yard without staggering payments, that are located within a short commute of places of employment thus allowing more leisure time, and that provide the ability to walk and interact with their neighborhood and the community, then we will do something fantastic. Small communities can provide opportunities for many of these solutions.

There appears to be a crisis today in the education and in the nurturing of community values; both contribute to the positive psychological sense and experience of place. Existing small communities have a positive community value structure based on mutual respect and concern for your neighbors and the community. This must be learned by example. New small communities with these values can generate a positive pride in their sense of community, schools, and neighborhood. As the adage instructs "Love thy neighbor as thyself."

Economists and advertisers tell us we have the highest standard of living in the world, with more and larger everything; but do we have a parallel standard of living, pride of place, sense of security, sense of well being, good neighbors, friends and sense of community, and lack of stress? No? If not, can we achieve it? Yes, I think we can, but it will require a change in the policies of consumption, in the provision of affordable housing, in the pattern of development and redevelopment along with a reevaluation of many of our current social conventions. It will require that the pattern of development create and enhance time, be more affordable, environmentally sensitive, and be an interesting place to live and work.

These are lofty goals. How can the planners, designers, architects, and politicians who are responsible for the urban and suburban codes implement these goals? Ask the residents of their township to generate a consensus vision for the most appropriate form of development. I am convinced that a more humanistic sense of place will emerge. Amend your master plans and change zoning codes to allow this alternative. Demand that the configuration and character of buildings, street patterns, and spaces be designed efficiently and economically to accommodate a range of household types. I am convinced that small communities will emerge which are beautiful and convenient, and will begin to meet many of these goals.

Have you ever driven through or visited a village, neighborhood, or town that made you think to yourself "What a great place this is!" Have you visited the "main street" in Princeton or Oldwick, Cranbury or Califon, and experienced a feeling of well-being; did you wonder why YOU live in a place without charm and character? Did you wonder why NOBODY creates these kinds of places today? **Did you realize that the zoning in your town probably DOES NOT ALLOW the creation of a traditional small community?**

After involving people in the Community Planning Process now for over 20 years, it is clear to me that most people think that the modern sprawl pattern of endless subdivisions, commercial strips, and deteriorated villages and cities is negative and inappropriate. But they don't know what to do about it. Some even think it is too late. IT'S NOT.

People fundamentally want places which are humane and livable--a good place to live, grow up, and die. They know that something is missing in their municipalities, their subdivisions, their office parks, and their commercial strip zones. Many people want a shared sense of stewardship of the land and water, as well as having a sense of community. Therein lies the reason for this handbook.

The country needs a new model of suburban development which will be more cost effective, with an improved quality of life. The old vision generated in the 1930s is clouding over. A new vision is emerging, one that will redefine the Old American Dream, using the best of the past and the technological and ecological advances of the present to create a more positive and secure future for everyone. Small communities activate this vision. Remember, almost every thing that is built is approved under a Master Plan, zoning ordinance, or code. Follow the process, create a common vision, change the Master Plan, the zoning, and you can start to implement the new American Dream.

Most of the ideas in this book are beginning to reach fruition in the real world because they are the common sense recommendations of so many people and are based on visions of real places which have withstood the test of time as they have evolved through the **Built-Form Evolutionary Spiral.**

Even though the politics and marketing of sprawl will continue into the future, the ethical, moral, and economic responsibility to plan, design, and build small communities is so intuitive in our nature that it will come to pass.

# THE PROCESS

The planning and design of hamlets, villages, and neighborhoods, or small communities as I will refer to them throughout the book, can focus either on new development or on the redevelopment of existing commercial, residential, and industrial areas.

All places are in a continuous evolutionary process, like the Built-Form Spiral. Starting with its early formation, a place grows to optimize the available resources, technology, perceptions, and financial capabilities. The spiral continues through deterioration and then redevelopment followed again by growth and optimization. The spiral is endless in this evolution. The important thing to remember is that as it evolves, we get multiple opportunities to intervene. Every decision we make effects the balance and the path of evolution. As the next cycle comes around, it relates back to the previous cycle and plans for the future.

Planning to create small communities must occur at both the macro scale of master planning and the micro scale of site planning and urban design. New hamlets, villages, or neighborhoods can achieve an even higher positive value than older ones when we combine the best of the past with a humanistic vision of the future. We must envision the potential and honestly attempt to solve the problems of the present. Planning communities on new, previously undeveloped land will be an easier task than redevelopment will be. Redevelopment and/or retrofitting of Euclidean zones of older industrial-retail areas is becoming more popular, challenging though it may be. Many of these places reach the limits of their economic and functional usefulness as predicted by the spiral diagram.

## The Built-Form Evolutionary Spiral

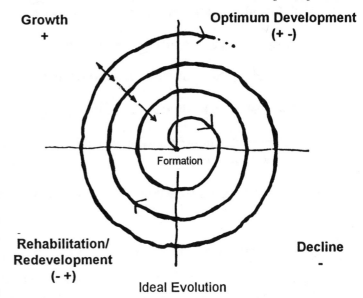

Growth
+

Optimum Development
(+ -)

Formation

Rehabilitation/
Redevelopment
(- +)

Decline
-

Ideal Evolution

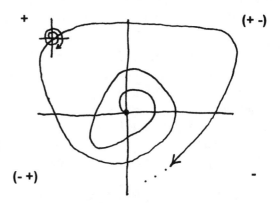

+

(+ -)

(- +)

-

Each quadrant describes the end result of events that occurred during the evolution of the built environment. These events produced forces that either extend or constrict the evolution in that quadrant, or cause a new spiral to form.

# A SEVEN STEP PLANNING AND DESIGN PROCESS

After years of planning and designing small and large projects, a process has emerged which reflects this evolutionary diagram. When this process is followed, opportunities to create small communities exist. The process consists of seven conceptual steps:

**I. Understanding the biography of the past**

**II. Analyzing and understanding the problems**

**III. Creating a common vision, Design by Democracy**

**IV. Analyzing and applying the potentials**

**V. Creating three- and four-dimensional plans**

**VI. Developing illustrated codes that reflect the common vision and the potentials**

**VII. Improving interaction between the community and the developers through submission and review of plans**

**These seven steps have been used to define the various sections in this book .**

## STEP I   THE BIOGRAPHY OF THE PAST

The biography of the past looks at a town's political, physical, and economic development over the life span of current generations. We must understand the historical development or growth of our municipality, document these changes over time, and analyze the impact of the total build-out pattern based on current zoning. We must understand the past policies at the national level as well as our personal conditioning. Chapters 3 and 4 review the history and evolution of suburban planning and design since the 1920s.

## STEP II   ANALYSIS OF PROBLEMS

The analysis of the physical problems at a local municipal level becomes apparent through the vision planning process.  Specific focus sessions with the elected officials, police, public works staff, legal council, neighborhood groups, or at town-wide meetings provide lists of the physical planning and related economic and social problems facing the area. In this stage there is an assessment of the most severe problems and what the participants recommend as solutions. This is particularly critical when the current master plan or zoning ordinance allows the physical characteristics which create the problems.

## STEP III   DETERMINING THE COMMON VISION

The common vision provides specific images of those places and examples of land use patterns that are positive and acceptable to the community, as well as those that are negative and unacceptable. I use both the VPS $^{TM}$ and Hands- On Model Workshops to help generate the vision.  These visual images should be used in the creation of the master plan's goals and objectives, in the land use, circulation, open space, and community facilities plans. They are particularly important to demonstrate the three-dimensional reality of the two-dimensional plan. The two-dimensional plan elements of the master plan can be given their three-dimensional image by using photographs and models to represent various land uses, points of interest, and attractive landscape characteristics. Images with positive ratings can be used to demonstrate the standards for streetscapes, housing densities, transit stops, parks, etc. The clearer and more understandable the vision of the master plan, the greater the probability that your municipality will get the quality of growth and/or redevelopment it desires. The negative images tell you specifically what to avoid. Chapter 5 describes the Vision Planning Process and the Hands-On Modeling technique.

## STEP IV  THE POTENTIALS

Using the positive images is the next step in the process. The potential of what the area wants to be in the future is generated through those images and model design workshops in the common vision step of the process. The range of characteristics which can be assessed in this process is dependent on those images used in the VPS $^{TM}$ and the results of the Hands-On Model Workshops. We typically include many images in the VPS $^{TM}$ which are further along on the evolution spiral or which have stood the test of time. If they come up positive, the potential for implementation exists. Sometimes the results of the Hands-On Model Workshops can be recycled directly into codes through figure ground plan and design standards. Chapter 6 looks at potentials for positive development and redevelopment and economic feasibility.

## STEP V  CREATING PLANS

Many of the potential images for future development duplicate pre-1938 streetscapes and land use patterns found in traditional places. To translate these potentials into master plans and zoning/development ordinances requires that they be more design specific and more three-dimensional. This does not mean that highly rated images, street form details, or building materials should be copied. Instead it means a sensitive understanding of the design principles inherent in the analysis of the positive images should form the basis of the master plan and design-development zoning ordinance. To the extent possible, the master plan should include the specific location and layout of all future roads, a conceptual-figure ground plan for all zones, and specific plans for the higher- density houses, mixed-use, and non-residential zones. Conceptual axonometric or positive photographic images can be used as guidelines. The normal two-dimensional plans must become more three-dimensional; the clearer the master plan, the easier the translation into the zoning and development ordinances. Chapter 7 contains the Ten Principles to design a small community.

## STEP VI  ILLUSTRATED CODES

It is critical that development ordinances be written and illustrated. Chapter 8 is an example of an illustrated ordinance which can be used in total or in parts for the creation of hamlet, villages, or neighborhoods.

## STEP VII  SUBMISSION AND REVIEW PROCESS

Chapter 9 describes the application process, with an emphasis on informal submissions and the submission requirements which hopefully fast-track the approval process.

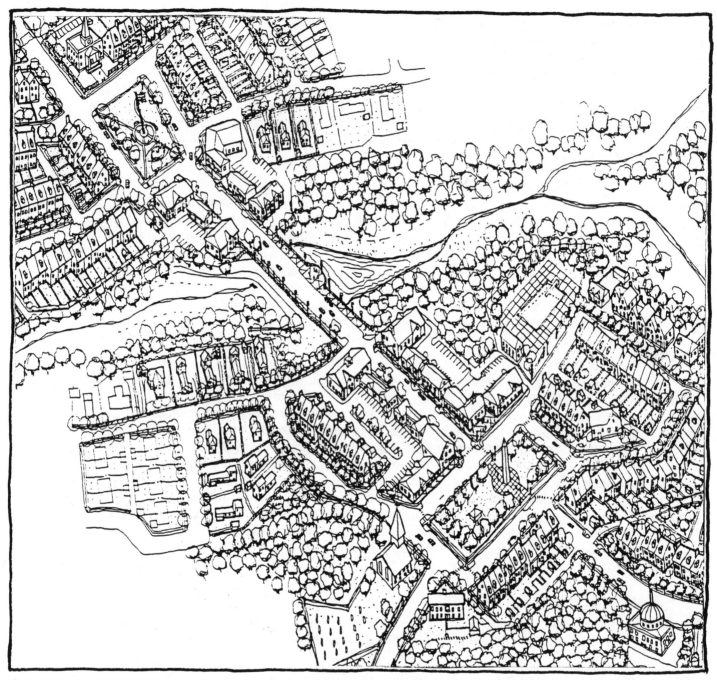

Axonometric sketch of the core for a new village community of Prince Georges County, MD.

# DEFINITIONS AND PROGRAM CHARACTERISTICS

## The Design of a Small Community

**Definition:**

*The art and science of the two-, three-, and four-dimensional spatial arrangements of buildings and structures, streets and roads, infrastructure and landscape elements, on the land, in harmonious and positive relationship to the human scale and the natural environment, in order to create and enhance a positive sense of community, neighborhood, and personal well-being.*

Anywhere Suburbia, USA.

This downtown street in Princeton, NJ, is a very successful pedestrian place.

## Sense of Community

Our basic intuitions and common sense seek a sense of community, a sense of place. People want and seek a sense of common friendships, a life that involves a neighborhood. People want to be able to walk to the post office, the pharmacy, the park, the school, and perhaps even their jobs; people want to feel safe; people need to have open spaces in which to play that are in close proximity to their homes. Unfortunately, existing planning has created undifferentiated sprawl development that does not satisfy most people's basic needs and desires. Today, and for the past fifty years, the location of new construction has been determined primarily by three key factors: the accessibility of a site to transportation routes, the availability of land, and the conservatism of the financial institutions and developers who believe that only the re-creation of the status quo will be financially beneficial. It is assumed that if a site can be reached by the privately owned automobile, consumers will appear.

Pedestrianism is not a mode of transportation that receives the attention it deserves in decisions about the location of such basic services as schools, grocery stores, post offices, or banks, to name but a few. Neo-traditional planners, inspired by traditional pre-1930 American towns, believe that this approach is wrong. Small communities, the kinds of places Neo-traditional planners design, emulate historic urban design compositions that have proven to be successful in a planning process that responds to the demands of contemporary life. Neo-traditional planners conceptualize communities whose fundamental requirement is that they encourage walking. They should be walkable with respect to both an aesthetically pleasing and inviting pedestrian nexus and the proximity of services, employment, mass transit, and residences. These communities should accommodate, but not surrender to, the automobile.

The Visual Preference Surveys ™ and Hands-On Workshops indicate that planners, government officials, the general public, and even traffic engineers now realize that people have come to desire a higher quality of place within an environmentally responsive framework. They realize that the quality and layout of place are intimately bound up with the quality of life. Small communities fulfill these basic human needs. They are the most efficient, harmonious, satisfying, and complete places to live, work, and play.

## The Two-, Three-, and Four-Dimensional Community

In the recent past planning has been viewed two dimensionally. Professionals work from drawings and technical manuals that obscure the complexities of a community. It should not be surprising then that flat, two-dimensional drawings and words inadequately express the multi-faceted aspects and problems of the built environment. Planning for small communities, in contrast, requires a comprehensive process that integrates traditional, two-dimensional land-use planning with the third and fourth dimensions of design. The third dimension defines the physical, spatial characteristics of a place. It asks, for example: How tall must a building be and what should define its relationship to other buildings in order to create an appropriate sense of enclosure? The fourth dimension is a time and perception factor as it relates to the experience of place. The fourth dimension is concerned with how people use and perceive their environment as they live in it and move through it.

One of the models produced at the Chester County, PA, 2000 symposium.

## Time

Time is one of the central human measurements for evaluating the operational characteristics of place. Time is required in order to complete the daily tasks of life, commute to work, get to the grocery store, take the children to school. In a world where time is a highly valued commodity, a typical suburban community, whose physical organization requires that large quantities of time be spent getting from place to place, squanders natural resources as well as human resources. Surely these resources could be used more effectively. This wastefulness, particularly the lost time, detracts from the quality of life. Conversely, a community that is structured so that many tasks may be performed without spending many hours in an automobile, on a crowded highway, or in frequent traffic jams will, as a result of its physical structure, add considerably to the quality of life.

Typical peak hour traffic flow currently on Route 1, New Brunswick, NJ. The average commute to work is currently 24 minutes or 200 hours per year in your car.

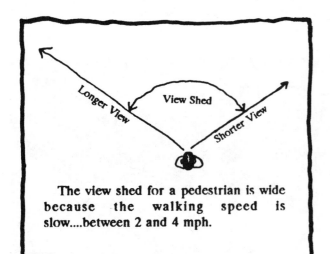

The view shed for a pedestrian is wide because the walking speed is slow....between 2 and 4 mph.

It is important for planners and designers to understand and integrate the fourth dimension of place into the planning and design process. By considering the many ways that people of all ages use and experience streets, public spaces, and buildings, we can better create places with positive visual and spacial characteristics. Drawing on a plan the paths people use and overlaying this with the viewshed of the pedestrian or the slow moving vehicle, allows one to more fully comprehend what is seen and then make the second- and third-dimensional changes in the design.

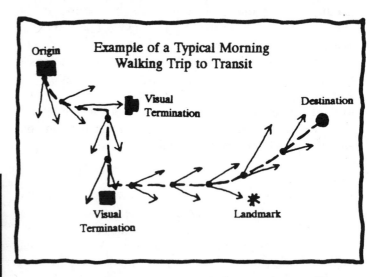

## Walking Speeds *
2 miles per hour=   176 ft/min
3 miles per hour=   264 ft/min
4 miles per hour=   317 ft/min

The average walking speed is approximately 3 miles per hour. In five minutes you can walk 1,500 ft.

*Elderly and small children walk slower.

We must consciously strive to avoid the conditioning of past land-use practices. Zoning and land-use regulations should not be implemented without a full consideration of the consequences and repercussions within the built environment. The two-dimensional methodology does not fully take into account the design implications of our actions. I contend that it is only through the use of thoughtful and deliberate design procedures that communities attempting to better the human condition will be successful.

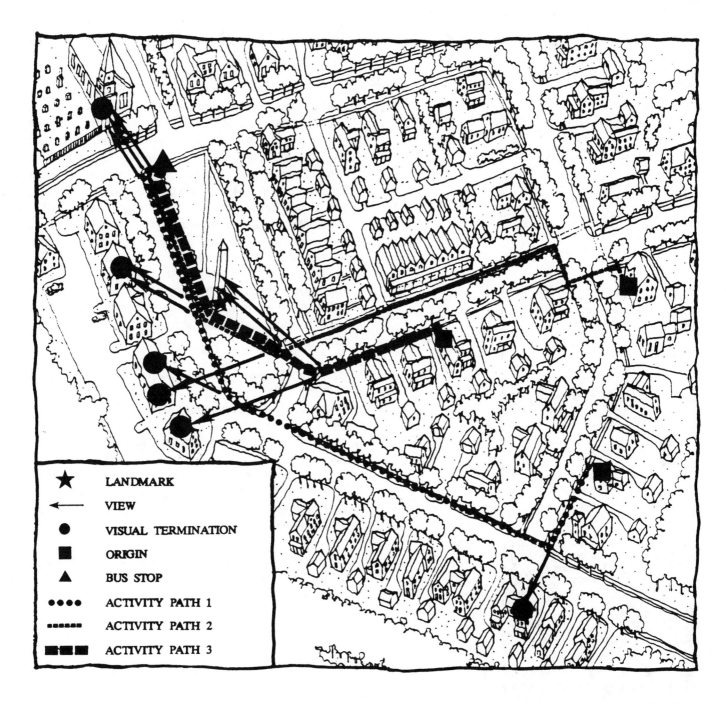

**LANDMARK**

**VIEW**

**VISUAL TERMINATION**

**ORIGIN**

**BUS STOP**

**ACTIVITY PATH 1**

**ACTIVITY PATH 2**

**ACTIVITY PATH 3**

Activity pattern diagram of the walking trip from home to the computer commuter mini bus stop. By overlapping activity paths of many people, the important visual and spatial characteristics of a small community become apparent.

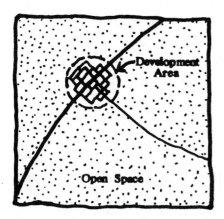

The Hamlet in a rural setting.

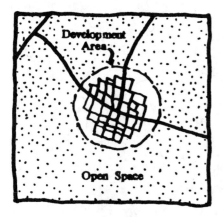

The Village in an exurban setting.

The Neighborhood in a town.

## What Are Small Communities in the Context of the State Plan?

### Communities of Place: The State Development and Redevelopment Plan for the State of New Jersey

The New Jersey State Development and Redevelopment Plan is fundamentally a very important and a very positive step towards better planning. It offers a definition of Communities of Place. But, more importantly from my perspective, it recommends that all future development and redevelopment in the State should be in the form of Centers, which at the smallest scale are hamlets, villages, and neighborhoods. The State, however, does not tell the concerned citizen and the developer exactly how one creates such a place. What are the procedures? What are the necessary processes that insure the creation of these communities? This book provides guidance in the creation of Communities of Place, small communities. I offer a process and principles for their design.

Before such a community can be created it must be defined.

The State of New Jersey Plan defines Community of Place as:

*"a dynamic, diverse, compact and efficient Center that has evolved and been maintained at a human scale, with an easily accessible central core of commercial and community services, residential units, and recognizable natural and built landmarks that provide a sense of place and orientation."*

I have found that this is a good, though general definition, but it requires very specific vision planning and design standards in order to be achieved.

## Program Characteristics of Small Communities

Small communities can take many forms, but I find three basic types--hamlets, villages, and neighborhoods--particularly applicable for the creation of new subdivisions or the retrofitting of existing strip commercial or residential development. Hamlets and villages correspond to types of centers identified by the State Planning Commission. These small communities share certain fundamental features, although they differ from each other primarily in size and intensity.

Small communities are designed with respect to the human scale, a scale which underscores a sense of community. They are distinguished from residence-only sprawl subdivisions and Edge City office-park malls by their compact form, their mixed use, their network of streets, their distinctive character, and their environmental sustainability.

This street in Princeton, NJ, is part of a network of streets that respect the human scale.

Small communities are ecologically responsible. They are located and developed according to capacity-based planning. The demand for development must be balanced with the limits of environmental and infrastructure constraints. These constraints include, but are not limited to, groundwater capacities, the impact of solid waste disposal, infrastructure systems, and sewer, water, air, and soil capacities.

Small communities are compact. The physical size and layout of the community is based upon comfortable, feasible walking distances. Shops, housing, schools, community services, recreation, jobs, and/or public transit can be reached by foot. Easing dependence upon the car fosters a higher quality, more richly detailed physical environment. As people walk, they inevitably notice architectural details. These, in turn, are part of the visual pleasure of walking. Walking with a goal (reaching a shop, for example) thus becomes an aesthetic experience that engenders interest and respect for one's community. It also augments a sense of responsibility and pride in the community.

This aerial of Blawenburg, NJ, illustrates a compact hamlet surrounded by open space.

The Village Common is the center of the community.

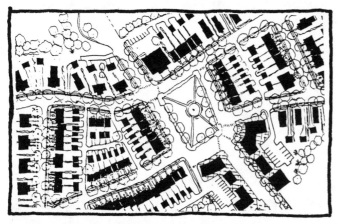

A network streets where every street intersects with at least two other streets.

Main Street of Basking Ridge, NJ, illustrates a good range of building sizes, shapes, and footprints.

Small communities are easily identifiable in the landscape. In rural situations they are surrounded by open space that defines the development boundary. This open space may be environmentally sensitive land or it may contain very low density uses such as recreational areas, large estates, or agricultural lands. Internal open spaces are fundamental to small communities. These spaces function as formal or informal public gathering places, they define neighborhoods and create recreation opportunities for all. When designed as infill in developed areas, new Communities of Place seek to integrate existing development with open spaces and a street network.

Small communities have a distinct physical identity, a community focus such as a village green or common, a mixed use core, or a simple crossroads. In larger small communities (villages, neighborhoods, or a town consisting of several neighborhoods), the community core or focus provides basic employment, shopping, and a mass-transit hub for residents as well as those living in surrounding areas.

Small communities contain a network of streets designed according to proven functional streetscape standards generated from the VPS ™ and user surveys. This network promotes walking by offering the possibility of multiple routes to destinations. Walking is further encouraged because of the many design standards, for example, sidewalk widths, street trees, and parallel parking that acts as a buffer between the pedestrian and moving traffic. These features were also created with the convenience of the private automobile and public transportation in mind; a network of streets provides multiple or alternative routes for an automobile as well as for the pedestrian.

Small communities are composed of buildings with a variety of footprints, heights, and scale. They contain a range of residential sizes and types affordable by a wide range of age and income groups. Lot sizes are mixed, with smaller housing units interspersed throughout the community. However, the majority of higher density, smaller lots are located near the core with larger lots nearer the periphery. Small communities are strengthened by the economic, social, and age diversity that such housing stock can provide. Behavior or the social contract is controlled through pride or the sense of community.

Small communities have a mix of uses. Buildings that contain uses other than residential units are located, primarily, in the community core. Mixed uses occur both horizontally, in adjacent buildings, and vertically, in offices and residences above shops and within certain height restrictions. Small communities contain a well-proportioned balance of jobs to housing; housing to recreation; housing to retail; housing to civic and social uses.

Small communities make use of a distinctive design vocabulary. This vocabulary is defined by a use of common materials, colors, and building-design relationships. Variation within the vocabulary gives richness and character.

Small communities prioritize maintenance of all kinds. Public facilities and services, including public community lands, are maintained to preserve the quality and character of a place. Personal and property safety must be maintained.

Small communities should be interrelated to form a hierarchy of places. This order of place, by size, includes hamlets in rural areas, as the smallest type, villages in rural, suburban and exurban areas, neighborhoods in suburban areas, which are part of towns. All small communities must be interconnected by roads, transit, and bicycle with all other small communities. Although small communities are discrete settlements, they need not be municipalities with taxing authority; many occur within existing townships. Their individuality and significance results from a spirit or sense of self engendered by their physical composition.

The Main Street of Cranbury has a distinctive design vocabulary. White painted clapboards, simple roof pitches, and shutters create a unity.

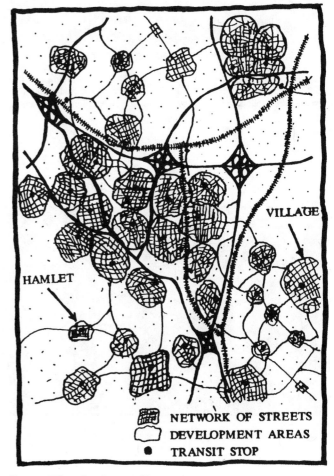

VILLAGE

HAMLET

🏠 NETWORK OF STREETS
⬡ DEVELOPMENT AREAS
● TRANSIT STOP

Connected hierarchy of communities.

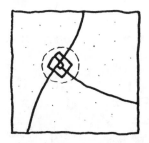

Mountainville Hamlet, Tewksbury Township, NJ. This represents the ideal small mixed-use core of a hamlet. Traffic is low and pedestrians feel comfortable. Notice how the snow defines the effect of the roadway.

## The Hamlet or Small Neighborhood:
### The Smallest of the Small Communities

Hamlets or small neighborhoods are the smallest communities; they have distinct identities, are identifiable in the landscape, and often possess a defined public space. In addition to residential sections, a hamlet has a compact nucleus that draws residents. This center may be nothing more than a green, tavern, day care facility, luncheonette, or mixed-use building that distinguishes it from the standard residence-only subdivision in form, use, and character. Hamlets have a distinctive architectural design vocabulary. Lots and buildings of varying sizes help to promote a range of family sizes, ages, and income levels in its inhabitants; they also offer visual variety. Specific streetscape standards are required and all streets should form a composite network. Sewage treatment can be provided by individual septic, individual septic with community treatment of gray water, small community treatment plants, or large regional treatment facilities. Hamlets have defined edges where there is a noticeable drop in housing density. This open space may be an area that requires specific site treatment; it may be composed of environmentally sensitive land, agricultural property, or recreational facilities, or it may contain estate housing with very large lots.

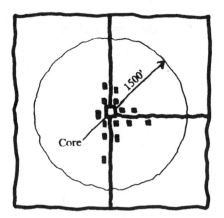

Hamlets are the settlement pattern for the smallest scale rural or exurban growth areas requiring small acreages of land. It is particularly important to note that hamlets can be sensitively developed in existing low-density rural areas without sacrificing the rural character of an area.

Aerial view of Mountainville Hamlet, Tewksbury Township, NJ.

# RECOMMENDED PROGRAM CHARACTERISTICS
# A HAMLET OR SMALL NEIGHBORHOOD

| | |
|---|---|
| Area (acres) gross | 10 -100 |
| Dwelling Units (D.U.) | 10 - 100 |
| Net D.U./Acre (lot size) | 1.0 - 6.0 |
| Population | 12 - 300 |
| JOBS: HOUSING RATIO @ 150 to 350 sq. ft. of building space per job | 0.25:1.0 - 1.0:1.0 |
| Open Space Ratio | .50 - .75 |
| Public Open Space Ratio | .03 - .05 |
| Local Retail | 26 - 52 S.F./D.U. |
| Civic Space* (minimum) | 300 S.F./D.U. |
| Green/Common Space (minimum) | 200 S.F./D.U. |
| Modal Split (auto: all other) | 90:10 - 60:40 |
| Water Treatment | Private or community wells |
| Sewage ** | Private Septic or Community Waste Water Treatment |

\* Land Area for Churches, Municipal Buildings, Library, Day Care, etc.
\*\* 50 units are the recommended minimum for an economically viable community waste water treatment facility.

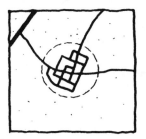

Village of Neshanic, Branchberg Township, NJ an ideal modified grid surrounded by open space.

Village scale commercial.

## Village in a Rural or Exurban Setting

Villages are mid-sized small communities. They offer a settlement-pattern model for small-scale rural and exurban growth. Villages require more land than hamlets and have a higher density. Although villages are intimate residential communities, they should offer the most basic employment, services, and shopping for their residents as well as for those living in surrounding low-density, rural, or exurban reserve areas.

Villages are characterized by a compact nature, a distinctive and unique building design vocabulary, a community focus, and perhaps a green or common defined by buildings. Housing and offices may be located above shops. A variety of community and social facilities are present. The low-density periphery of the village is no more than a 1/4 mile walking distance from the end of the commercial spine, community center, or Main Street.

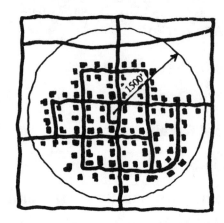

Specific streetscape standards are required; all streets should form a composite network. A village should be served by inter-community transit. The highest net density housing is located in the center of the village with lower density on the periphery. It should be identifiable in the landscape by open space surrounding the village. The open spaces can be environmentally sensitive areas, agricultural land, recreational-use land, and/or very large estate lot housing requiring specific site treatment. Sewage treatment can be provided by individual septic with community gray water treatment, by community treatment plant, or by regional treatment.

# RECOMMENDED PROGRAM CHARACTERISTICS
# A VILLAGE

| | |
|---|---|
| **Area (acres) gross** | **100 - 500** |
| Dwelling Units (D.U.) | 100 - 600 |
| Net D.U./Acre (lot area) | 1.0 - 8.0 |
| Population | 200 - 1,800 |
| Jobs: Housing Ratio @ 200 to 350 sq. ft. of building space per job | 0.75:1.0 - 1.75:1 |
| Open Space Ratio | .45 - .70 |
| Public Open Space Ratio | .03 - .08 |
| Local Retail** | 26 - 52 S.F./D.U. |
| Civic Space*** (minimum) | 300 S.F./D.U. |
| Green/Common Space (minimum) | 200 S.F./D.U. |
| Modal Split (auto: all other) | 70:30 - 50:50 |
| Water Treatment | Community or regional well(s) |
| Sewage | Community or Regional Waste Water Treatment |

\*   347 square feet U.L.I 1991 national standard for office space
\*\*   Additional retail required as it becomes more of a regional center
\*\*\* Land Area for Churches, Municipal Buildings, Libraries, Daycare, etc.

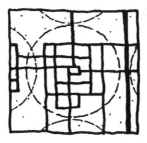

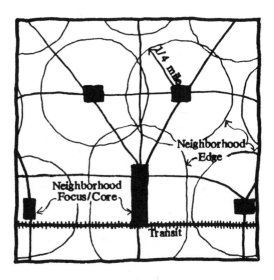

## Neighborhoods within an Urban Village or Town

Neighborhoods are the primary development forms that create larger regional centers like towns or urban villages. They can occur or be developed in leftover/underpopulated urban pockets. They can be models for retrofitting suburban development and exurban areas. Neighborhoods can be created in existing strip commercial areas; they can be incorporated in the planning of corridor centers, or in the redevelopment of existing villages that expect significant growth. Towns or large urban villages are the largest models for small communities. They are composed of two or more interconnected neighborhoods. These individual neighborhoods share many of the characteristics of the hamlet or village--each contains an appropriately scaled core of neighborhood-related services. However, unlike a hamlet or village, each neighborhood is in close physical proximity to another neighborhood, and all neighborhoods relate to a larger, common core.

Each neighborhood is contained within a 1/4 mile walking distance from the end of the commercial spine or community focus to the periphery. The town core and all related neighborhoods must be connected by sidewalks, bike paths, and on-grade transit. Traditional streetscape standards are required; all streets should form a composite network. Some mixed-use buildings, housing and offices located above shops, exist in the community focus. A range of housing types and densities exist, with an optimal net density of 5 du/ac. The highest net density is located near the center of the neighborhood with lower density on the periphery. A neighborhood should be identifiable in the landscape; the periphery can be defined by open space. The open spaces may contain natural features, environmentally sensitive land, and/or recreational areas. The periphery can be a low-density transition to another neighborhood, or it can be a seam formed by a major roadway with institutional or civic uses.

A town core is larger in scale and character than the individual neighborhood core. This image illustrates the scale and character of a village core at Lake Forest, Il.

# RECOMMENDED PROGRAM CHARACTERISTICS
# A NEIGHBORHOOD WITHIN A TOWN

| | |
|---|---|
| Area (acres) | 175 - 300 |
| Dwelling Units (D.U.) | 400 - 2,100 |
| Net D.U./Acre (lot area) | 4.0 - 15.0 |
| Population | 1,000 - 6,000 |
| Jobs: Housing Ratio @ 150 to 250 sq. ft. of building space per job | 0.5:1.0 - 1.0:1.0 |
| Open Space Ratio | .10 - .35% |
| Public Open Space Ratio | .03 - .08 |
| Local Retail* | 26 - 52 S.F./D.U. |
| Civic Space** (minimum) | 300 S.F./D.U. |
| Green/Common Space (minimum) | 200 S.F./D.U. |
| Modal Split (auto: all other) | 40:60 - 20:80 |
| Water Treatment | Regional Treatment |
| Sewage | Regional Waste Water Treatment |

\* Additional retail required as it becomes more of a regional center
\** Churches, Municipal Buildings, Libraries, Daycare, etc.

New high-density neighborhood in Harbortown, Memphis, TN.

The neighborhood within the town is characterized by a compact nature, a distinctive and consistent architectural design vocabulary, a community focus, and a green or common defined by buildings. The core of this settlement pattern contains retail, service, and office uses as well as large-scale community and service facilities. Towns and urban villages are mixed-use communities with all of the commercial and civic functions commonly required on a weekly basis, including food stores, grade schools, post offices, and retail shopping. They contain employment opportunities and a wide range of services used by residents and those who live in outlying areas. The urban village or town core contains an intermodal transportation node, where bus, or light or heavy rail lines are available to maximize the opportunities for private automobile-trip reduction. They offer public transit to other areas of concentrated jobs, such as existing office parks and other community cores. Sewage treatment is by regional treatment plants.

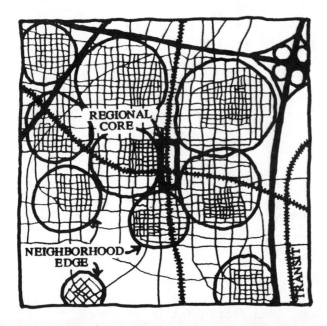

REGIONAL CORE

NEIGHBORHOOD EDGE

TRANSIT

Interconnected neighborhoods create a town or regional center. The relationship of the various neighborhoods to each other depends on the ecology of the site and the existing land use features.

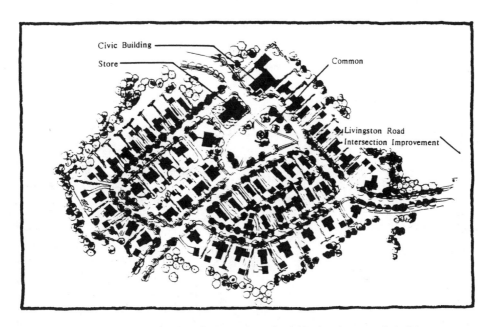

Figure ground plan of proposed small neighborhood community in Prince Georges County MD. Designed by ANA.

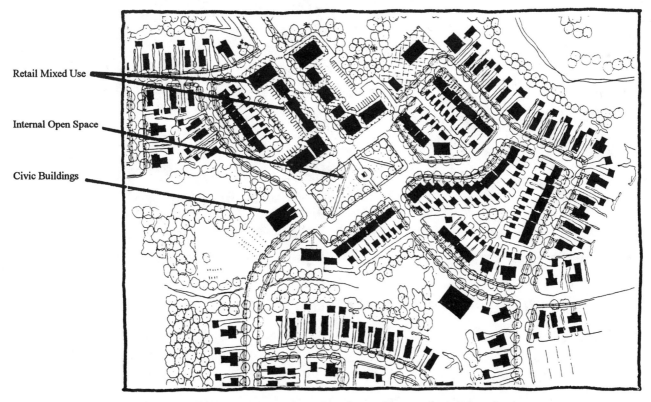

Figure ground plan of a portion of a small town center in Prince Georges County, MD. Designed by ANA. The center serves several small neighborhood communities.

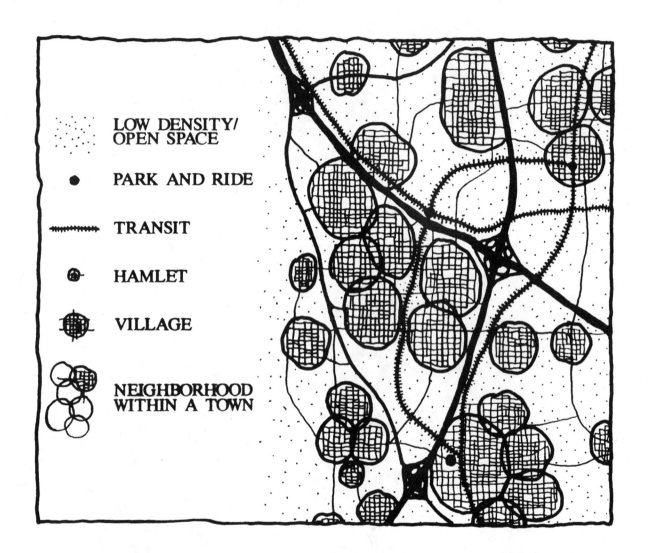

**LOW DENSITY/ OPEN SPACE**

**PARK AND RIDE**

**TRANSIT**

**HAMLET**

**VILLAGE**

**NEIGHBORHOOD WITHIN A TOWN**

Regional hierarchy of small interconnected communities.

## TABLE OF COMBINED
## RECOMMENDED PROGRAM CHARACTERISTICS FOR SMALL COMMUNITIES

|  | HAMLET | VILLAGE | NEIGHBORHOOD |
|---|---|---|---|
| AREA (acres) | 10- 100 | 100 - 500 | 175 - 300 |
| DWELLING UNITS | 4 - 100 | 100 - 600 | 400 - 2,100 |
| NET D.U./ACRE (lot size) | 1.0 - 6.0 | 1.0 - 8.0 | 4.0 - 15.0 |
| POPULATION | 12 - 300 | 200 - 1,800 | 1,000 - 6,000 |
| JOBS: HOUSING RATIO<br>150 to 350 sq. ft. of building space per job | 0.25:1.0 - 1.0-1.0 | 0.5:1.0 - 1.0:1.0 | 0.5:1.0 - 1.0:1.0 |
| OPEN SPACE RATIO<br>PUBLIC OPEN SPACE RATIO | .50 - .75<br>.03 - .08 | .45 - .70<br>.03 - .08 | .10 - .25<br>.03 - .08 |
| LOCAL RETAIL* | 26 - 52 S.F./D.U. | 26 - 52 S.F./D.U. | 26 -52 S.F./D.U. |
| CIVIC SPACE** (minimum) | 300 S.F./D.U. | 300 S.F./D.U. | 300 S.F./D.U. |
| GREEN/COMMON SPACE<br>(minimum)*** | 200 S.F./D.U. | 200 S.F./D.U. | 200 S.F./D.U. |
| MODAL SPLIT<br>(auto: all other) | 90:10 - 60:40 | 70:30 - 50:50 | 40:60 - 20:80 |
| WATER | Private/Community Wells | Community Well<br>Regional Supply | Regional Supply |
| SEWAGE | Septic or Community<br>Treatment | Community or<br>Regional Treatment | Regional Treatment |

*    Additional retail required as it becomes more of a regional center

**   Land area required for Churches, Municipal Buildings, Library, Day Care, etc.

*** This is included in the total public open space

# PROCESS STEP I AND II
UNDERSTANDING THE BIOGRAPHY OF THE  PAST
ANALYZING AND UNDERSTANDING THE PROBLEMS

This image taken in the early 1950s is a clear vision of future strip commercial land use.

# A BIOGRAPHY OF THE PAST

## Introduction

Understanding the biography of the past is the first step in the process of designing small communities. We must understand the relationship between the rational and the personal programming that contributes to the current physical condition. We carry our past with us. By combining the most positive aspect of our past programming with a clean rejection of the negative, the future is more clearly defined. In this Chapter, I offer my perspective on the evolution of sprawl development through a brief description of the roles of federal and local policies, planning movements, and social, political, and economic trends as they relate to land use. I examine the inefficiencies of sprawl, the disparate demands on local infrastructure, and the social impact of living in developments that are strictly utilitarian areas with no sense of place--the Edge Cities, residential subdivisions, office parks and strip malls. Through a realization of the negative effects of sprawl, we come to understand that much of the pattern formulated in the 1930s has reached optimization and is beginning to deteriorate. This is exacerbated by building new sprawl development and approving additional plans, some of which is not yet built. What is required is a new vision, application, and process. In short, we must understand what sprawl is so that we may implement a more thoughtful and responsive planning process.

Typical sprawl pattern with separated land uses.

An image that always receives a negative/unacceptable rating.

## An Historical View of Forces Affecting Land Use

The following analysis is a synopsis of events that have conditioned our thinking about the pattern and consequences of sprawl. It is presented to provide a basic understanding and chronology of the planning biography of our past. It highlights some of the most significant legislation and records the events and policies that clearly reveal the reasons why many land planners, bankers, and transportation planners continue to encourage sprawl today. Readers should consider what role these played in the planning of their towns and the surrounding region.

## An Older America

In the late 1800s the country consisted primarily of vibrant and fundamentally positive villages, towns, and farms. These villages and towns were the center of social and community life. There were also a few large cities, like New York and Chicago, where large groups of immigrants lived in very crowded and congested conditions. In the late nineteenth and early twentieth centuries, the City Beautiful Movement sought to improve the urban image through the construction of monumental public facilities in the center of cities. This was a time when streetcars were heavily used and most needs were within walking distance of the home or the streetcar stop. Throughout the twentieth century, the private automobile became increasingly popular. Although it began as a recreational vehicle for the affluent, it soon became affordable because of the efficiencies of the assembly-line and mass production. Increasingly, there were signs that the popularization of this mode of transportation would have an impact on the design of places. The familiar images of the 1920s indicate a love affair with this new technology. Just how far reaching the impact would be could hardly have been foreseen.

## Early Suburbs

Places that developed in the late 19th or early 20th century have a slightly different development pattern. During this time, streetcars and interurban transit facilitated the growth of towns and cities beyond their original boundaries. New streetcar suburbs sprang up at unprecedented distances from the city or town center. On a very limited scale, development began to sprawl. In the streetcar suburb, the detached house was popular and possible because of available land. Perhaps more important, however, the street-

For a short while cities and towns were able to have a balance of transit and automobiles.

car made increasingly distant residences possible because householders could more quickly reach jobs, services, and cultural sites within the metropolitan area. Although streetcar suburbs could be placed at great distances from town, the community continued to be fairly compact. People still had to live within walking distance of the streetcar; it was their primary means of transportation. Thus, the streetcar suburb could not experience rampant and unchecked growth.

At the same time as the developing streetcar suburb, during the period roughly between 1870 and 1930, rail lines, streetcars, and the emerging automobile offered a freedom in town design that had not been known before. This freedom gave an impetus to design for new towns. Such newly designed residential towns made possible an escape from the 19th century industrial city, often a foul and unhealthy place. Town planners saw an opportunity to offer a better life away from the tenements, they espoused country living, while endowing their plans with the community and cultural facilities of the city. Radburn, (c. 1929) by Wright and Stein, has been one of the most influential of these suburbs. Radburn attempted to combine the growing dependence on the private automobile with the ability to walk to a train station and to school without crossing a road. The basis of the plan was a complete multiple-use community. This plan departed from the traditional community form with the use of cul-de-sacs off loop roads and internal walkways and parks. Because of the stock market crash in 1929, Radburn was never completed. Consequently, it has never been properly repeated. However, many of its individual features have been adopted without an understanding of the whole concept. The cul-de-sac, for instance, is the most used and abused feature in current suburban subdivisions. We now see cul-de-sacs without the walkways or the internal parks. Houses do not front on parks, one can not easily walk to community facilities.

The internal park of Radburn, NJ, created at the ends of the cul-de-sacs.

This is an aerial view of Radburn, (c. 1930) provided by Radburn Association.

## The Evolution of Sprawl from 1900 - 1992: Why Did It Occur?

Sprawl is the product of federal programs and policies and the corresponding state and local land use policies. It is an economic program of personal consumption, reinforced by court decisions. It is the result of a premeditated set of planning policies that were developed during the New Deal era in order to create consumer investment activity though infrastructure and policy incentives provided by the Federal Government. The federal programs supporting the 30-year mortgage guarantee and new highway construction opened previously inaccessible land to speculators. The highways were needed to provide access to land and to give the middle class their piece of the media-programmed American dream, a small lot, a house, a T.V., and a car, the image reinforced by the 1939 World Fair. The marketing campaigns worked. The new consumer society loved the new houses, new cars, and new appliances. Dad worked, Mom stayed at home. They left the farm and the old neighborhood. They moved to the country. Now the limitations of this vision are becoming evident. Now we see that these policies entailed pollution, the degradation of the countryside and a style of life neither convenient nor problem free. Now we see that that American dream consumes an unprecedented amount of exurban land, requires millions of cars, millions of miles of highways, and billion of barrels of oil. While these policies were undertaken in order to create market demands from the New Deal Era through the 1980s, it is now clear that this economic policy created serious ecological and economic problems. Furthermore, the price of housing and cost of living have outpaced many personal incomes.

Mom, Dad, Dick, Jane, and Spot. The traditional nuclear family, for which sprawl was planned and designed, has changed radically.

### Village of Euclid v. Ambler Realty

This landmark 1927 court decision upheld the constitutionality of single-use zoning, thereby rationalizing its universal application. Protection of the health and the safety of the community justified the separation of residential, commercial, and industrial land-uses from which one or another use was excluded. This ruling became the basis of all comprehensive zoning and planning in the United States, making single-use zoning the norm and mixed-uses zones illegal in many places. Euclidean zoning is the prime land-use regulating characteristic of sprawl. As evidence of the pervasiveness of such sprawl consider whether you know of any municipalities that permit a mix of uses in a single zone.

Land separated into Euclidean zones.

1950s style subdivisions

The vision of the smiling driver of a new car on the multi-deck roadway c.1950.

## Federal Housing Administration (FHA)

In response to the poverty and consequent neglect of municipal facilities during the Depression, government programs were enacted to stimulate economic growth. The National Housing Act, adopted in June, 1934, created a program to stimulate building activity. To facilitate home financing, the FHA provided insurance for long-term mortgages, extending repayment periods for up to 30 years. The market for home ownership was vastly expanded, and housing starts grew from 93,000 in 1933 to 619,000 in 1941. The FHA was mostly concerned with "economic soundness"; consequently, it tended to favor new construction, suburban development, rather than urban redevelopment. The FHA also established minimum standards for home construction. These uniform standards became the basis for residential construction during a time of unprecedented growth. The cookie-cutter subdivision was created, producing acres of similar houses on uniform lot sizes with similar layouts and mortgages.

## Federal Highway Administration

In 1937 the Federal Highway Administration was established; it called for new road types to accommodate the individual ownership of cars and trucks. The American Association of State Highway and Transportation Officials (AASHTO) manual, first published in 1937, was soon to become the "Bible" for all road design standards. It provided standards for the modern freeways, highways, arterials, collectors, intersections, and ramps we know today. Subsidized by the Federal Government through a tax on gasoline, massive highway building programs were encouraged. Highways became a symbol of progress and development along them followed shortly. Strip commercial and residential subdivisions grew up along these thoroughfares, steadily gobbling up the countryside. The economic engine of the country was gearing up. Such development proceeded unchecked and without any rational plan. Such unchecked development was only reinforced by the Federal Aid Highway Act of 1956.

## The Elimination of the Streetcar

Most of our larger cities and towns once had a network of street cars. The village I grew up in had a street car system connecting the center of several villages like a string of pearls. But streetcars lost their popularity, dismantled by a coalition of automobile and oil companies, when automobiles, which moved faster than streetcars, became a requisite component of the American dream. Gasoline was cheap, and the convenience of getting in the car and driving off became part of everyday life. Even Los Angeles once had a remarkable system of trolley cars, that is now being replaced after billions of dollars of investments in roads and freeways. New Orleans, Boston, and San Francisco are among the best known American cities that maintained their streetcar systems. Today the systems in New Orleans and Boston are looked upon as valuable models of low technology transport, and San Francisco's well known cable cars are a major tourist attraction as well as a functional component of the city. Street cars provide structure and order to the neighborhoods, villages, and cities that they service.

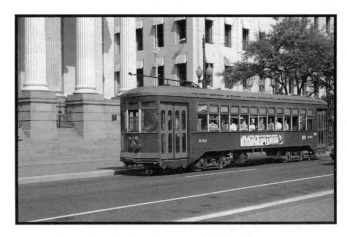
The streetcar, functional, efficient and fully occupied.

## The New York World's Fair, 1939-1940

The New York World's Fair fostered the vision of the American Dream. It popularized the new highways and sprawl pattern by heralding the city of the future, one that was laid out along a string of super highways. In GM's Futurama, visitors marveled at the future while traveling above a huge model. The aerodynamic cars of the future promised even greater freedom. The fair was only one of the widely publicized definitions of life in the future. Immensely popular, it introduced Americans to many of the artifacts we now take for granted. For the first time many Americans saw television and heard of air conditioning, two technological marvels that have played their part in defining the American home. These inventions made the neighborhood movie obsolete and the cooling front porch a less-than-necessary amenity.

The vision of the new highway system.

## World War II and the National Resources Planning Board (NRPB)

Even before the war's end, deteriorating cities were seen by planners as the ultimate challenge. The NRPB brought a new intensity to our thinking about the future of cities, and vast changes were seen for the post-war society.

One of the many Levittowns.

Urban renewal in New Brunswick, NJ.

Urban riots of the late 1960s

## After the War

With the return of veterans and the baby boom's larger families, farmland was re-evaluated for its development potential. New housing was required. Villages began to expand. Random cul-de-sacs and curving street patterns, patterns that paid no heed to the terrain requirements, appeared in former fields outside of the traditional walkable villages and neighborhoods. Large cities began to lose their middle- and upper-income populations as FHA programs were strengthened. Through television and marketing, the expectations of Americans grew. A house in the suburbs and a car, or two, in the garage became the definition of the good life. The suburbanization of America began in earnest when Levittown was started, in 1947, on 1,400 acres of Long Island. At a rate of 35 per day, more than 17,000 identical houses were built within the next few years. Levittown demonstrated to the housing industry how to work on an unprecedented scale; it paved the way for other even larger Levittowns, as well as smaller clones, across the country.

## Urban Renewal

The National Housing Act of 1949 addressed "the elimination of substandard and other inadequate housing through the clearance of slums and blighted areas." The Housing Act of 1954 expanded Urban Renewal to establish "a broad unified front to accomplish the renewal of our towns and cities," by establishing redevelopment procedures. However, Urban Renewal programs dealt only in physical renewal and did not strive to redevelop the community as a whole. The empty lots cleared by Urban Renewal are still visible in many of our cities and urban centers. In terms of community planning these acts have proved to be a dead-end. They neither ended the degradation of the inner city nor promoted the creation of healthy environments.

## Late 1965

Inner city riots demonstrated the pent up frustrations in the cities, and led to additional economic flight from cities. Fear, excessive drug use, low educational attainment, and high unemployment have contributed to additional urban flight and subsequent suburban growth.

## Federal 701 Comprehensive Planning Act

This act subsidized the creation of comprehensive master plans during the 1960s and 1970s. The resulting plans mirrored the current thinking in the area of land-use management, and they encouraged urban sprawl. They typically required single-use zoning and highway development, both of which underscore and enhance the importance of the automobile. Where possible, in order to decrease taxes and to pay for infrastructure, municipalities encouraged large-lot zoning. How many of your towns were planned for sprawl development with 701 Federal funding?

## Federal New Communities Assistance Program

The New Communities Act of 1968 instituted federal loans for the infrastructure of new communities across the country. By providing more affordable housing, jobs in proximity to homes, and community services this act was seen as an antidote to the continued high cost of suburban sprawl. Unfortunately, only a few new communities were funded. The HUD New Communities Project, which I worked on as a graduate student created a prototype new community as a response to the negative impacts of the sprawl pattern and the deterioration of the economic, social and educational fabric.

However, what evolved out of the new communities movement was the Planned Unit Development (P.U.D.). This is a generalized land-use pattern that allows multiple uses on a tract of land. A large parcel could be developed in conformity with a general plan that specifies development areas, open spaces, commercial uses, etc. Unfortunately, these P.U.D.s simply continued the separate land-use patterns of sprawl. Commercial developments in a P.U.D. are essentially strip malls; the open spaces are those lands that contain environmental constraints and so cannot be built upon; the single-family residences are located within pods; and the garden apartments and townhouses are located in different pods. It is still, primarily, automobile oriented.

A P.U.D. could be a small community if properly designed. The intent was to plan a well designed place. Unfortunately there were no clear design principles available to direct the three- and four-dimensional characteristics into a small community, rather it became, as its title suggests, Planned Unit Development.

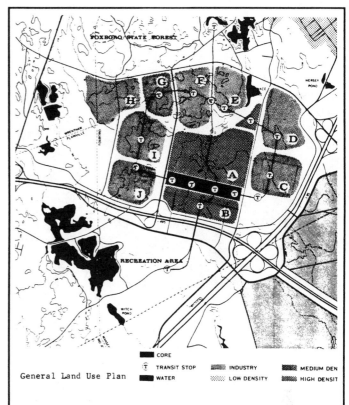

General Land Use Plan

CORE
TRANSIT STOP    INDUSTRY    MEDIUM DEN
WATER    LOW DENSITY    HIGH DENSIT

Eight neighborhoods with a town and regional center connected by looped transit.

**HUD New Community.    250,000 people on approximately 2,500 acres.**

A P.U.D. could have a town green with a residential and mixed-use core.

We are now beginning to realize that most of the physical design features which make communities livable were in front of us all the time in many of our villages, small towns, and neighborhoods.

## Environmental Movement

Growing environmental awareness stimulated many concerned citizens and citizen groups to pressure legislative and zoning officials to consider environmental and natural features as the basis for land-use controls. The resulting New Jersey legislation includes the Pinelands Act (which puts development controls on approximately 25% of the State of New Jersey), flood plain legislation, runoff retention and sediment control, the Wetlands Act (which sets standards for the preservation of wetlands because of the deterioration of water quality), and the Coastal Area Facilities Review Act (CAFRA).

Protecting low lands, marshes, and land with high water table is critical now and in the future.

As a by-product of the space program, we saw in 1968 for the first time a photograph of the entire planet as it appears in space. This photographic image crystallized what had previously been an abstraction: that we live on a small and fragile blue planet, and it is the only one we have. This event sparked concern for the earth as an ecological entity, and the beginning of a world wide ecological movement.

One year later, Ian McHarg created a system for incorporating ecological concerns in the planning and design process. In *Design With Nature* he illustrated an overlay-mapping technique as it applies to the environmental features of sites and entire regions. This is a technique that can be, and has been, used for identifying land that is environmentally suited for development or, conversely, land that by virtue of environmental constraints is unsuited for development. It became the basis of the current GIS system and the shocking realization that land characteristics were organic while zoning lines were typically geometric. Somehow these two characteristics needed to be rationalized.

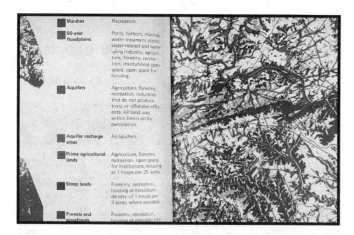

McHarg's technique revolutionized site planning by indicating which lands must be protected and which could be built on with the least constraints.

This photograph by NASA provided the unified vision which has been used by the environmental movement around the world. The photographic reality transformed the abstraction of place. We are all living on one small blue planet, our home, Earth.

## *The Costs of Sprawl* Report and the Energy Crisis

In 1974, The Real Estate Research Corporation published a report detailing the inefficiencies of sprawl development. The report was a rallying cry for some, but its effect has been short-lived. Sprawl and a crowded highway are lucrative short-term money makers for financial institutions and developers who resist the kinds of controls needed for long-range planning for small communities.

The energy crisis in 1973 required that the United States rethink its priorities about the consumption of its natural resources. In response, the size and weight of cars was reduced, as was the speed limit on the interstate highways. For the first time energy efficiency became a matter of concern. It became clear that oil, a non-renewable resource, would become more expensive and, perhaps, less obtainable. People began to understand that burning oil substantially contributes to air pollution and, therefore, a community with a more compact development pattern could reduce transportation demands, and consume less energy--oil. The life-style of the average American requires more fuel consumption than people of any other country anywhere else in the world. Should our patterns of development be examined in the light of these factors?

## Municipal Land Use Law (MLUL) and the Historic Preservation Act

The State of New Jersey enacted the MLUL in 1975. This act takes a major step toward the proper regulation of land. The MLUL also legislated, for the first time, the importance of aesthetic considerations with the following statement: " to promote a desirable visual environment through creative development techniques and good civic design and arrangements." The MLUL is a positive tool, but it still encourages sprawl.

The National Historic Preservation Act of 1966 helped in the rediscovery of historic patterns and traditional building and streetscape forms. Tax credits offered an incentive to preservation and spurred acceptance of the Act. The typical analysis of a historic district reveals that its functioning, building fabric and streetscapes present a significant contrast to the typical modern sprawl pattern. It is a promising development in the education of the electorate, focusing as it does on maintaining and preserving our heritage. It also offers models from an earlier time, models that are relevant

Cars lined up for gas in 1973.

Classic mixed use on main street Bordentown, NJ.

to some of today's problems. These models offer a different perspective on the issues regarding the location of development and what directions those developments should take.

## Mount Laurel and Mount Laurel II

The 1978 Mount Laurel Decision, by the New Jersey Supreme Court, states that all municipalities must accept their fair share of low and moderate income housing. This decision requires many municipalities to revise their master plans and zoning ordinances. The decision helps to define the categories of low and moderate income, and creates a formula for calculating each municipality's fair share. A builder's remedy establishes that 20% of any new development must be affordable. Consequently, many municipalities have begun to rethink the kind of master plan that encourages urban sprawl, a building pattern that discriminates against lower income people because of the high cost of land as well as the concomitant reliance upon the private automobile. Planners must recognize that such housing is to be integrated within communities where zoning is not single use exclusionary. Furthermore, people of low and moderate incomes frequently need transportation to jobs and other services, consequently transportation issues must be considered in the location of this housing. Such factors have made neo-traditonal planning more attractive. Its principles address these problems. In 1983, the New Jersey Supreme Court strengthened its 1978 decision after determining that communities were ignoring the original mandate. Mount Laurel II has become the impetus for the development of a state plan.

## Visual Preference Survey ™

I first used the Visual Preference Survey ™ technique in 1979. Initial surveys indicated an almost universal negative reaction to sprawl and a positive response to traditional settlement patterns. The technique has since been applied to master plans, redevelopment plans, and town-center design plans, and is now being used for vision planning across the country. The mandate is clear; citizens who are concerned, who participate in the Visual Preference Surveys™, see sprawl and urban deterioration as the primary land-use evil.

## What is a Low and Moderate household?

**Low:** a household having 0-50% of the regional median household income.

**Moderate:** a household having 50.1% to 80% of the regional median household income.

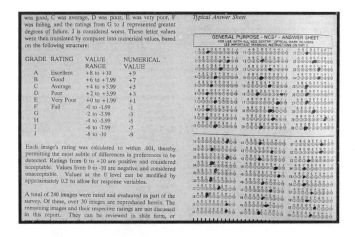

Response from a Visual Preference Surveys ™.

Applying the concept of the small neighborhood community to existing suburban areas.

New commercial/retail under construction, too much is still empty.

## State Planning Act and the Fair Housing Act

New Jersey passed the State Planning Act in 1985. This Act calls for a state-wide master plan for growth that includes the development and redevelopment of our cities and suburbs. The process of cross-acceptance (a process that calls for municipalities to be involved in the plan's development) is mandated to assure that all levels of government, as well as the general public, participate in preparing and adopting the plan. The plan supports managed growth in centers and seeks to abate sprawl.

The 1985 Fair Housing Act grew out of the Mount Laurel decisions as well. The growth management considerations of the State Plan became the basis of fair share calculations under the Fair Housing Act, legally connecting the two acts.

## National Building Bust

In the late 1980s the economy began to slow, and a recession loomed. Between 1980 and 1989 more sprawl development was created than at any time in the our history, a boom fueled by the deregulation of the banking industry. One consequence of this overbuilding is a high vacancy rate in offices and retail centers and high numbers of approved, though not yet built projects. Buildings are sitting empty all over the state. Another, is that in the early 1990's building starts are at their lowest point since World War II. Economist believe that the growth sector of the spiral is over and that we are going to have to become more efficient, to modify our life styles. James Dale Davidson and Lord William Rees-Mogg in their book, The Great Reckoning, state,

> Consumerism cannot be the center of life for long. It is always shallow because it relates to the creation in people's minds of wants that suit the manufacturer rather than the consumer of goals.

A new opportunity to plan emerges. We have time to take stock of what we have and how to maintain or, better yet, improve it. It is time to ask the people for a collective vision, to revise our master plans and zoning ordinances. Boards that have approved plans permitting sprawl should reconsider these decisions; perhaps they can offer incentives on unbuilt projects so that land will instead be developed to create small communities. To do nothing is to continue the sprawl pattern; neither the county nor the common man can continue to afford that.

## The Negative Effects of Sprawl

The effects of sprawl are visible everywhere, for sprawl consumes valuable land and resources. Between 1950 and 1980 New Jersey lost 50% of its farmland to development. Of course, speculators, transportation engineers, bankers, real estate brokers, and many farmers approved and supported this development. Many politicians saw nothing but ratable dollars to build new town halls, bigger police departments, and bigger public works departments, and the potential to assume more power and influence. In the process, we have compromised the quality of life and of the environment for many. This is not to say that we should not have accommodated growth. On the contrary, I am only criticizing the way in which growth proceeded.

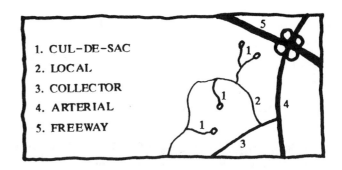

1. CUL-DE-SAC
2. LOCAL
3. COLLECTOR
4. ARTERIAL
5. FREEWAY

In the sprawl pattern, goods and services are scattered throughout the region. This arrangement requires elaborate road systems to link all areas. The conventional sprawl road-system relies on a hierarchy that begins with small, local roads and cul-de-sacs that feed into collectors which, in turn, dump traffic onto multi-lane arterials and major highways. This system, that lacks centers, produces excessive congestion and waste. Furthermore, because retail establishments are located along major arterials, the automobile is necessary for even the most basic of daily requirements, a quart of milk or a loaf of bread. Nearly all of the landscape is developed, even if the population remains sparse.

Automobile dependence results in air pollution; therefore, it is not surprising that much of the State of New Jersey fails to meet Federal clean air standards. The Federal Clean Air Act and the New Jersey Rand Bill target automobiles as significant contributors to air pollution, and mandate that New Jersey create a plan to reduce dependence on the automobile. Low-density sprawl feeds on over-use of the automobile and makes transit impossible. Without logical centers or concentrations of mixed use, transit cannot be efficient and effective.

Sprawl is characterized, in part, by an economic mindset that, often times, places taxes and ratables above everything. Municipalities need to expend funds for the planning of small communities so that land use plans can be more efficient and economical for the user and the town. Somehow, there is seldom enough money for planning. Municipalities continue to engineer and build or repair roads, but

A typical cul-de-sac without the parks, open space, and pedestrian connections envisioned by Radburn.

fail to understand the necessity of planning parks, community centers, public spaces, and buildings which could enhance the sense of community and place. Roads and sprawled office parks and strip malls are good ratables. As one planning board chairman recently noted, "We don't want any single family houses because they generate kids, and we cannot afford to have any more kids in this town." Another chairman said, "We only want large expensive houses in this town. They're good ratables."

Sprawl does not create a balanced community, rather, sprawl discourages it. Jobs can be well integrated with housing. A balance between jobs and housing would allow a percentage of the population to walk or ride a bicycle to work, saving $5,000 in personal cost and $10,000 to $15,000 in public costs per year, but this is seldom considered. Imagine what $5,000 more each year to spend on the house or to save for that special need would mean to householders.

New Jersey's demographics are changing. Families are becoming smaller and less traditional. There are more single parents and dual income families whose work schedules make chauffeuring children to after-school activities and medical appointments a hardship. The sprawling suburb no longer responds to the needs of its population. Instead it makes the activities of daily life burdensome. Once attending a child's performance in a play or sporting event was a pleasurable part of life; now it requires a level of scheduling that characterizes a military campaign. How many parents can walk over to the playing fields when a child is playing on the soccer team or even come to watch the soccer game because they have no time? How many sons or daughters can walk to a job downtown?

Many individuals, corporations, and organizations think that the period of steady economic growth that began in the 1950s was an extremely prosperous one, the embodiment of the American dream, the consumer society. The standard of living, based on the number of cars, televisions, and the size of houses (number of rooms per person) did indeed increase dramatically for most people during that period of time. But it is clear the quality of public spaces--communities, neighborhoods, and streets--and the spiritual and social quality of life, showed no commensurate improvement. In fact, based on survey work we have done in New Jersey and in other municipalities across the country, the public

This image depicts a separation between residential and commercial uses making them accessible by car only. The positive feature of this image is the proximity to the school.

The modern, underutilized parking lot with 5% to 7% landscaping.

place has deteriorated physically, emotionally, and financially.

People are aware of the biography of the past fifty years, and concerned about the deterioration of the environment, the disastrous effects of traffic, and the high social costs that have come with rampant sprawl. People are becoming increasingly anti-development. Fear is fueled by an apprehension that future development will be as socially and environmentally destructive and negative as existing sprawl. They fear more of the same, and find that the same is unacceptable. What people want is an alternative that incorporates the features and financing of modern life with a greater sense of community, of place, of neighborhood: a place that is more affordable.

Unfortunately, this alternative is not available in most presently approved forms of development. Master plans must be amended to encourage it; zoning laws must be written and illustrated to allow it. Submission processes and application documents must be simple and comprehensive to allow rapid passage and assurances of quality small communities. We have realized the vision set forth in the 1930s and what was good then and through the 1980s seems not to be appropriate now. We require a new vision for future spatial evolution; an updated vision in which we will learn from our problems, the biography of our collective past, the potentials of technology and community, and design a more life-enhancing environment.

The basic small community design in model form created by ordinary people.

The results of Visual Preference Surveys [TM], and Hands-On Model Building workshops from all over the country indicate a clear mandate to re-think sprawl. A new planning model is emerging, a physical, social, and financial four-dimensional plan for the development and redevelopment of the future. It is time to design small communities built on valid contemporary human and ecological considerations, not on outdated social and economic policies. It is a form of development modeled after more traditional communities and neighborhoods, but updated for the twenty-first century.

*We are a product of our past, our present, and our vision of the future.*

The historic fabric which has survived the test of time, provides an excellent opportunity to understand positive visual and spacial relationships.

# ANALYZING THE PAST TO BETTER DESIGN THE FUTURE

CHAPTER
FOUR

## Introduction

The historic communities in New Jersey provide some excellent examples of small communities . This chapter analyzes several historic communities that have withstood the test of time and continue to thrive. The analysis of these places has contributed to a set of neo-traditional design principles that will be presented later in this handbook. I firmly believe that the existence of these design features, in these historic small communities, is in no small measure related to the continuing prosperity and popularity of these places. It must be remembered that these case studies are not an exhaustive listing of desirable hamlets or villages in New Jersey, nor is the list a random compilation. Rather, these case studies are to be regarded as good examples of communities that work, communities that have taught us valuable design lessons.

Cranbury, NJ., Main St., Residential.

As planners and designers, we face the challenge of creating and maintaining communities which are affordable, efficient, scaled to human proportions, and environmentally sound. When searching for design solutions within these constraints, it is important to consider and learn from the past, from its successes and its failures. The past can reveal suggestions and alternatives for the future. Most planners operate as if anything over 50 years old does not exist, as if it should not be consulted, let alone repeated. I, to the contrary, believe that we should realize that our past is usable, that it can provide concrete examples of the kinds of communities that provide the services and pleasures of civilization.

When we examine what has happened to our urban pattern in the last fifty years, we see a trend towards decentralization. However, this trend encompasses only a minuscule period in a larger history of urbanization, 50 out of 4,000 years. For the most part, the history of civilization revolves around two

Street facade, Frenchtown, NJ.

Main Plaza, Santa Fe, NM, is based on the earliest building code in the Americas, The Laws of the Indies - 1545.

realms, the urban and the rural. Although we as people and as a society have changed with time, it is evident that we are still drawn toward urban places; this is a worldwide attitude. We still have a need for community, for the amenities such places provide, and for places where many people meet, congregate, do business and play.

There are many elements of the past that are important to planning for the future--these include the history of development, and the measurement of existing historical places, structures, and archeological sites. Related to the history of development is the history of land use and zoning regulations which were put in place to guide development or to restrict it. Social, economic, and political forces should also be recognized as they contributed to development or to the regulation of development.

This chapter provides a methodology for analyzing the past in any community. Traditional settlement patterns common to the central New Jersey region are described. Several traditional hamlets and villages costitute our case studies.

The following case studies illustrate how traditional places have been able to adapt to modern demands without losing their sense of place or limiting the quality of life of their inhabitants. These are places that are not museums but have indeed adapted to modern technology and life styles.

## Traditional Settlement Patterns

The traditional small communities that exist today developed long before the current pattern of sprawl emerged. A vision for the future, one that has evolved through Visual Preference Surveys ™ and Hands-On Model Workshops administered throughout the nation, is based upon the physical and visual characteristics of the places that people feel offer the best alternative to current development patterns.

Before 1938, most of New Jersey's settlements were organized within a clear hierarchy of places. Cities, boroughs, hamlets, villages, towns, farmlands and open space were interrelated and connected by roads, railways, and streetcars. Each community type had specific social and economic functions. These places functioned as discrete communities, yet they were also part of a larger regional community anchored by a town or city.

Smaller settlements, generally hamlets, provided a focus such as a church, general store, specialty shop, or even just a crossroads drawing the community together. Villages provided for some of the daily needs of residents, and offered a small amount of employment. Towns offered a larger source of employment and provided for regional needs. The inhabitants of surrounding hamlets and villages came to town on a regular basis for shopping, professional services, and entertainment.

The neo-traditional pattern maintains the positive qualities of the traditional pattern, yet it responds to contemporary demands. The neo-traditional pattern requires that each small community have a core, a base of commercial space to satisfy some, if not the majority, of the commercial demands of its residents. It can satisfy many of the recreational and some of the job demands of residents. Each time residents have an opportunity to avail themselves of these amenities trips are reduced, traffic congestion is mitigated, and a greater sense of community occurs.

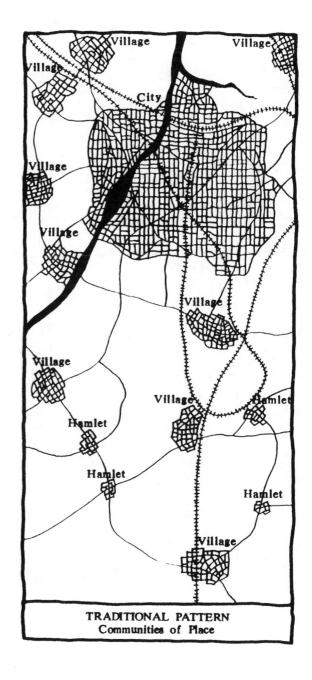

**TRADITIONAL PATTERN**
Communities of Place

# FOUR NEW JERSEY CASE STUDIES

**These places have survived 50 years of sprawl. They are cherished by the people who live in them.**

**They are everything a contemporary subdivision is not but should be.**

Hamlets, villages, and small towns make up the majority of New Jersey's traditional settlement patterns. By examining the common elements of these places, as well as the elements which make each place unique, we can understand the fundamental spatial qualities that must be incorporated to create small communities. Existing historical settlements also demonstrate how their evolution has accommodated changing times, technology, and life-style. The following case studies provide a look at historic settlements in New Jersey which have retained their character. Some have endured intense development pressures, incorporating growth into the village pattern. Others have been surrounded by faceless subdivisions, yet have protected their own sense of place. Some have adapted to changing demands, successfully integrating the automobile without losing the village character.

Each case study reveals the current state of the original settlement, including expansions which respect the original pattern. The study area consists of all areas within 1,500 feet, the most comfortable walking distance, of the edge of the community focus or core. Most of the settlements studied are completely contained within the study area. The four case studies are Califon, Cranbury, Oldwick, and Crosswicks. Each case study documents the basic plan showing residential and non-residential buildings, as well as the designation of the basic area of the community. They contain illustrated descriptions of the settlement patterns and histories. I have also included street sections which demonstrate the variation of street sections, including pavement widths, curbing, build-to and build-up lines, parking, and other street scape elements.

# Califon, Hunterton Co., NJ

### Location
Califon is located along the South Branch of the Raritan River in Hunterdon County, New Jersey. It is surrounded by steep wooded slopes and farmland. Several county roads access the village, and a county highway lies just beyond.

### Development History
Califon was settled as an agricultural community in the 18th century. As the village grew in the 1800s, the river was dammed and became a source of power for several mills. Califon became an export center for local agricultural products and small cottage industries. The arrival of the railroad in 1875 spurred the last major growth phase of the village proper. The core of the village has changed little since the turn of the century, with new growth restricted to outlying areas since World War II.

# Califon

## VITAL STATISTICS

| | |
|---|---|
| STUDY AREA: | 162 Acres |
| OPEN: | 77 Acres(48%) |
| DEVELOPED: | ± 85 Acres |
| DU: | 156 |
| GROSS DENSITY: | 1.0 DU/Acre over study area |
| NET DENSITY: | 4.2-8.7 DU/Acre |

## DESIGN CHARACTERISTICS

| | |
|---|---|
| LOT SIZE: | 5,000 - 10,500 Sq. Ft. |
| LOT WIDTH: | 30 - 70 Ft. |
| LOT DEPTH: | 90 - 225 Ft. |
| SETBACK: | 12 - 20 Ft. |
| SIDEYARD: | 5 - 20 Ft. |
| FOOTPRINT: | 800 - 1,500 Sq. Ft. |
| BLDG. HEIGHT: | 2 - 2 1/2 Stories |
| PARKING: | On-Street & Rear-Yard Garages |

VITAL STATISTICS ARE APPROXIMATIONS
DESIGN CHARACTERISTICS INDICATE TYPICAL CONDITIONS IN THE STUDY AREA
A SETBACK IS MEASURED FROM CURB OR EDGE OF ROADWAY

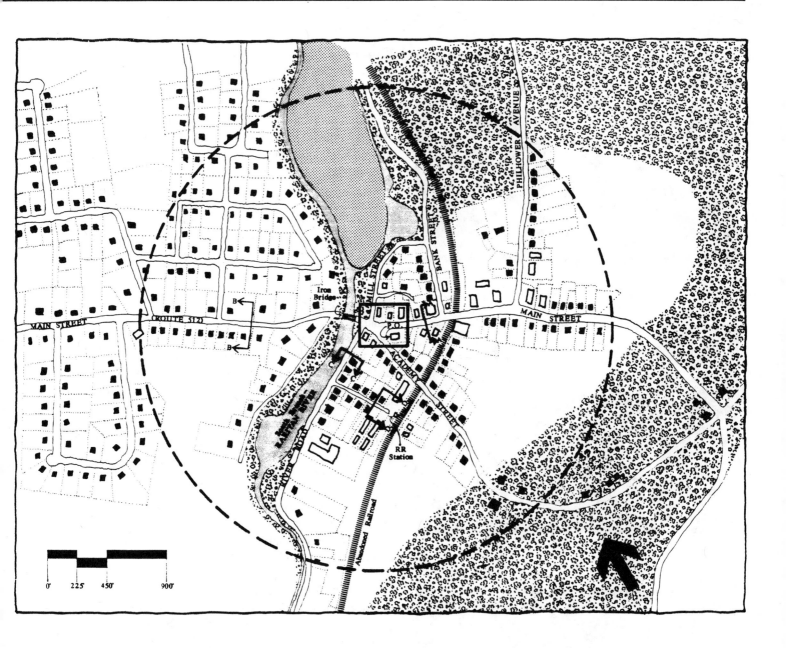

# LEGEND

RESIDENTIAL

COMMERCIAL/PUBLIC

MIXED USE CORE

WOODS/OPEN SPACE

STREET SECTIONS

## Community Character

The character of Califon has been shaped by the river. Although the village developed on both banks, the river forms a natural boundary to Califon's central area. An iron bridge creates both a sense of arrival and entry to the village's commercial area. Within this mixed-use core there are several retail establishments, some with offices or apartments above shops. The post office is also located within the core, at the junction of the two main roads. Services within the community are oriented toward the needs of the residents, reflecting the village's working nature. Califon is not a retail or tourist destination, and its character suits it as a residential community with identity.

## Design Elements

Califon is a compact community. Steep slopes define the location of buildings and the layout of roads throughout the village. The form of Califon's roadways may be its most distinctive design element. Streets in the village are generally curved, creating anticipation for what is around the bend. Visual termination is evident throughout the village, often created by means of these curving roads. Many other streets end at a perpendicular street where a larger building has been placed. Some streets terminate at the river, creating a park-like vista.

Because a wide range of lot widths are interspersed throughout the village, there is an interesting variation between building sizes. Architectural styles are also varied, but Colonial and Victorian predominate.

## Land Uses

Commercial uses include restaurants, a bookstore, lumber yard, tackle shop, clothing, antiques, general store, bank, and an legal office. There is an abandoned factory or warehouse at the railroad, as well as a functioning basket factory.

## Open Spaces

Much of the wooded, steep terrain surrounding Califon on two sides remains undeveloped, as do lands along the river. Because of the terrain, entering the village from the hills above can be a dramatic experience. Califon unfolds before you as you negotiate roads winding into the village. The South Branch of the Raritan River is a major element of Califon's character, creating internal open space. Large areas of undeveloped lands remain within the village; they cannot be developed because of steep slopes. These lots are not maintained as public parks. An abandoned railroad bed cuts through the center of the village and has great potential as an internal park. The old train station already houses the local historical society.

## Community Focus

The core of Califon is defined as the commercial area extending up from the river. The core contains a mix of uses, with apartments located above several shops, and interspersed residence-only structures.

## Walking Distances

The original village of Califon provides a clear example of the importance of walking distances. The village extends just 1,500 feet from the core in two directions, and extends just beyond this distance in a third. At the time Califon developed, it was not practical to live more than a few minutes walk from the village focus. Although subsequent, post World War II, development has extended beyond 1,500 feet from the core to the north of the village, it has not become a part of the village character. One reason may be that it was not within walking distance of the core, and it has become more closely associated with automobile-oriented strip centers outside the village.

## Typical street character with sections for a range of street types in Califon, New Jersey.

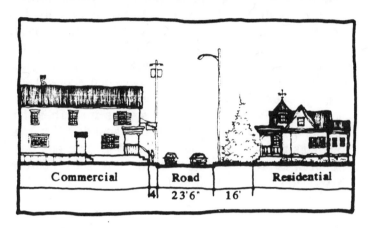

Section A - A',
Main Street
Moderate to low ADT

Section A - A'

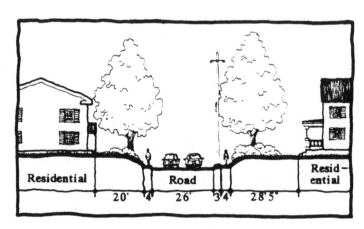

Section B - B',
Route 512
moderate ADT

Section B - B'

Section C - C,
River Road

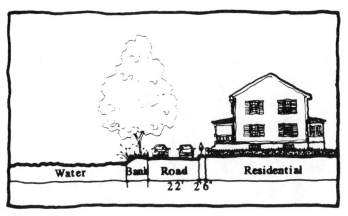

Section C - C

Section D - D',
Center Street.
Low ADT

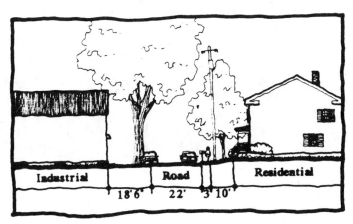

Section D - D'

# Case Study Two
# Cranbury, Middlesex Co., NJ

**Main Street**

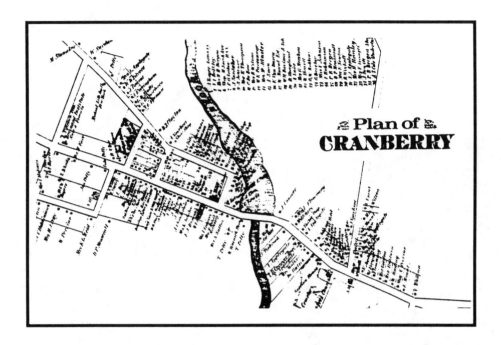

# Cranbury

### Location

Cranbury is located in Middlesex County, New Jersey. It is situated within a predominantly agricultural area which includes some low-density exurban development. The surrounding topography is generally flat to gently rolling hills. The village developed next to a brook, which provided power for a mill, and at the junction of major transportation routes, the primary Philadelphia-New York stage coach route and the Amboy-Trenton route. Several main county and state roads continue to pass through or near Cranbury village, including Highway 130 and the New Jersey Turnpike.

# Cranbury

## VITAL STATISTICS

| | |
|---|---|
| STUDY AREA: | 230 Acres |
| OPEN: | 110 Acres(48%) |
| DEVELOPED: | 120 Acres |
| DU: | 265 |
| GROSS DENSITY: | 1.2 DU/Acres |
| NET DENSITY: | 1.7-11.6 DU/Acre |

## DESIGN CHARACTERISTICS

| | |
|---|---|
| LOT SIZE: | 4,500 - 16,000 Sq. Ft. |
| LOT WIDTH: | 30 - 100 Ft. |
| LOT DEPTH: | 125 - 250 Ft. |
| SETBACK: | 12 - 25 Ft. |
| SIDEYARD: | 0 - 15 Ft. |
| FOOTPRINT: | 800 - 1,500 Sq. Ft. |
| BLDG. HEIGHT: | 2 - 3 Stories |
| PARKING: | On-Street & Rearyard Garages/Lots |

VITAL STATISTICS ARE APPROXIMATIONS
DESIGN CHARACTERISTICS INDICATE TYPICAL CONDITIONS IN STUDY AREA
SETBACK IS MEASURED FROM CURB OR EDGE OF ROADWAY

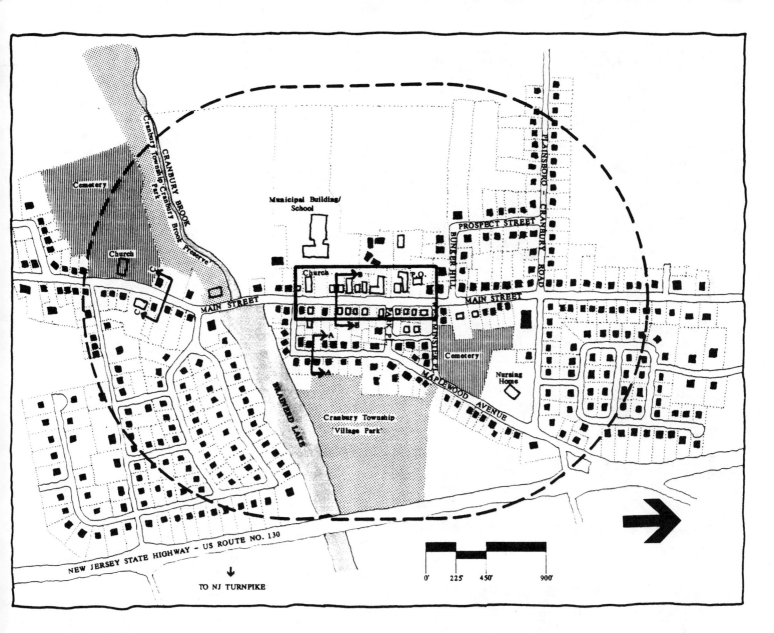

LEGEND

| | |
|---|---|
| RESIDENTIAL | |
| COMMERCIAL/PUBLIC | |
| MIXED USE CORE | |
| STUDY AREA | 1500 FT. from the core |
| STREET SECTION | |

## Development History

The village of Cranbury was originally settled, in the 17th century, at the junction of the Philadelphia-New York transportation route (now Main Street) and Cranbury Brook. This original settlement was located south of the brook and remained very small. It consisted of a mill and a cooper's shop. By 1800, Cranbury had grown to about 25 houses, and included a church, tavern, and post house to service residents. As travel between New York and Philadelphia grew in frequency, inns and taverns became an important element of Cranbury's development. In the mid-1800s commercial growth pushed the village to the north of the brook, which is where the commercial area of the village remains. A way-station for travelers, Cranbury became the business center of a predominantly agricultural area, with trade in agricultural commodities as well as industries such as milling, tanning, and apple-distilling.

The village has experienced little new internal development, but two residential areas have expanded adjacent to the village since World War II. These neighborhoods have been successfully woven into the community fabric, although their character is distinct from that of the village proper.

## Community Character

Cranbury's identity is based upon Main Street, which is the linear spine of the community. Main Street is the center of community, social, and commercial life in the village. The automobile is ever present on Main Street, but it is well integrated. Cranbury presents a varied character which consists of a mixed-use community focus (Main Street) and a range of residential lot and building sizes.

## Community Focus

Main Street serves as a mixed-use area with a seamless commercial frontage of about 900 linear feet. Housing is located above many of the ground level retail shops, with offices above others. Brainerd Lake and Cranbury Brook lie just south of the mixed use area.

## Walking Distance

Most of the village is within 1,500 feet of the edge of the community focus. However, development along Main Street has extended beyond this distance in either direction. Portions of the original development south of the Brook extend beyond 1,500 feet of the core, but development beyond 2,500 feet tends to bear no relation to the village. There is an extensive sidewalk network that connects most residential units to the core and community facilities.

## Open Spaces

Cranbury has both internal and peripheral open spaces. A village park, adjacent to the Lake, the Brook, and the school site provides internal public space. There are two sizable cemeteries within the village. Much of the land around the village continues to be used for agriculture.  Cranbury remains a distinct community defined by open space.

## Land Uses

Cranbury is a residential village; the predominant land use is residential. Community uses (school, municipal building, and museum) are located in the center of the village behind a mixed-use area. They are accessed from Main Street. The post office is located on Main Street, along with most churches and commercial facilities. A commercial green house is the sole manufacturing industrial use within the village proper.

**Typical street character with sections for a range of street types in Cranbury, New Jersey.**

Section A - A',
Maple Avenue
Low ADT

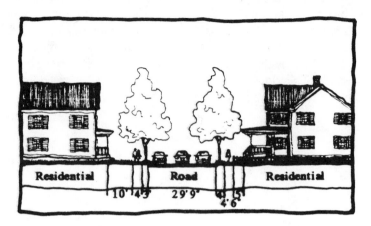

Section A - A'

Section B - B',
Main Street
Moderate to High ADT with low speed.

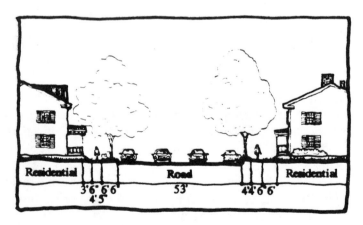

Section B - B'

Section C - C,
South Main Street

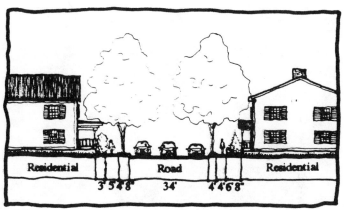

Section C - C

Section D - D',
Park Place .
Low ADT

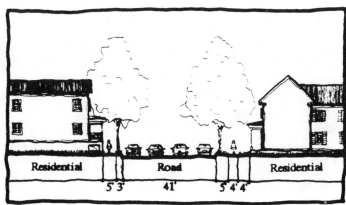

Section D - D'

## CASE STUDY THREE
# Crosswicks, Burlington Co., NJ

# Crosswicks

### Location
Crosswicks is located in Chesterfield Township in Burlington County, New Jersey within a rural agricultural area. Several county regional roads intersect at the village. It is located close to the New Jersey Turnpike and State Highway 130, although access is not direct.

### Development History
Crosswicks was the site of a Lenni-Lenape Indian settlement called "Crossweeksung." In 1677 a group of Quakers settled along the creek near the Lenni-Lenape settlement. The Quakers built their first meeting house in Crosswicks in 1692. The village developed along the Assinpink Trail both where it crossed the creek and on the hill above the creek where the present village is located. Much of the initial development in Crosswicks occurred in the early 1700s with the Friends Meeting House, whose present structure was built in 1773, acting as the focal point of the community. The village became a way station containing an inn and tavern along the Trail. The original structures along the curving Main Street were built prior to 1750. A brick schoolhouse was erected next to the Meeting House in 1784. The primary commerce in Crosswicks was agricultural trade, and in the mid 19th century it contained wheelwrights, blacksmiths, and saw and flour mills (located below the village along the creek).

# Crosswicks

## VITAL STATISTICS

| STUDY AREA: | 160 Acres |
| --- | --- |
| OPEN: | 105 Acres(65%) |
| DEVELOPED: | 55 Acres |
| DU: | 110 |
| GROSS DENSITY: | 0.7 DU/Acre |
| NET DENSITY: | 2.9 TO 14.5 DU/Acre |

## DESIGN CHARACTERISTICS

| LOT SIZE: | 3,000 - 15,000 Sq. Ft. |
| --- | --- |
| LOT WIDTH: | 30 - 80 Ft. |
| LOT DEPTH: | 75 - 235 Ft. |
| SETBACK: | 8 - 40 Ft. |
| SIDEYARD: | 5 - 15 Ft. |
| FOOTPRINT: | 600 - 1,750 Sq. Ft. |
| BLDG. HEIGHT: | 2 - 2 1/2 Stories |
| PARKING: | On-Street & Rearyard Garages |

VITAL STATISTICS ARE APPROXIMATIONS
DESIGN CHARACTERISTICS INDICATE TYPICAL CONDITIONS IN STUDY AREA
SETBACK IS MEASURED FROM CURB OR EDGE OF ROADWAY

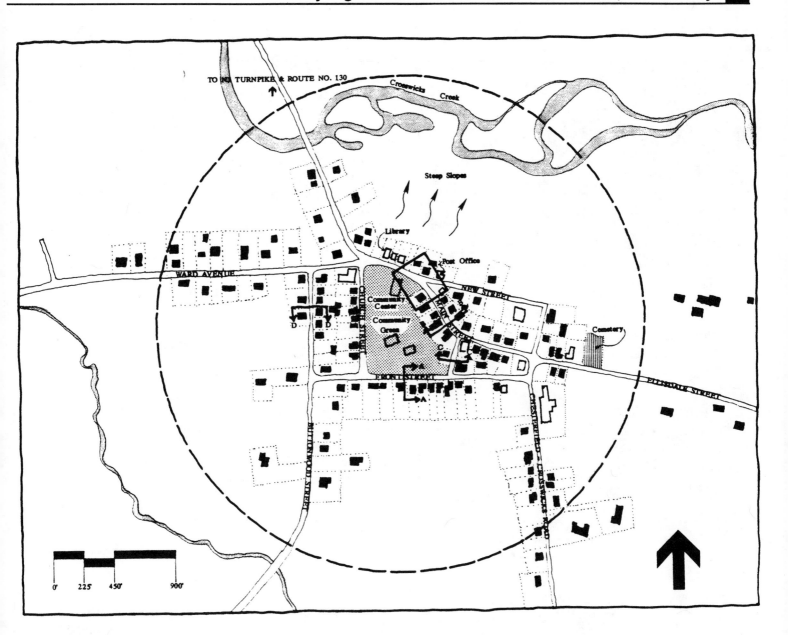

## LEGEND

| | |
|---|---|
| RESIDENTIAL | |
| COMMERCIAL/PUBLIC | |
| MIXED USE | |
| STUDY AREA (1,500' FROM THE CORE) | |
| INTERNAL OPEN SPACE | |
| ILLUSTRATIVE STREET SECTIONS | |

## Community Character

Crosswicks provides a sense of urbanity within a predominantly rural setting. Physically it is a very tight community. Streets are well defined by closely spaced houses set close to the street. A community green defines the center of the village; it is bounded by homes and community facilities such as the library and community center. The green also brings another dimension to this community, suggesting that it is tight-knit socially as well as physically. The neighborhood-like feel of the community is strong, with the community park serving as the focus.

## Design Elements

The social character of Crosswicks is evident in the architecture of the village. The importance of social interaction in the community is seen in the relationship of homes to the street. Many houses, particularly along Main street, are built within four feet of the sidewalk. Porches extend toward the public domain on houses with larger setbacks. A notable design element is the closely spaced row of single family houses along the bend in Main street. The placement of these structures defines the street at a critical location.

## Land Uses

Crosswicks is primarily residential, yet there are a small number of retail and a variety of community uses. The public library (located in the old firehouse), post office, and community center are located at the northern edge of the community green. Along Main Street there are two antique shops, a general store, and a restaurant with apartments on the second floor. There are also two day-care centers within the village, each located within residential areas at the village periphery.

## Community Focus

Crosswick's community center is not commercial in nature. Rather, it is composed mainly of community services and facilities. The community green provides the physical and social focus of the community. Retail and community facilities are located on the northern edge of the green along Main street. Within this 6.5 acre community park stands the historic Friends Meeting House.

## Walking Distances

The entire village of Crosswicks is within 1,500 feet of the community focus. Most of the village is, in fact, within 500 feet of the edge of the community park.

## Open Spaces

The land surrounding Crosswicks has for the most part remained undeveloped beyond agricultural uses. The most notable peripheral open space lies between the village and Crosswicks Creek to the north. This area is characterized by a steep slope, and the lack of development provides scenic vistas from the village. The community park is the major internal open space, and contains a playground and sports courts for active recreation. A cemetery is located adjacent to the eastern edge of the village.

## Typical street character with sections for a range of street types in Crosswick, New Jersey.

Section A - A',
Front Street
Low ADT

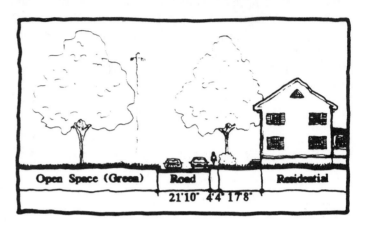

Section A - A'

Section B - B',
"Main Street"
Moderate to High ADT with low speed for this character of street.

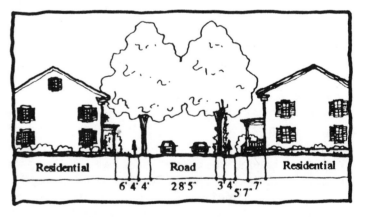

Section B - B'

Section C - C
Small Street connecting Front Street and the Main Street.

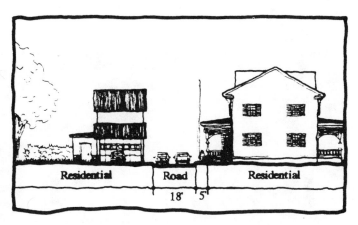

Section C - C

Section D - D',
Button Wood Street

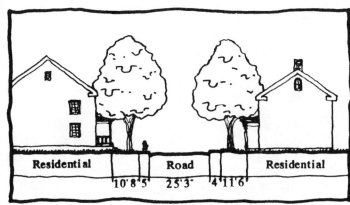

Section D - D'

# CASE STUDY FOUR
# Oldwick, Hunterton Co., NJ

# Oldwick

### Location
Oldwick is located in a relatively rural area of Tewksbury Township, Hunterdon County, NJ. The village is bisected by a fairly heavily traveled county road (Route 723) which provides access from nearby Interstate 78. The topography of the surrounding region is characterized by rolling to steep hills.

### Development History
Oldwick was first settled as New Germantown early in the 18th century, and town meeting records date back to 1735. Like many small settlements of the time, Oldwick prospered as a center for agricultural commerce. Most of the village's development occurred in the early 1800s. By the 1880s, Oldwick boasted 55 dwellings, two churches, an academy, four stores, and numerous services such as cobblers, tailors, blacksmiths, saddlers, a tannery and a cooper. The village itself has seen very little development in the 20th century, and its development pattern closely resembles that of the late 19th century.

# Oldwick

## VITAL STATISTICS

| | |
|---|---|
| STUDY AREA: | 230 Acres |
| OPEN: | 175 Acres(76%) |
| DEVELOPED: | 55 Acres |
| DU: | 60 |
| GROSS DENSITY: | 0.3 DU/Acre |
| NET DENSITY: | 2.9 TO 8.7 DU/Acre |

## DESIGN CHARACTERISTICS

| | |
|---|---|
| LOT SIZE: | 5,000 - 15,000 Sq. Ft. |
| LOT WIDTH: | 40 - 80 Ft. |
| LOT DEPTH: | 135 - 200 Ft. |
| SETBACK: | 6 - 24 Ft. |
| SIDEYARD: | 5 - 20 Ft. |
| FOOTPRINT: | 600 - 1,200 Sq. Ft. |
| BLDG. HEIGHT: | 2 1/2 - 3 Stories |
| PARKING: | On Street & Rear yard Garages/Lots |

VITAL STATISTICS ARE APPROXIMATIONS

DESIGN CHARACTERISTICS INDICATE TYPICAL CONDITIONS IN STUDY AREA

SETBACK IS MEASURED FROM CURB OR EDGE OF ROADWAY

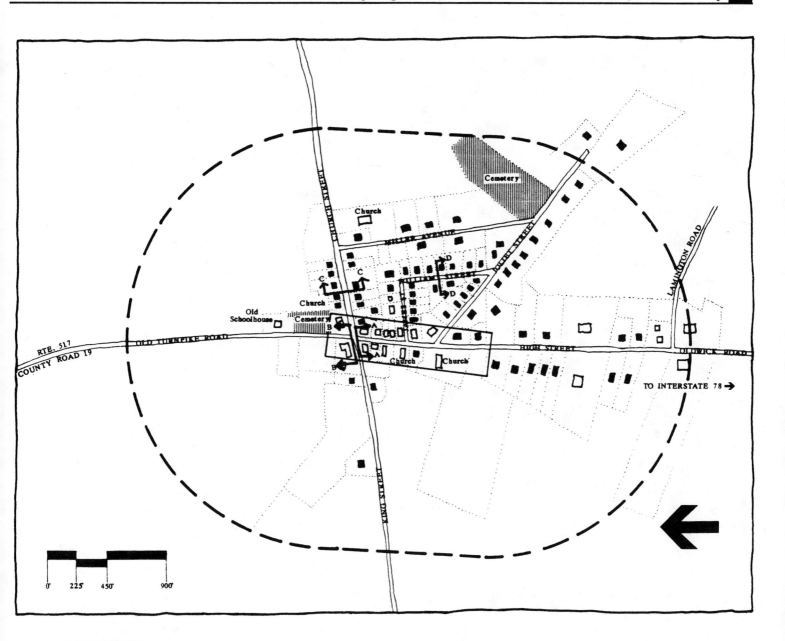

**LEGEND**

RESIDENTIAL

COMMERCIAL/PUBLIC

MIXED USE CORE

STUDY AREA - 1,500 ft. FROM THE CORE

ILLUSTRATIVE STREET SECTION

## Community Character

Oldwick is a mixed use village. This character of the village is largely defined by the area along High Street, the main thoroughfare in the village which leads to Interstate 78 and to other communities in the Township. The commercial activity along High Street gives Oldwick a rich vitality for a relatively small village. The residential areas of the village, outside the central core, are almost rural in character.

## Design Elements

The most notable design element in Oldwick is the placement of buildings in relation to the street. Throughout the residential areas of the village, buildings are set back 15 to 20 feet from the road edge. Although houses in some areas are spaced quite far apart, the placement of buildings close to the street maintains a pleasant streetscape. At the center of the village, buildings are not only placed closer to the street, about six feet from the curb, but they are much more closely spaced. Lot sizes, and thus the space between structures, increases with distance from the center of Oldwick. Lots at the periphery of the village are quite large, and the community blends with the surrounding agricultural land.

## Community Focus

The center of community life in Oldwick lies along High Street, particularly at its intersection with Church Street. Most commercial activity in the village is focused at, or near, this crossroads. A church, general store/deli, restaurant (former inn), several stores, and professional services are located within the community focus. Oldwick continues to serve as the center of activity for the surrounding area much as it did when the village was a center of agricultural commerce in the past. The population of the village alone cannot support the level of economic activity in Oldwick, but it functions as a center for the region.

## Walking Distances

All residents of the village of Oldwick are well within 1,500 feet of the community focus. A network of sidewalks parallels the main roads, those with higher ADTs. The buildings along these roads are located close to each other with narrow front yards. As roads decrease in ADT the buildings are spaced farther apart, the sidewalks disappear, and people walk on the road surface.

## Open Spaces

Oldwick's boundaries are well defined by peripheral open space. Most of the surrounding land is used for agricultural purposes or contains residences in former farmhouses on very large lots. There are two cemeteries in the village, one of which is located within the community focus. This cemetery, in conjunction with the yard of the former schoolhouse, creates internal open space. The other cemetery is located at the edge of the village, and functions as peripheral open space.

## Typical street character with sections for a range of street types in Oldwick, New Jersey.

Section A - A',
Old Turnpike Road at Church Street, the Main Street of Oldwick.
Very high peak hour traffic, speed limit is too high.

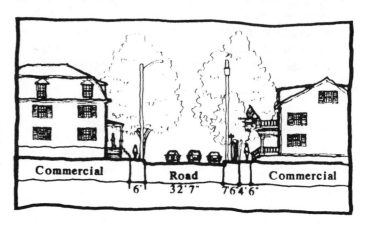

Section A - A'

Section B - B',
Old Turnpike Road at Church Street.

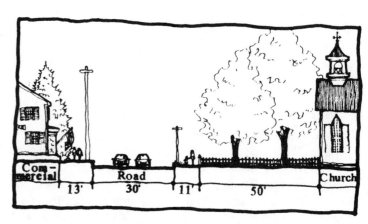

Section B - B'

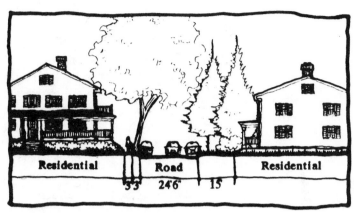

Section C - C
Church Street, moderate to low ADT

Section C - C

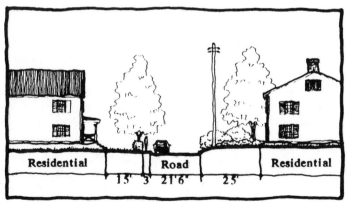

Section D - D',
Willcom Street.
Very low ADT
Residents can safely walk on the edge of the road.

Section D - D'

# S U M M A R Y

These case studies illustrate the design elements of several historic settlements that are both functional and economically viable today. They are important because they demonstrate that traditional design can be adapted to accommodate the changing needs of the community, while also pointing out which elements are important to the experience of place. The traditional elements which may have been used for very different reasons in the past are what make these villages successful, thriving small communities. It is my belief that by understanding and studying these visual and spatial characteristics, we understand those principles that are fundamental and must be incorporated in order to achieve the human scale and sense of place at all levels of small community. Once we understand these, it is possible to apply them to new, and larger places. If one does not understand planning and nurturing the social fabric at this basic level it will never be understood on a large scale, the neighborhood in a town or the urban village.

For the most part, the characteristics of the previous case studies match the elements of the small communities definition found in the Introduction. These communities are compact. They have streets which often accommodate curbside parking, yet are not over designed. Community facilities are often a part of the community focus, and open spaces are found both internally and externally. They all display a variety of building and lot sizes and contain a core that accommodates a mix of uses. All of these design features contribute to and underscore the individual sense of community.

Despite the many factors encouraging urban sprawl, a few communities have managed to escape these pernicious forces. In turning to them we are reminded not only of what life was like before the sprawl, but we can discover those elements that make it possible and desirable to revise our current practices. When we do so, we discover design elements and attributes that markedly contribute to the quality of life in these highly desirable and much admired communities. In them, inhabitants have staunchly fought against contemporary ideas of progress in order to preserve the community as the inhabitants want it to be, and as they see it. I believe that this dedication to historic development patterns should be an inspiration to all planners. We must carefully consider the design principles so prevalent in these communities and learn to apply them, learn to use them to restructure our thinking about design, planning, and zoning. I believe that these general design principles must be incorporated into our current and future design and planning processes if our labors are to succeed in creating and building truly livable communities. In doing so, I do not assume that we duplicate these places, but rather that we learn from the patterns and principles inherent in their forms and patterns. Planners can do a better job of designing new or retrofit places than current practice suggests.

These traditional villages are very important to future generations to see and experience. It is critical that those places be protected to preserve the streetscape and building fabric. Roads should not be widened, the building vernacular must be respected.

I have used many of these traditional places, which have received positive evaluations in the VPS^TM, to illustrate many principles of good design and balanced planning. Many lay planners are concerned that these are old places and therefore cannot be recreated. I agree that the patina cannot be recreated, but certainly these places contain specific scales, proportions, densities, street scape standards, and design vocabularies which can be used and interpreted in new materials and building techniques. They contain a balance of residential to non-residential and uses which should be required in all communities.

New small communities designed with these inherent principles can be charming, interesting, affordable, and sustainable in their early stages and will mature to achieve greater value, worth, and status.

## SUMMARY CHART OF DESIGN FEATURES
APPROXIMATIONS BASED ON AVAILABLE DATA AND FIELD INSPECTION

|  | Califon | Cranbury | Crosswicks | Oldwick |
|---|---|---|---|---|
| Study Area | 162 acres | 230 acres | 160 acres | 230 acres |
| Open space | 77 acres (48%) | 110 acres (48%) | 105 acres(65%) | 175 acres (76%) |
| Developed | 85 acres | 120 acres | 55 acres | 55 acres |
| Dwelling units | 156 | 265 | 110 | 60 |
| Gross density | 1.0 du/acre | 1.2 du/acre | 0.7 du/acre | 0.3 du/acre |
| Net Density | 4.2-8.7 du/acre | 1.7-11.6 du/acre | 2.9 - 14.5 du/acre | 2.9 to 8.7 du/acre |
| Lot size | 5,000-10,500 sq ft. | 4,500-16,00 sq ft. | 3000-15,000 sq ft. | 5000-15,000 sq ft. |
| Width | 30-70 ft. | 30-100 ft. | 30-80 ft. | 40-80 ft. |
| Depth | 90-225 ft. | 125-250 ft. | 75-235 ft. | 135-200 ft. |
| Setback | 12-20 ft. | 12-25 ft. | 8-40 ft. | 6-24 ft. |
| Sideyard | 5-20 ft. | 0-15 ft. | 5-15 ft. | 5-20 ft. |
| Footprint | 800-1500 sq ft. | 800-1500 sq ft. | 6000-1750 sq ft. | 600-1200 sq ft. |
| Building Height (stories) | 2-2 1/2 | 2-3 | 2-2 1/2 | 2 1/2-3 |
| Parking | on-street rear yard | on-street rear yard | on-street rear yard | on-street rear yard |
| Pavement Width | 22' - 26' | 29' - 53' | 18' - 25' | 21' - 32' |

# PROCESS STEP III
## CREATING A COMMON VISION

*It is impossible to think without a mental picture.* Aristotle

*Where there is no vision, the people shall perish.* Proverbs

Workshop participants starting to design a small community in a Hands-On Model Workshop.

# CREATING A COMMON VISION
## -- DESIGN BY DEMOCRACY

CHAPTER
FIVE

## Introduction

**Creating a Common Vision** explains how to use community participation in the planning process. The neo-traditional planning and design process will not bear fruit if we cannot bring people--municipal officials and developers, engineers and planners, the community at large and the body politic--together to effect real choice. This section details how using the results of this process to develop plans and standards will result in small communities being planned, designed and built.

The community's understanding of its value can be generated through a Visual Preference Survey ™ and Hands-On Models model building workshops. If planners are to create the types of places in which people really want to live, then the concerns and desires of the inhabitants must be taken into consideration, for they, the residents, are the ultimate users.  Participation not only helps the planning process work more smoothly, it is the only insurance a community has that its preferences will be considered. The results of Visual Preference Surveys ™ have had a tremendous impact on planning and design in many of the communities that have used it.

 The VPS ™ is a way of evaluating a range of images and places with various intensities, uses and designs. Positive evaluation indicates that potentials exist in communities for these types and design of buildings, parks, or spaces. The conceptual three-dimensional site plans that result from Hands-On Model Workshops demonstrate three- and four-dimensional site planning alternatives that are acceptable to the community. If we could plan, zone, and design for the characteristics most people want, the resulting built places would contain these positive characteristics.  A critical observation after tens of thousands have participated in the Visual Preference Survey ™ and the Hands-On Model

Filling out a Visual Preference Survey ™ (VPS) form is easy and stimulating.

exercise is that there is an intuitive and fundamental insight which directs people to desire a small community. Consequently it is from their surveys and models that the design principles have emerged.

## Master Planning with a Vision

The master plan is the primary tool used by municipalities to define goals and objectives, and land-use and circulation patterns of a community. The master plan is the foundation of zoning and development policies. Zoning contains most of the rules and regulations that determine the three- and four-dimensional forms. Most master plans, however, take no cognizance of the residents' image of their town. They use words or phrases that may have multiple interpretations depending upon the experience or understanding of the readers.

In order for the master plan to be effective, it must represent a clear vision of the future appearance and character of the town. It should be a specific statement and not just generalized goals such as those in the Municipal Land Use Legislation, for example to protect health, safety and welfare; these are implicit. The master plan must provide a vision; it must include specific statements and images of both those places and landscapes identified as positive and desirable and those identified as negative and unacceptable. The vision is best formed through community consensus. The goal of formulating community consensus is to determine, with respect to the master plan, the goals, physical character, appropriate intensity, street types, and design vocabulary desired by the residents for the future of their community. Once determined, the vision of the community must be coded. The community vision must become a part of planning documentation.

Most planners now practicing have little or no design training. They cannot think three- or four-dimensionally. They can not visualize, in their mind's eye, how their two-dimensional zoning ordinances will translate into a three- and four-dimensional environment. We know, of course, that most zoning ordinances are cut and paste jobs, and are seldom pre-tested before they are published. In contrast, the results of the VPS ™, tailor-made by each community, illustrate what should be avoided or encouraged in order to provide for the desired design and details.

This image received a negative rating in the Manhiem, PA, VPS ™. The negative rating results primarily from the overly wide asphalt roadway.

This image received a positive rating in the Manheim, PA, VPS ™.

The vision plan recognizes that much of the image of a community results from the land development controls which the municipality has enforced. Therefore, the ultimate goal of the vision plan is to define how these controls should be restructured in order to reflect the preferences and expectations of the community.

## The Visual Preference Survey ™

The Visual Preference Survey (VPS) is a research and visioning technique consisting of photographic images, evaluation forms, optional questionnaires, and evaluation/ analysis techniques to understand and present the results. The purpose of the VPS is to articulate the residents' impression of the present community image and to build consensus for its future character. The conclusion of the process is called a Vision Plan.

Vision planning involves the participation of community residents, who are asked to numerically rate images of their town and other places as either acceptable or unacceptable. This common vision (consensus on positive and negative images) enables the planning process to work more efficiently. It provides agreement concerning the present visual, physical character of the community and the desired design of future development. Potential developers can use the results to understand what the community wants and will accept. With the vision plan in hand, planners also have a logical basis, an immediately comprehensible, illustrated reference document, for the development and design-review processes.

A Community Visual Preference Survey expands database generation. It can have two sections: (1) a Visual Preference Survey and (2) a community based questionnaire. The Visual Preference Survey is the most important component because participants rank images of places, spaces, and land uses. An optional questionnaire offers participants a forum for providing demographic and marketing information as well as written comments, ideas, opinions, and suggestions regarding past development, the quality of existing zoning, and preferred future directions.

## The Visual Preference Survey ™ Techniques

Images that illustrate the visual and spatial qualities and the functional characteristics of the community's existing zoning should be selected for the survey. Images must reflect

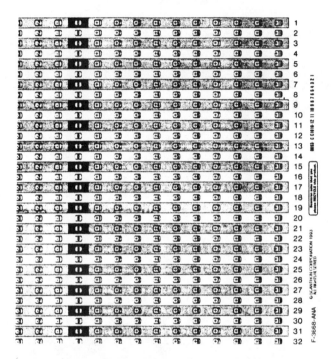

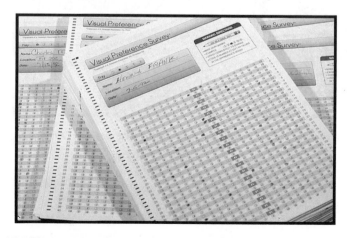

VPS ™ information can be processed quickly because of special scanned answering sheets. Unlimited numbers of people can particapate. Everyone's vision is important.

This shopping district in Chatam, NJ, consistently receives negative ratings.

This image of the core of Madison, NJ, consistently receives positive ratings.

what people see when they move through the study area, along streets, sidewalks, and public spaces, all of the integral components of the public viewshed. They should illustrate such aspects as building form, density, a sense of enclosure, setback, scale, massing, spatial definition, architectural style, colors, textures, materials, landscaping, road types, streetscape elements, types of land use, level of human activity, and development density that occur both in the study area or elsewhere in the region. Images that suggest alternative approaches to land use and design solutions other than those which occur in the study area should also be included for the community response; if they test positive they have applicability. Specific analysis of these images can extract such specific positive and negative design and planning features as:

- style and massing of the buildings
- walls and materials
- eaves and canopies
- net density
- setbacks
- streetscape elements
- colors
- windows
- roof pitches
- doors and entrances
- composition and grain of adjacent buildings.
- signing
- decorative elements
- landscaping
- treatment of parking

These elements can be translated by architects into specific building designs that are new but reflect the character of the vision.

The VPS ™ survey does not, however, consist entirely of images that strongly contrast. Images which appear closely related can reveal the slight variations that distinguish a positive image from a negative one. The purpose is to review a sufficient number of images so that a common preference and consensus vision begin to emerge. The common vision offers huge benefits by revealing the desired community image in the positive images, and what should be avoided in the negative images. This should be the fundamental reason for a master plan. In too many master plans the desired municipal fiscal benefits outweigh the physical, visual, psychological, and ecological considerations. The visual is particularly difficult to deal with. The Visual Preference Survey ™ can provide a balance. Results have confirmed that those spaces and places which are evaluated as positive also generate high economic value.

Respondents are asked to rate images from +10 to -10. They are asked to give a positive rating to those images they would want to see in their town and negative ratings to those they do not. The degree to which an image is positive or negative is reflected in the value (ie. +3 versus +9 or -2 versus -8). It also speaks to the question: Is this image appropriate for my township? Images that people do not feel strongly about are rated as zero. Respondents understand that the results of each image will be mathematically reviewed. Results are tabulated, analyzed and reported back to the participants. Finally, the images that best represent the community's vision are incorporated into the master plan. Prior to the survey it is made clear to the participants that the results will be used to shape future regulations.

This image of new multi-family housing received very high VPS ™ ratings.

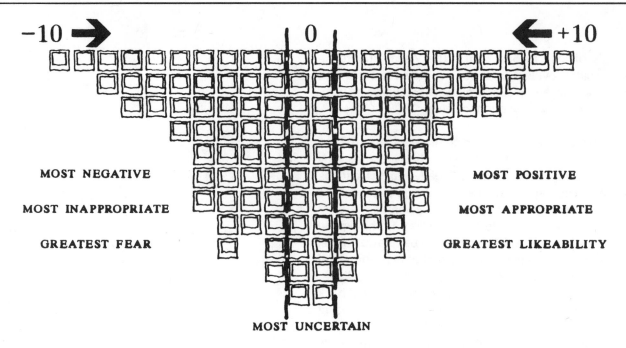

$-10 \rightarrow$　　　0　　　$\leftarrow +10$

MOST NEGATIVE

MOST INAPPROPRIATE

GREATEST FEAR

MOST POSITIVE

MOST APPROPRIATE

GREATEST LIKEABILITY

MOST UNCERTAIN

Once the VPS ™ results are generated, the calculated image value is recorded on each slide. The slides are then arranged on a light table from the most negative to the most positive; from the most unacceptable to the most acceptable. There will be one image with the most positive score and one image with the most negative rating. These two images represent the most desirable/acceptability and the most undesirable/feared image.

The specific characteristics of these images must be analyzed. Many or most of the positive and negative features will be seen in the adjacent positive or negative images. These images must be reviewed for general and specific planning and design content. It is also critical to understand if the characteristics contained in the negative image are generated by the existing zoning and development regulations. By analyzing each image in this form, the appropriate design and planning response to the negative images can be found in the positive rated images.

The most difficult to interpret and of greatest political implication are the images in the center, 0, or neutral category, neither positive, or negative. These images require the most sensitive review of the range of scores. The standards deviations must be carefully reviewed for these images if they are to be of great use.

## Community Surveys

The second, optional, portion of the survey requires responses to specific questions. These questions are used to obtain various demographic and market data about the respondents, as well as to target specific policy questions, concerning the community. The last pages of this portion of the survey are write-in responses. We evaluate the responses, then compile a Book of Public Comments from them. Maps of the area can also be included which ask people to notate traffic problems, pedestrian flow patterns and other problem areas. All of their results and comments can be correlated with the results of the image ratings.

Results of the VPS ™ and the survey, if used, should be presented to the community. The response sheets can also be returned to individuals in order to help them understand their values relative to average scores. There must also be an opportunity for community discussion. Such discussion helps to clarify the strong opinions and leads to an understanding of strategic decisions that may have to be implemented. Discussion also strengthens the community's vision and helps generate consensus and commitment. Once the community has reviewed the recommended images and conclusions, the vision can be translated into the master plan and later into the development regulations.

The master plan provides a guide and framework to direct the actions of the Municipal Council, Planning Board, Board of Adjustment, and other agencies. It defines policies and the police power of zoning. It recommends priorities and changes in zoning ordinances, capital improvements, and redevelopment and preservation programs. Therefore, it must be a collective image of the citizens' concerns. In order to be representative, it must contain the results of the Visual Preference Survey ™. These results should be converted into reproducible photographs and be included in the goals and objectives, land use, circulation plan and all other optional plans within the Master Plan. These images will explicitly illustrate what the language of the master plan stipulates. Hence, all of the specifications will be readily comprehensible to professionals and laymen alike.

In most municipalities which have completed the vision planning process, the current zoning and land development policies must be revised where images from within the municipality received negative ratings and where positive

58. ON A BIG SHOPPING TRIP, HOW FAR DO YOU WALK?
(CONSIDER THE DISTANCE TO AND FROM YOUR MODE OF TRANSPO
OR, IF YOU WALK FROM HOME, THE FULL DISTANCE FROM AND
YOUR HOME. THE AVERAGE PERSON CAN WALK 250 FEET PER MIN

| | | | |
|---|---|---|---|
| A. Less than 250 feet | 8% | B. 250 - 500 feet | 12% |
| C. 501 - 750 feet | 21% | D. 751 - 1,000 feet | 8% |
| E. 1,001 to 1,500 feet | 12% | F. 1,501 - 2,000 feet | 10% |
| G. 2,001 2,500 feet | 8% | H. 2,501 - 3,000 feet | 4% |
| I. 3,001 to 3,500 feet | 4% | J. Over 3,500 feet | 17% |

59. WHAT IS THE MAXIMUM WALKING DISTANCE YOU WILL TOLERATE I
WHERE YOU PARK YOUR CAR AND YOUR SHOPPING DESTINATION

| | | | |
|---|---|---|---|
| A. Less than 250 feet | 5% | B. 250 - 500 feet | 15% |
| C. 501 - 750 feet | 24% | D. 751 - 1,000 feet | 15% |
| E. 1,001 to 1,500 feet | 13% | F. 1,501 - 2,000 feet | 12% |
| G. 2,001 to 2,500 feet | 5% | H. 2,501 - 3,000 feet | 4% |
| I. 3,001 to 3,500 feet | 0% | J. Over 3,500 feet | 8% |

60. HOW LONG DOES IT TAKE YOU TO FIND A PARKING SPACE WHEN Y
TO SHOP OR USE SERVICES IN HIGHLAND PARK?

| | | | |
|---|---|---|---|
| A. Less than one minute | 33% | B. One to two minutes | 21% |
| C. Two to three minutes | 25% | D. Three to four minutes | 4% |
| E. Four to five minutes | 11% | F. Five to six minutes | 4% |
| H. Six to eight minutes | 5% | I. Eight to ten minutes | 4% |
| J. Over ten minutes | 0% | | |

61. SHOULD THE CONSTRUCTION OF NEW HOUSING BE ENCOURAGE
BOROUGH?

| | |
|---|---|
| A. Yes | 29% |
| B. No | 71% |

For questions 62 to 64, consider Highland's Park Central Business District as Ran
between Adelaide and 6th Avenue.

62. SHOULD THE CONSTRUCTION OF ADDITIONAL TOWNHOUSES OR APA
IN THE CENTRAL BUSINESS DISTRICT BE ENCOURAGED?

| | |
|---|---|
| A. Yes | 16% |
| B. No | 84% |

63. SHOULD THE CONSTRUCTION OF ADDITIONAL SPECIALIZED RETA
CENTRAL BUSINESS DISTRICT BE ENCOURAGED?

| | |
|---|---|
| A. Yes | 78% |
| B. No | 22% |

64. SHOULD THE CONSTRUCTION OF ADDITIONAL OFFICE SPACE IN THE
BUSINESS DISTRICT BE ENCOURAGED?

| | |
|---|---|
| A. Yes | 34% |
| B. No | 66% |

Highland Park CBD Community Character Survey: Questionnaire

Page 8

images cannot be achieved because existing zoning does not allow for them. Uses and images which create a positive community character should not only be included in the goals and objectives of the master plan, they should guide and develop specific community design plans within the master plan. They should be used in the ordinance to illustrate specific land use designs. The results of the Visual Preference Survey ™ can also be translated into design guidelines. They will be extremely effective in design reviews, if a community wishes to establish such a process.

These photographs will be easier for all developers, planners, politicians, and laymen to use and to understand than are the typical words and tables zoning ordinance.

With the vision plan in hand, planners also have a logical basis for the development and design review process. The common vision reflected in the vision plan enables the planning process to work more efficiently. It provides agreement as to the desired character of the community and future development. Potential developers can use the results to understand what the community wants and will accept.

## Emergence of a National Consensus of Visual Preference Surveys ™

Our firm has conducted and analyzed approximately 50,000 surveys. A broad spectrum of people, ranging in age from 17 to 88, with the mean age of 44, and an almost equal number of men and women have participated. The participants have included planners, municipal officials, developers, architects, traffic engineers, students, and concerned citizens. Most of the earlier surveys were performed within New Jersey, but recently they been administered throughout the country, in such diverse places as California, New Mexico, Washington, Minnesota, Florida, Oregon, Arkansas, New York, and Pennsylvania. The surveys have been for master plans, specific site plans, downtown redevelopment projects, circulation plans, classes, workshops, and seminars.

A clear visual and spatial preference has emerged from these surveys, what I call the American vision survey, or the vision of a new American dream." Although every region has an individual opinion on its positive vernacular and a solidarity of opinion regarding the negative images, overall the survey results have been fairly unanimous. In general, I have found that most people reject the current pattern and

This image typically rates on or near the top when it is used in a survey. It represents the strong held association of a small house, a private rear yard, and a well landscaped surroundings. The pitched roof and the chimney are desired detail features.

spatial characteristics of sprawl in favor of more traditional or neo-traditional small communities, the New American Dream.

The next few pages are filled with images from various Visual Preference Surveys ™. This is an extremely small sample of over approximately 7,000 images which have been tested. Each image has appeared in a number of surveys and is identified as positive, neutral, or negative. Below each image is a comment about the image synthesizing the comments and responses much as it would appear in a vision plan.

This image from the universal set typically receives the most negative rating. It is most feared; it is to be avoided. This unkept image of trash in the street reveals a total lack of concern. Trash and litter on any street will lower its value, especially when combined with an overly wide street, deteriorated buildings and steel window covers.

All arterial roads which have been engineered for only the maximum accommodation of traffic receive very negative ratings.

All remaining natural areas receive very positive rating. Preserving natural and environmentally sensitive areas, or adding landscaping to street and parking lots, always results in a more positive rating.

Single family units set far from the road receive a negative rating. The unsecured back of the unit is the most negative feature.

The traditional relationship of house to street receives very positive rating. This classic relationship includes parallel parking, parkway, sidewalk, small front yard, and porch or portico to defining the semi- public space.

This image contains 18 units in the contemporary cookie-cutter pattern prescribed by zoning. It is a single-use zone with overly wide streets, similar sized lots and standardized setbacks. It typically receives negative ratings.

This image of a hamlet contains 18 units of various lot and building sizes with a mixed-use center. The roads are narrow, and it is well integrated into its natural setting. It typically receives a positive rating and cannot be repeated because it is not allowed by zoning.

Strip commercial building with frontyard parking always receives very negative ratings. This area is prime for renewal.

This image of a rehabilitated shopping center, Mashapee Commons, receives positive ratings. It contains all the traditional Main Street features including parallel parking, lights, and awnings.

This new retail area is zoned as neighborhood commercial. It always receives negative ratings. It is a pad of concrete surrounded by asphalt. It is exclusively auto oriented. Parking lot is conveniently located in front of the front doors. No pedestrian amenities.

This image consistently receives a positive rating. It depicts a new mixed-use neighborhood commercial building with retail on the ground floor and housing and offices above. The positive design features include the two story height, pitched roof, signage, rigid canopy with clerestory, sidewalk, shade trees, and on-street parking.

This image of multi-family housing is consistently rated negative. Even though it has a low net density, it contains many design elements that people find unacceptable. Some of the undesirable features are front-yard parking, on-grade ground floor rooms, and a lacking of semi-public space.

This image is always positive. It contains every design feature that is right for high density multi-family housing (40 -60 DU/acre) including a well defined pedestrian realm, fenced semi-public space, first floor raised above street level, five story height, and consistent design vocabulary.

This image of a state highway always receives a negative rating. The low intensity use, the signing, and character of the edges contribute to the negative rating.

This state highway receives positive ratings. With an equal amount of traffic, the differences are in the scale and character of the edges. The height of the buildings, the proportion of the street, and the landscaping create a pleasant and urban street.

This type of office building always receives a negative rating. The strip windows, the primary design feature, contribute to its negative appearance. This building receives lower negative ratings the closer one gets to it. Only glass box buildings receive lower ratings; these should be avoided.

This office park has the feeling of a campus, particularity with the clock/water tower as a focal point. The pitched roofs, individually- scaled widows, and brick exterior generate the high positive ratings.

This roadway provides the primary access to the units. The image is of a garagescape; only cars live here. Where are the doors for people, or do they, too, go through the garage. All garagescape images receive negative ratings and consequently should be avoided.

This parking lot, with an extensive canopy of trees, receives positive ratings. One tree should be planted for each four to six parking spaces. Trees in a parking lot provide both shade for the cars and aesthetic relief. Peripheral landscaping visually screens the lot from the roadway or sidewalk.

All town greens, commons, and piazzas receive positive ratings. They are appropriate for all community types. Generally bordered by mixed-use and public buildings, they are spaces which define the center of the community. When a tower or high architectural element is present the value of the image increases.

In conclusion, the VPS ™ provides the pictures/vision of what your community wants and what it does not want on its land. The images are not arbitrary; they are not unreasonable. They are a product of a public process. They represent public consensus from people who have experienced the place. They provide insight and reasoned responses. They represent a consensus vision. It is planning and design by democracy.

Now you must have the will to translate this vision into your master plan and ordinances. It is only through implementation that your vision will become the new reality.

The small community is the basic DNA of planning.

The basic structure of small community evolving at a Hands-On Model Workshop.

# THE HANDS-ON MODEL BUILDING WORKSHOPS

The second component to create a common vision, in conjunction with the Visual Preference Survey ™, is the Hands-On Models. Individuals, teams of designers, developers, or councilmen/women are asked to design a small community. The underlying belief is if you understand community design on a small scale, hamlet or village, then you can better understand the basic principles, dimensions, and figure-ground patterns needed to create small communities at any level, size or scale. I call it the DNA of planning.

Architects have long used models and perspectives to study and to present design solutions. Models are ideal design tools to help visualize site plans for those who are unaccustomed to reading two-dimensional drawings.

The Association of New Jersey Environmental Commissions (ANJEC) sponered a series of workshops to teach the elements of design to planners and engineers. Using three-dimensional models of residential, commercial, and institutional, participants move the pieces, or buildings, in response to the environment and infrastructure, until they feel comfortable with the site design. These models are an ideal substitute for drawings because most people cannot read a two dimensional plan, find it even harder to draw a site plan, and don't have access to expensive CAD technology. Consequently, models are an effective tool for teaching non-designers how to think visually and three-dimensionly.

We researched both basic residential and non-residential building types common in New Jersey's villages and hamlets and those that received high ratings in the Visual Preference Surveys ™. After experimenting with several scales, the models were built to 1 inch equals 20 foot scale. This seemed to be the easiest scale to understand, to hold in your hand, to create visually comprehensible space, and to visualize distances. In total thirty-two building types were produced from the original grant. This repertoire has been expanded to include several vernacular styles ranging from New England, Southwestern pueblo, and Northwestern bungalow, strip malls, office parks, and fast food outlets. The non-residential building types provide additional challenges when modeling the redevelopment and retro-fitting of suburban areas. Trip generation/trip mitigation analysis

The first ANJEC workshop in Newton, NJ.

Workshop participants look over models at the beginning of an exercise.

> A team will always produce a traditional small community, never a cookie cutter or a cul-de-sac subdivision.

Model layout created in the Chester County, PA, 2000 design symposium.

has been added as part of the evaluation criteria so people can also understand that trip reduction can be significant in a properly designed small community. The Hands-On Model workshops can now be tailored for rural communities, for suburban communities, or for the infill of older neighborhoods.

Participants are introduced to the Hands-On Model workshops by completing an exercise in which they site one residence and one garage on a parcel of land. They move the two model pieces around until they are comfortable with the layout. Then, they draw lines around the base of the models and complete the site plan using simple graphic notations.

Following this exercise, groups of individuals, typically 8 to 10, team up to create a small hamlet on a site with various ecological constraints and road layouts. All teams begin with a design discussion moving the models into a variety of configurations until all or a majority of members agree on a design. Again, once the building models are appropriately located, the participants draw lines around the base of the models. Finally they draw in the other essential elements such as pavements, sidewalks, driveways, trees, hedges, and other landscaping, and property lines. After the design group has penciled in the layout, the site plans can be analyzed to tabulate the necessary bulk, yards, setbacks, and road standards, etc.

After hundreds of workshops using this technique, some fundamental observation and principles emerge. The most basic is that **no two places are alike**. However, **most exhibit many features that are similar** to the design principles elaborated later in this handbook. The most important observation is: **when left on their own to design, after minimal orientation, a team will always produce a small hamlet that looks like a traditional community, never a cookie-cutter subdivision.** Incidentally, **no group has ever laid out the models in cul-de-sacs!**

That people intuitively create this type of community says: anyone can create a site plan that is better than the typical cookie-cutter or dead-worm subdivision that results from a strict variance-free interpretation of modern zoning. In some workshops these models are compared with an existing ordinance. Typically, the participants discover that the type of small community that they have intuitively designed cannot be built in their community because it fails to conform to all of the subdivision standards. Only when this is brought home to the respondents do they come to understand the impact of zoning laws, the lack of design in the planning process, and the forces that impede the developments they want to see.

As has been pointed out the small hamlet is essentially the DNA of urban design. The hamlet is primarily applicable to rural and exurban locations without the additional constraints inherent in suburban retrofit applications. A typical positive hamlet will exhibit the following characteristics:

Hamlets for a rural municipality completed in a workshop.

> ●Small communities have a center green, core, or focus
> ●Non-residential, civic, and community buildings are located in the center of the focus area
> ●Taller, landmark buildings are always located in the center
> ●The density in the built up area of the site ranges from 4 to 9 dwelling units per acre, net density
> ●Environmental resources are protected and enhanced
> ●Roads are narrow
> ●The periphery of the community is surrounded by low-density, large lots, agricultural lands, environmentally sensitive lands, or open space

Typical suburban sprawl of 30 units on a cu-de-sac.

The workshops repeatedly prove that individuals can create a positive design of a small small community. They begin to see site planning at the three and four-dimensional scale. People see the relationship of building elements to the street, to the community, and to the open spaces. Planning is, thereby, moved from the abstraction of two-dimensional land use into three- and four-dimensional visualization.

Hamlet for a rural municipality created in a Hands-On Model Building Workshop.

Typical cookie-cutter suburban pattern.

Model of neighborhood center for Washington Township, NJ. (Designed by A. Nelessen Associates).

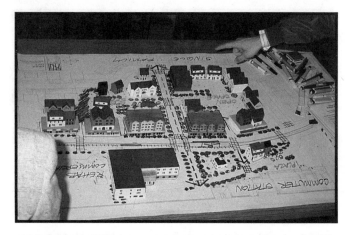

This model was completed in a Hands-On Model Workshop in Portland for a Community Light Rail Transit Station Area.

Final evaluation of the many small hamlets and neighborhoods that have been designed indicates that small communities are visually and spatially more comfortable than sprawl; people like them and want to live there. They are environmentally and economically sustainable and will create a positive sense of neighborhood and community. The developed areas in the models typically have a net density 4 to 9 dwelling units per acre. This suggests that people do not intuitively reject dense development. Most of the models show peripheral open space which has been protected in some way from development. The combination of high net density plus peripheral and internal open space suggests that a layout in a more traditional form in small communities should be mandatory in all existing lower density subdivision zones. This might be particularly applicable for the redesign of the many cookie-cutter subdivisions which have been approved and not yet built.

So as not to leave you with the impression that this modeling technique is only applicable at the rural scale, the following examples show how the technique has been used for the design of a small town, for the retrofitting of a strip and for designing a community light rail transit station area.

# Using the Model Workshop and the Visual Preference Survey ™ Together

There is an interesting correlation between the Hands-On Model workshops and the Visual Preference Survey ™. The visual and spatial characteristics of the figure-ground plans of the hamlets created in the workshops often match those in the images which receive high ratings in the Visual Preference Surveys ™. In other words, people intuitively create places in the Hands-On Model workshops that are identical to those places which call forth positive responses in the VPS ™. This relationship also indicates that generating figure-ground plans from VPS ™ images is an exercise that is extremely helpful in order to determine the appropriate spatial relationship between buildings. The figure-ground plan can then be used in generating ordinances.

Photographs of the models can be used in both Master Plans and in Ordinances. It is recommended that developers and planning boards use these techniques. The VPS ™ can determine a visual and spatial consensus, a common vision of the desired results, while the block Hands-On modeling building technique, using real sites, assures that the site plan will assume the desired three- and four-dimensional form.

By planning and designing small communities, using the Hands - On Model and the VPS ™ as guides, people begin to understand how their vision can improve the quality of life, and enhance the quality of the environment, and thereby reduce economic and social stress.

"Tell me, I forget;
Show me, I remember;
Involve me, I understand."

Eastern Proverb

# PROCESS STEP IV
## ANALYZING AND APPLYING THE POTENTIAL

New housing surrounding a neighborhood green in Harbortown, TN receives very high VPS ™ ratings.

# POTENTIALS FOR POSITIVE DEVELOPMENT AND REDEVELOPMENT

CHAPTER
SIX

**Identifying the Potentials** is the fourth step in the planning and design process. Most of us can enumerate problems. However, generating potentials is more difficult. The potentials for new development and redevelopment are based on the consensus vision, on local and state policies, on environmental conditions, on access and linkages, on the character of existing settlement patterns, on the projected balance of residential to non-residential uses, on the road network and transit, and on the proper location in a hierarchy of places. It also depends on the positive fiscal impacts that provide additional incentives for implementing the small communities concept.

Highly rated, new moderate-density single family housing in Natchez, MS.

This step determines the design features of the potentials for positive development. Vision planning provides images of positive places and place designs through the use of VPS TM, Hands-On Model Workshops, and discussions. It identifies the type and character of development preferred by or acceptable to the community. It identifies existing models and alternatives for development; it can indicate appropriate locations for development or redevelopment, e.g. existing places which receive negative ratings might be ripe for redevelopment. Positive potentials arise from policy decisions at the federal, state, or local level. Because small communities will be planned, approved, and built at the local level, local participation in the process of developing potentials is critical.

We now face the challenge of transforming community desires into affordable visions for the future. We must see to it that these visions become a reality through planning policies and development plans that will allow them to occur.

A street in Princeton, NJ, that always receives positive ratings.

## The Emerging Alternatives to Sprawl

In recent years, a few planners, reacting to community will and environmental need, have sought alternatives to archaic zoning and land-use practices. Land-use concepts such as planned developments, clustering, and mixed-use centers have grown in popularity. Zoning practices such as performance zoning, T.D.R., capacity-based planning, transit-oriented development, and traditional neighborhood development have emerged in an attempt to better guide development. Some of these concepts have begun to control sprawl; others have actually encouraged it. Recently, more and more research has been completed on the impact of sprawl and the development of alternatives. The pedestrian pocket concept, the transit-oriented development of Peter Calthorpe, and the Traditional Neighborhood Development (TND) of Andres Duany and Elizabeth Plater-Zyberk have received national attention.

The resort community of Seaside, Florida, and its principal designers Andres Duany and Elizabeth Plater-Zyberk have come to symbolize the popular neo-traditional movement. Harbortown, a new community by RTKL, Laguna West, by Peter Calthorpe, and Kentlands, by Duany/Plater-Zyberk, are being built. Indeed, Seaside and Harbortown are considered by many to be two of the better examples of new American community planning and architecture created in recent years. In Seaside, traditional standards of urbanism have been joined with the regional architectural vernacular in order to create a design vocabulary, one of the main components of small communities. Sometimes heavily criticized because of the "resort" nature of the community, it has, nonetheless, set the tone for the neo-traditional movement. In 1989 Peter Calthorpe and others presented the results of a design charette at the University of Washington in The Pedestrian Pocket Book: A New Suburban Design Strategy. This book reinforces the concept of traditional urbanism linked to transit and walking distances. It stresses the need for a three-dimensional urban design plan as the basis for future zoning. Pedestrian pockets are compact communities sized to place all residents within walking distance of a fixed-rail transit line which links together communities of higher and lower orders. Transit-oriented development is now being reconsidered all over the country.

New single family housing in the Kentlands embodies traditional community designs.

Hundreds of these neo-traditional communities, or traditional neighborhoods, have been and are being designed and constructed. Approval of these communities has occurred despite the fact that there are more anti-development groups. When presented with thoughtful alternatives to sprawl, people often see the potential positive impacts, understand the fiscal and economic impacts, and can then accept these alternatives. Although neo-traditionalism has only recently received wide public attention and professional scrutiny, its roots lie in tried and true planning practices. It is not--as critics claim--an attempt to impose an idealistic vision of "the good ol' days" upon modern society. Nor does it try to simply create cute places by copying the past. The neo-traditional movement is about integrating those elements which have historically proven to be important to the community in a planning process which responds to modern demands. It is a direct manifestation of people's desires as reflected in the vision planning results.

A new street in Seaside, FL.

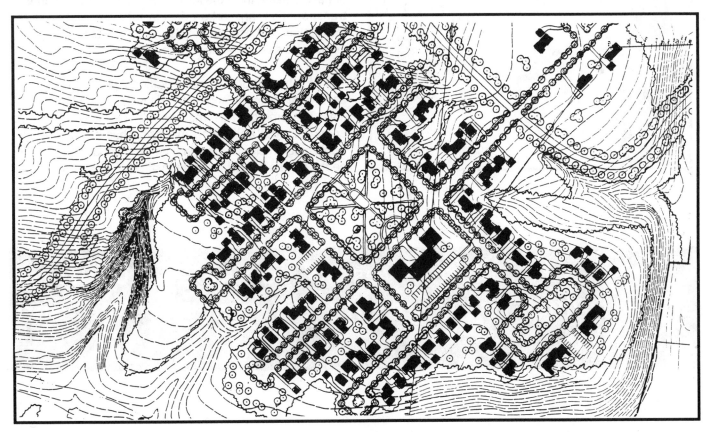

The figure ground plan for a new neighborhood in Frenchtown, NJ, designed by A. Nelessen Associates.

In New Jersey. The Middlesex-Somerset-Mercer Regional Council (MSM) has contributed much research to the role of land-use regulations in the evolution of sprawl. They have disseminated information on planning and growth management to planners, municipal officials, and the general public. One on-going project of MSM and USDOT has been research on compact, walkable communities clustered around transit nodes to decrease future highway travel demands.

Through many workshops and presentations in the past few years, the hamlet and village concept has now struck a positive and receptive chord in New Jersey as well as in the rest of the nation. In 1990, the American Planning Association (APA) and the American Institute of Certified Planners (AICP) began a series of national workshops called *Neo-traditional town planning.* In two full days of presentations and workshops, local government officials, planners, engineers, and developers delved into all aspects of neo-traditional planning, from the impact of sprawl, to site planning, transportation, and urban design for new villages to the translation of these standards into workable zoning concepts, and associated legal concerns.

The APA has embraced neo-traditional planning principles as have many traffic engineers, developers, and municipalities. The emerging alternatives are receiving positive responses. APA's *Planning* magazine has begun regularly publishing articles addressing neo-traditional planning concepts, as has the Urban Land Institute.

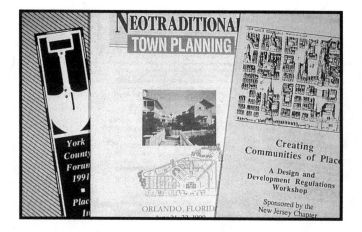

There are alternatives to continued suburban sprawl which are more efficient, cost effective, and profitable.

## The New Jersey Development and Redevelopment Plan (The State Plan)

The New Jersey State Plan places the concept of centers into state policy. The State Plan purposefully does not contain a specific vision of what these centers are or should be. Large regional areas have been designated, and the conceptual frame has been set. However, it leaves municipalities and counties the opportunity to craft their own vision and physical potential. In each of the 567 municipalities, multiple centers are possible through development of open land or retrofitting of residential and commercial areas.

The State Plan provides a unique potential for implementing the small community types that have emerged through the vision planning process. There are many objectives of the State Plan which are inherent elements of small communities and the neo-traditional planning and design process. The State Plan provides delineation criteria and policy objectives for each planning area. Several policy objectives are common to the planning areas in which new communities of place will most likely be located (suburban, fringe, and rural planning areas). The primary objective of the State Plan is to guide development into what it calls community development boundaries or service areas. Within these areas a series of centers must be defined in order to prevent further aimless sprawl and environmental degradation. A second objective is the provision of a variety of housing choices, provisions that encourage municipalities and developers to confront the challenge of affordable housing. The New Jersey State Plan also supports the use of public and alternative travel systems that link new and existing centers to metropolitan areas. The conservation of open space and the provision of buffers for environmentally sensitive areas is another objective which is inherent in Communities of Place. Finally, the State Plan recommends regional approaches to planning and to the provision of services for development in centers.

### Planning Areas and Policy Objectives

The Plan's statewide policies are applied through the designation of Planning Areas. Each area "reflects distinct geographic and economic units within the State."

PA1 -- Metropolitan Planning Area
PA2 -- Suburban Planning Area

Planning designation in the State Plan.

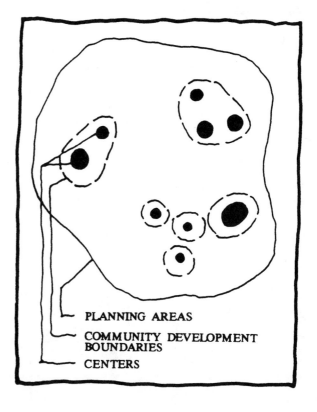

PLANNING AREAS
COMMUNITY DEVELOPMENT BOUNDARIES
CENTERS

A typical suburban planning area

Suburban strip commercial has a high land bank of underutilized and inefficient parking lots.

PA3 -- Fringe Planning Area
PA4 -- Rural Planning Area
PA5-- Environmentally Sensitive Planning Area

Each Planning Area is characterized by the kinds and intensities of existing development, the character of the existing environment, proximity to existing areas of development, and the character and location of public and private infrastructure. With the exception of the Metropolitan Planning Area, Planning Areas do not coincide with municipal or county boundaries, but define discrete geographic areas which are suitable for common application of public policy.

Four of the five planning areas are likely candidates to receive development or redevelopment/infill using the planning and design principles recommended in this book. These are the suburban, fringe, rural, and environmentally sensitive planning areas. These areas can, without a doubt, be improved or preserved through the use of neo-traditional designs.

The specific character of the area determines the magnitude and location of future growth. Policy objectives of the Planning Area should guide municipal and county planning in general. Several policy objectives are common to three of the planning areas in which new Communities of Place are the most likely to occur: the suburban, fringe, and rural planning areas. Several objectives of the State Plan are central to neo-traditional planning and design: reinforcing and enhancing existing centers; rehabilitating and completing the center concept in existing suburban areas (retrofitting; and the creation of new centers.

## Suburban Planning Area

Suburban Planning Areas lack high intensity centers and have available vacant developable land usually served by urban infrastructure. They lack transportation alternatives to the private automobile. They lack the compact settlement pattern of the older suburbs in the Metropolitan Planning Area. There are few focal points for community interaction. Their existing patterns of sprawled development are inefficient in terms of the cost of facilities and services, unless they have a high ratio of jobs to housing. When jobs and housing are out of balance (a low ratio of jobs to housing) high property taxes result. When there is an overabundance of jobs to housing, the consequences are characterized by traffic congestion, a lack of affordable housing, and the destruction of open space that is critical to define a community's character and sense of place. This is the policy of ratables (i.e. high numbers of jobs to housing); it is anti-Community of Place, which seeks a balance between jobs and housing.

The underdeveloped lands in the Suburban Planning Area are sufficient to accommodate much of the market demand for future growth and development in the State. The State Plan must guide development into more efficient and serviceable patterns for the Suburban Planning Areas. An extension of public services from neighboring Metropolitan Planning Areas can help to create compact centers of development that support public transportation systems. The retro-fitting of existing subdivisions and strip commercial zones provides additional opportunities to accommodate this growth.

New development in the Suburban Area should be planned to eliminate sprawl; no new strip malls, subdivisions, or office parks should be built  unless they are integrated into a Community of Place. Existing strip malls, office parks, and subdivisions must be retro-fitted, over time, into Communities of Place. Internally-oriented, mixed-use centers that promote a sense of community should be designed for this Area. These centers should be surrounded by open space systems that protect environmentally sensitive resources and provide regionally significant passive recreational opportunities. Transfer of Development Rights and Credits can be a helpful tool. However, the legislature will have to allow such rights in these areas. The state should allow municipalities the discretionary power to decide whether or not to allow T.D.R. and T.D.C.

## Fringe Planning Area
Fringe areas are, primarily, served by rural, two-lane road networks and on-site well water and waste water systems, not by an urban level of infrastructure. They have no plans to become part of urban utility systems. The Fringe Planning Area is predominantly a rural landscape with scattered small communities, and free-standing residential and commercial developments. Agricultural operations may still be active.

Suburban zoning characterized by leap frog  development patterns.

Fringe area surrounding an existing compact village.

An effort is needed to manage growth in such areas in order to avoid the current pattern of dispersed development. Compact, deliberately designed community patterns can reduce land conflicts and encourage the preservation of an area's rural character. The area should act as a green preserve between the more intensely developed urban and suburban areas and the agricultural and environmentally sensitive lands. Development should be concentrated in or at the edges of existing communities or in well planned self-sufficient new small communities. The character, location, and magnitude of new development should be based on the capacities of the existing environmental systems. Infrastructure should primarily be provided by the private sector. Growth should be concentrated in existing centers or well-designed new centers.

## Rural Planning Area

Rural Planning Areas contain most of the state's farmland, as well as land related to other economic activities such as fishing or mining. Healthy soil, adequate water supplies, and contiguous plots of land devoid of land-use conflicts are essential to sustaining farmland productivity.

Rural areas characterized by active, productive farmland.

For these areas planners must encourage rural development in a form that supports agriculture. The State Plan supports the "right to farm" within Rural Planning Areas. The location of goods and services essential to farming should be in convenient proximity to agricultural lands but concentrated in discrete centers. New and existing development and growth should be guided into these discrete centers, and creative land preservation tools, such as the transfer of development rights, should be used to ensure future growth is compatible with ongoing agricultural operations. No subdivision or strip commercial development should be allowed. New development must be as part of a small community.

## Environmentally Sensitive Planning Area

Environmentally Sensitive Planning Areas contain large contiguous land areas with valuable ecosystems and habitats that have remained relatively undeveloped and rural in character. These critical natural resources should be protected through extremely low density allowance, between one unit to six and one unit to fifty or more acres of land, depending upon environmental constraints. Critical environmental areas should not be built upon; development credits must be transferable. The location, character, and magnitude of development should be linked to the capacity of the natural and man-made environment to support new growth and development.

Rediscovery of the small community--the hamlet and village in rural and suburban locations, the neighborhood and urban village in the urban setting--is occurring all over the country. All of the Hands-On workshops, Visual Preference Surveys ™, lectures, presentations, magazines and newspaper articles, new marketing studies, and forthcoming books are giving voice to an impulse for change, for redefining the American Dream. A small community provides the best opportunity for a logical, rational alternative to sprawl. The fact that this vision is embraced by the State of New Jersey in its development and redevelopment plan, and the accompanying financial and economic analysis conducted by the Rutgers Center for Urban Policy Research, signals the potential economic viability of the concept.

Environmentally sensitive areas.

A hamlet/ small neighborhood.

# Potential Locations for Small Communities
# 4 Criteria

While the State Plan advocates centers as the primary target for new development and growth in the state, it does not address the more specific issues related to the location of centers. Many municipalities do not know where these centers would best be located, and without operational criteria the location of centers could be counter-productive. The location of new small communities or the retrofitting of existing strip malls or residential tracts into small communities must meet some basic criteria. Four basic criteria are outlined which will be expanded later in this chapter.

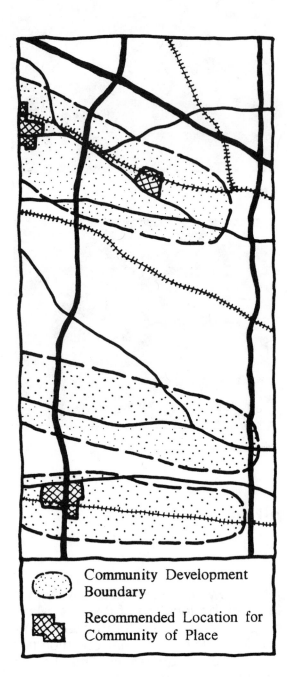

Community Development Boundary

Recommended Location for Community of Place

## 1. Ecological Responsibility

Future development, or redevelopment, of centers can only be located on parcels of land within defined growth or redevelopment areas where ecological analysis indicates development suitability. The ecological development characteristics of the land and the base zoning will determine the number of units possible. The number of units is then used to determine the amount of internal and peripheral open space, the amount of non-residential uses, the amount of civic and institutional spaces, and the amount of job generating spaces required.

The design and construction of a small community must not degrade the natural environment or such ecological characteristics as steep slopes or sensitive water areas. It must achieve a sustainable environmental quality. The air and water quality and the biological and ecological pollution output must be balanced with remediation and purification. All future small communities must be sewered, with the exception of small hamlets with pie shaped or deep rear lot configurations, estates, farmettes, or farms. Furthermore, areas which currently have septic failures should be sewered to eliminate this environmental problem.

## 2. Mobility and Linkages

The location of small communities must permit a high level of mobility for everyone. Movement must be accommodated through a network of streets, sidewalks, and bicycle paths. Opportunities for public and alternative modes of transportation must be supported and provided. The core of every center must be linked to all other cores by roads and transit. In the lower orders of place, such as the hamlet, an on-demand small bus, or what I call a computer commuter similar to a dial-a-bus network, must be provided. This should be incorporated with existing school bus networks, senior citizen buses, local buses, or taxis. If a small community is properly designed it will have a balance of jobs to houses. It will provide jobs within walking distance or a short bus commute of residences.

## 3. Settlement Patterns

There must be sufficient separation between hamlets and villages to achieve individual identity. The location of a small community must also be responsive to the design character of local historic settlement patterns, vernacular architecture, and streetscape design. Each small community should have its own design vocabulary based upon the site location, the adjacent vernacular architecture, and the physiography of the site.

## 4. Balance

The location must allow a balance of retail to housing, jobs to housing, open space to housing, and civic space to housing within a defined community size. A small community must create a logical node in the hierarchy of places. Each must relate to all the other small communities, both large and small, in the regional hierarchy of places.

## First Locational Criteria
## Development on Ecologically Suitable Land

A development suitability map of a municipality is generated from soils maps, geological conditions, biological field studies, aerial photographs, and topographic studies. When all of these characteristics are overlaid and the specific positive and negative characteristics are isolated, a single map can be produced which indicates those areas most suitable for development, those moderately suitable for development, and those with severe development limitations. Ideally small communities should only be developed, or redeveloped, on land most suited for development. Development must be restricted on lands with severe development constraints and limited on lands with moderate development constraints. The number of units assigned to the severe and moderate constraint areas should be transferred to those areas with the least constraints.

A development suitability map with assigned intensity of development must be completed in the master plan phase of the planning and design process in order to avoid potential litigation. The master plan must assign the holding capacity, or yield, of the various parcels in the municipality based on the ecological characteristics of the parcel, which then must be translated into zoning. If zoning follows property lines in generally straight lines, then there must be factors to assess the holding capacity for each parcel, or zoning lines might have to follow ecological lines. It should be remembered that ecological definition lines are never straight like contemporary zone lines, they are organic; they must be specifically measured and calibrated for each parcel.

Development Suitability

| 1/2 | suitable |
| 3 | develop with guidelines |
| 4/5 | unsuitable |

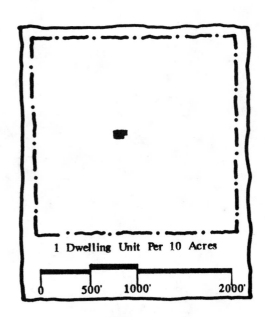

1 Dwelling Unit Per 10 Acres

| 0 | 500' | 1000' | 2000' |

0.1 dwelling unit per acre = 1 unit per 10 acres, as shown above.

EXAMPLE: A site of 100 acres might have only 50 acres which are developable, with the remainder in severe constraint categories (e.g. wetlands, water, steep slopes). If the zoning calls for 1 unit per 2 acres, without specifying the environmental constraint limitation, the land owner assumes that the land will yield 50 units. If only 50 acres are fully developable, and the remainder is ecologically constrained, the land holding capacity is 25 units not 50!

Based on recent court cases in New Jersey, the gross density for the site still determines the yield. The gross density must factor in environmental constraints.

The following are recommendations for determining holding capacity.

## HIGHEST CONSTRAINTS
The characteristics of areas which generate the most constraints and areas where development is <u>not permitted</u> are:
1. flood ways
2. wetlands
3. open water
4. areas with high levels of toxic waste

**Recommended Gross Holding Capacity: 0 to 1 Dwelling Units per Acre** (to be transferred to developable portion of the site)

## SEVERE CONSTRAINTS
Areas with severe constraints that restrict development (except as modified by D.E.P.E. or Core of Engineers) are:
1. flood plains
2. slopes greater then 24% and ridge tops
3. areas of 0 - 1.5 foot seasonal high water
4. buffer areas to fish streams and wetlands
5. rock outcrop areas and non-rippable bedrock within 2 feet of surface
6. major aquifer recharge areas
7. historic or archaeologic sites
8. soils or locations with severe septic suitability, ground waste water recharge or streams discharge problems.

9. land with toxic chemicals
10. class I agricultural soils in an active farming community

**Recommended Holding Capacity: .1 to .2 Dwelling Units per Acre**

These areas should be preserved as open space. Any development density assigned to these areas should be extremely low and transferred to another location. Any development credits generated from these areas must be transferred to a more suitable portion of the site or to an adjacent site under joint ownership.

## MODERATE CONSTRAINTS
Areas with moderate constraints with limited development at low densities are:

1. slopes between 15 - 24%, and ridge tops
2. class II agricultural soils, if in an existing agricultural community
3. aquifer recharge, secondary
4. soils or locations with moderate septic suitability, ground waste water recharge, or stream discharge problems
5. areas of mature and/or climax vegetation
6. land with low level toxic contamination with clean-up or treatment possibilities
7. major viewsheds

**Recommended Gross Holding Capacity: .2 to .4 Dwelling Units per Acre**

## NON-CONSTRAINED LAND:
Non - constrained lands are relatively flat and well drained. Highest net densities are encouraged.

**Recommended Gross Holding Capacity: greater than 2.0 Dwelling Unit per Acre**

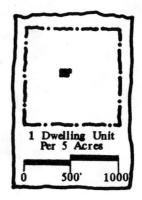

0.4 dwelling units per acre = 1 unit per 2.5 acres, as shown above.

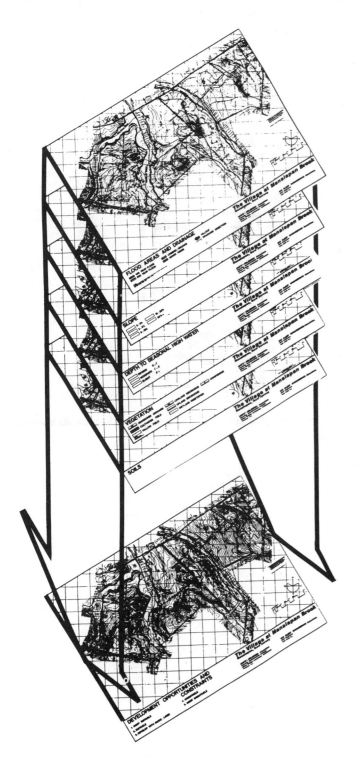

The geological soil and surface characteristics are mapped separately and then overlaid. Overlay technique results in a development suitability map.

## MAPPING OF CONSTRAINTS TO DETERMINE AREAS MOST SUITABLE FOR DEVELOPMENT

All of the factors need to be individually mapped to determine the exact location of each characteristic. Overlays have been used since 1968, but the new GIS systems will soon replace this manual graphic technique. Zoning should establish and reflect this technique, but the land owners must have the opportunity to do field analysis of the data to determine the exact location and area of various restraining characteristics. A soil composite Development Suitability Map can be created by overlaying the series of maps and analyzing the results on all areas of the map. All areas should be labeled according to their suitability for development.

The holding capacity, or total number of units (site yield), should be determined by the ecological features of the site. Typically, sites do not have all unconstrained land; portions of a site will be highly developable while others are moderately or non-developable. Too many of the current land use laws have involved an attempt to control the location and intensity of development through zoning without proper development suitability analysis and assignment of development intensity at the master plan stage.

Many communities have assigned factors to limit development. Some have approved cluster development which uses the holding capacity of the entire site before considering environmental constraints. This has resulted in high-density clusters that are unacceptable to many. A site holding capacity based on environmental factors will reduce the number of units over previous zoning without factoring-in environmental constraints. Too many municipalities have reverted to one unit on two to three acres, with a verifiable perk test on each lot in order to determine the total number of units or holding capacity of a parcel. Unfortunately, because developers are required to lay out the subdivision and complete tests on each lot, the advantages of creating a small community are diminished from the beginning.

The total number of units projected for a location will determine the functional classification of the community into a hamlet, village, neighborhood, or town. It is the net density that determines the visual and spatial character of a place. The size will depend on the total number of attainable units.

Pre-1960 zoning, zoning without environmental analysis, blanket zoned much of the land in New Jersey without regard for the underlying constraints. Unfortunately, this established expectations for financial yield. New technology and an increasing body of scientific evidence will inevitably continue to disappoint many of these expectations. Much of this early zoning has been litigated. Much of the land has environmental constraints, such as wetlands. To develop at appropriate intensities, all such areas must first be analyzed and described in terms of the various constraints as indicated earlier. This must be completed at master plan level and further refined at specific plan stages. Laying out a regulating plan is the key to sensitive utilization of constrained lands. It is not sufficient to simply zone lots over gross areas knowing that various environmental constraints exist.

The housing pattern which characterizes sprawl zoning always receives negative ratings.

## ZONING WITHOUT ENVIRONMENTAL CONSTRAINTS

If your municipality has zoning not based on an environmental analysis, then the following set of factors are recommended at your next master plan re-examination, assuming that your municipality has completed a thorough development suitability analysis. These factors will help create a responsive ecological balance on land which was previously zoned without considering environmental constraints.

The various constraints of a site should be measured and then multiplied against the existing gross site zoning. When constraints overlap the most severe constraint factor should be used. These multipliers are particularly important if the existing zoning is greater than 0.3 to 0.5 dwelling units per acre to prevent overdevelopment of non-constrained land.

| Environmental Features | Multiplication Factor | |
|---|---|---|
| Open Water on Site | 0.0 | units |
| Wetlands | 0.05 | units |
| 0" to 1" SHW | 0.1 | units |
| Wetlands Buffer | 0.2 | units |
| Flood Plain | 0.2 | units |
| Slopes over 24% | 0.2 | units |
| Non-Constrained Land | 1.0 | units |
| Preserved Historic or Archaeological Site | 2.0 | units |
| Aquifer recharge | 0.2 | units |

Example of a 100 acre site

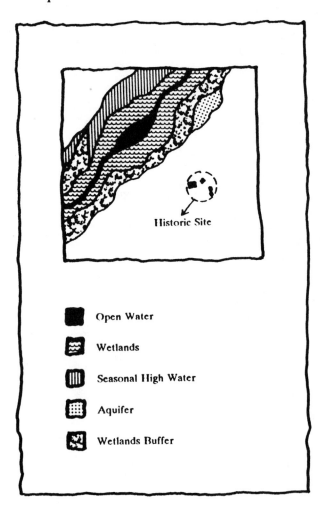

Open Water

Wetlands

Seasonal High Water

Aquifer

Wetlands Buffer

**EXAMPLE:**
   Site Area is 100 acres
   Current Zoning  3 DU per acre

| Site Characteristics | Area (Acreage) | Density (DU/A) | MFactor | Holding # of units |
|---|---|---|---|---|
| Open water | 3 A | 3 | .0 | 0 |
| Wetlands | 10 A | 3 | .0 | 0 |
| 0-1 SHW (partially included in wetlands) | 10 A | 3 | .1 | 3 |
| Wetlands buffer (partially included in SHW) | 8 A | 3 | .2 | 5 |
| Floodplain (Included in SHW) | 5 A | 3 | .2 | overlap |
| Slopes over 24% | 0 | 3 | .2 | 0 |
| Aquifer | 1 A | 3 | .2 | .6 |
| Non-Constrained | 67A | 3 | 1 | 201 |
| Historic | 1 A | 3 | 2 | 6 |

**TOTAL HOLDING CAPACITY**                    **216 Units**

The parcels should be zoned for 216 units. The new GIS system, which can contain all the ecological, zoning, and tax information, will allow any one to enter a lot and block number and see the number of permitted units for a site. An owner or potential purchaser will have to field verify the ecological characteristics.

If this site was planned and designed as a small community the 216 units would be used to determine the number of non-residential uses and amount of open space required for a small community. The provision for non-residential uses offers an additional incentive for the creation of a small community. Preservation of open space is one of the greatest incentives for a municipality to allow or encourage small communities .

The loss of open space and the protection of environmentally sensitive and agricultural lands, and aquifer recharge areas are of great concern. Land suitability analysis has been upheld by our courts. In New Jersey, Mount Laurel housing cannot be built on land with a high water table or steep slopes. Development on flood plains and wetlands has been controlled by federal, and state governments for years. The ecological responsibility in locating a small community is to protect and preserve sensitive lands. Because water drainage areas, streams, and underground aquifers are connected they do not necessarily respect geometric property lines. The uniform protection of these important environmental features must be considered in site location and development intensity.

Rural zoning that has destroyed the rural character.

Many townships have zoned for large lots in an attempt to be environmentally sensitive.  Many of these municipalities have been sued as exclusionary or have begun to understand that .5 to.3 or.2 dwelling units per acre destroys the fundamental character of the township.  Respecting the ecological constraints and transferring the capacity to a small community provides a win-win opportunity for the environment and for the people.

## TRANSFER OF UNITS

There are three basic ways in which environmentally sensitive lands can be preserved while encouraging development. The first two are variation on Transfer of Development Credits (TDC)

### 1. On-Site Transfer

Typically this is single site or tax lot. This technique maps the constrained lands and determines the holding capacity. Units allocated to the constrained lands are transferred to other portion of the site with few or no constraints.

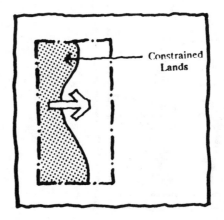

On-site transfer.

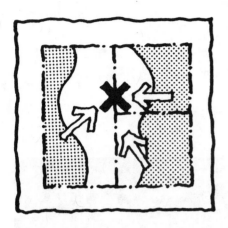

Adjacent lots transfer through joint ventures.

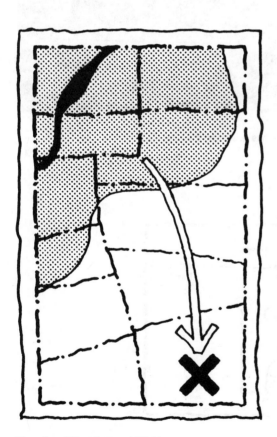

Transfer of Development Rights.

## 2. Adjacent Site Transfer

Two or more adjacent or contiguous sites with individual owners are encouraged to enter into a joint venture in order to create a small community. The location of the community should be sited on the most suitable land with a great amount of preserved open space . One large hamlet or village is always better than several small ones. The incentive to the individual owners is that they may transfer some or all of their units yet still achieve the non-residential bonus.  Sometimes, in rural municipalities, I recommend that a very low density development ( 1 du per 15 acres) can be retained on the sending site.

## 3. Transfer of Development Rights (TDR)

This technique is allowed in New Jersey by legislative empowerment in the Pinelands and Burlington County. It has been used for years in many other towns and counties throughout this country. This technique establishes sending areas that the township wishes to preserve but have been previously zoned for sprawl development. Receiving areas are also designated as places in which Communities of Place may be constructed. In order to preserve land in the receiving zone, the owner is allowed to sell some or all of the development rights of his or her farm to a buyer who will build them in the receiving area. If the land owner in the receiving area sells the development rights, then the land will be restricted to open space/agricultural use and very limited building. This process becomes more complicated when there is a mandatory restriction of subdividing the sending zone. A farmer, for example, wants to sell the rights to his or her land, but can find no willing buyer. Because he or she could previously subdivide it, there must be a guaranteed source of money available to purchase these development credits by a third party or bank. The up-front money to purchase and hold development rights is the economic problem in this mandatory TDR scheme. This is less of a problem in voluntary TDR.

Municipalities must allow both forms of Transfer of Development Credits (TDC), particularly when there are islands of uplands or non-constrained lands in a sea of constrained lands. Adjacent site transfers should be actively encouraged. Municipalities should prepare their own GIS of environmental constraints and location of access roads. Master plans should designate areas where small communities are recommended. Lists of adjacent land owners should be prepared from the tax record and contacted. The concept should be discussed and illustrated. Municipalities must begin to take a proactive role in the development of their communities if they wish to be environmentally responsible.

In order for Transfer of Development Right to work, there must be legislation, and money must be allocated to make it work on a mandatory basis. In the mean time, it should be implemented on a volunteer basis in all remaining rural and suburban towns.

A historic small community with buildings clustered to preserve environmentally sensitive areas. This creates a public amenity.

## Second Locational Criteria
## Mobility and Linkages in Potential Centers

Mobility must be understood in the potential location or redevelopment of small communities . It is possible to grow and develop with only minimal negative impact upon the existing roadways while, at the same time, we decrease levels of pollution and noise. If properly designed and located, centers can significantly reduce the negative impact of additional vehicles, improve the quality of trips, increase access to more facilities without the use of a car, and reduce pollution. All this will require less road widening as it improves the quality of life and provides more time for personal activities.

When compared to the typical sprawl pattern, hamlets, villages, and properly designed neighborhoods generate significantly reduced travel demands. P.U.D.s have consistently produced 20% fewer trips than the same number of units planned as sprawl. Small communities can play an important part in further reduction of trips. Hamlets and villages offer increased opportunities for proximity between homes and all uses which are now auto bound, such as recreational facilities, retail, commercial buildings, and em-

**TRIP GENERATION**
Conventional Street Pattern
PLANNED UNIT DEVELOPMENTS

|  | Average Trip Rate | Maximum Rate | Minimum Rate |
|---|---|---|---|
| Per Unit (Weekday) | 7.9 | 10.0 | 6.2 |

Traffic Generation Source ITE(driveway volumes entering and exiting)

Disaggregated trips: Source ANA

| | | | |
|---|---|---|---|
| Job | 3 | 4 | 3 |
| Shopping | 1 | 1 | 1 |
| Social and recreation | 2 | 2.5 | 2 |
| Children service | 1.9 | 2.5 | .2 |

Small buses are ideal for the computer commuter network.

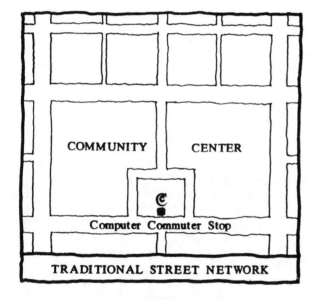

COMMUNITY    CENTER

Computer Commuter Stop

TRADITIONAL STREET NETWORK

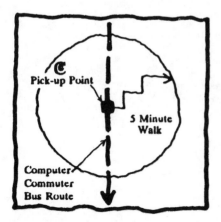

Pick-up Point

5 Minute
Walk

Computer
Commuter
Bus Route

ployment.  Small communities can and should be planned and designed around transportation nodes or pick-up points for buses, vans, and commuter shuttles.  Small communities allow pedestrian and auto movement to co-exist; they are not places where the automobile dominates life.  Furthermore, the use of a road network retains traffic within the system and, therefore, reduces the impact on arterial roads.

Access to small communities should occur off arterial roads. Multiple access points should be provided.  Centers must be designed to complete or create a network of small two lane streets connected to arterials or highways. All roads must link to other roads; this creates a choice of routes from any origin to any destination.

A small community is a compact development form that requires specific road and access design parameters. This more compact form provides the opportunity for greater mobility through walking, bicycling, small electric vehicles, and the possibility for car, van pools, and computer controlled shuttle buses. There must also be an appropriate mix of housing, jobs, recreation, and civic uses all within walking distance, or by a short drive or shuttle bus connection.

### The Ideal Suburban Transit:
### The Computer-Commuter

Larger centers, villages, and neighborhoods are more intensive and should have direct connections to transit. To quote the State Plan, "Capitalize on the high density settlement patterns that encourage the use of public transit systems and alternative modes of transportation to improve travel among major population centers and transportation terminals." For example, every small community could have a commuter bus pick-up point. This point must be within a five to eight minute, or 1200 - 1500 feet maximum walking distance from all houses. When a small community achieves a five-dwelling unit per acre net density, a bus system can achieve a significant reduction of auto trips. Furthermore, it provides a significant reduction in personal costs by alleviating the need for more than one vehicle per household. The recommended system is one with small, 18 to 30 passenger, shuttle buses, the type you typically see used in airports or as senior citizen buses. The system is based on the concept of dial-a-bus, however; instead of direct home pick-up, buses would only stop at designated community center pick-up points and would be confined to a field approximately 24 minutes ride from the pick-up point. In order for this to work, there must be a pre-determined network of pick-up and drop off points. Ideally the computer-commuter stop contains a bench, a covered waiting area, an adjacent retail store to pick up coffee and a paper, a clock, a garbage container, a bulletin board, a telephone, a diagram of the local network, and an indentation in the curb for convenient bus pull-over.

When you enroll in the system, you are given a code number for origins and destinations within your commuting range/network. Then you simply dial the computer, punch in your identification number, origin, and destination. The computer tells you when the bus will arrive. By the time you take a short, healthy walk to your origin point, the bus arrives, and 10 - 20 minutes later you are at your destination.

Most municipalities currently have a public school bus system, a senior citizen bus system, taxi service, and/or car pooling. Many municipalities are served by local or regional bus systems. By my own observation, most of these systems run at extremely low utilization rates costing large amounts of public money. A more coordinated and programmed transportation network, like the computer-commuter system could incorporate existing rolling stock that would be replaced, over time, by more efficient vehicles. The addition of a two-way radio system in each vehicle and a main control computer activated by touch-tone telephone are the basic requirements. This coordinated system could forge a new public/private system that would be considerably more cost effective and efficient for both the private and the public sectors. I am saddened when I see only a handful of people on those large buses. What a waste of energy and resources!

Larger small communities can use something like the commuter computer but must also rely upon line haul systems, like link buses, street cars, and light and/or heavy rail to service surrounding small communities.

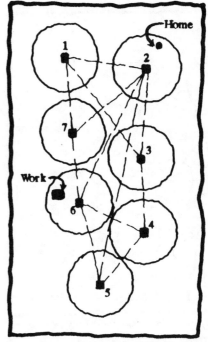

The computer-commuter stops in the middle of all small communities. creating a network.

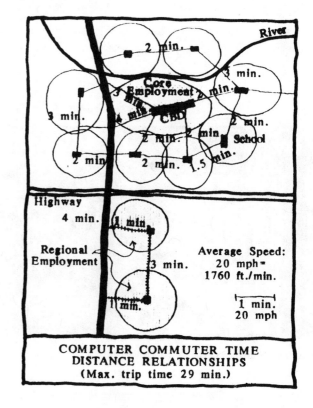

COMPUTER COMMUTER TIME
DISTANCE RELATIONSHIPS
(Max. trip time 29 min.)

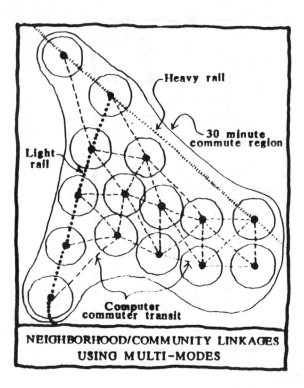

Heavy rail

30 minute
commute region

Light
rail

Computer
commuter transit

**NEIGHBORHOOD/COMMUNITY LINKAGES
USING MULTI-MODES**

The New York City based Regional Plan Association recommends developing or revitalizing centers adjacent to rail lines. Pedestrian Pockets and Transit Oriented Development (T.O.D.) guidelines on the West Coast have resulted in the design of several communities using existing and proposed train lines. New rapid transit lines incorporated within the computer-commuter systems could provide tens of millions of dollars for personal consumption, home ownership, and education. Transportation networks could achieve an unprecedented sense of community when total reliance on the second and third vehicle is reduced.

Larger scale small communities should utilize heavy rail systems. Existing and planned train stations should be used as a focus of mixed- and multiple-use development. Redevelopment to the greatest extent possible should be focused on and around the train lines. Existing rail lines offer the most promising locations for new centers within the existing suburban sprawl context.

The process of retrofitting our sprawled areas will pivot on the use of all types of public transit. All neighborhoods, villages and hamlets must be linked by some type of public transit ranging from the computer commuter to light rail. Those towns which have existing rail service must make them more pedestrian accessible and an inviting experience. Art and design skills must be relearned in order to make walking efficient, enjoyable, and desirable.

The success of street car lines in cities like Sacramento, Portland, San Diego, and New Orleans has led to a renewed interest in streetcars. Streetcars are low tech, inexpensive to build, and appropriate for short linear configurations. A two mile section of line connecting a series of neighborhoods or villages can increase the pedestrian range five times. If a jobs-to-housing balance of 1:1 is achieved within an area with a net density of four to six d.u./acre (gross density is dependent upon environment, open space, etc.) the need for more than one car per family is eliminated. If only 30% of the costs typically associated with the second or third car were allocated to streetcar transit fees the system would pay for itself in a short period and provide millions of dollars for personal consumption, home ownership, and education. Walking, trains and trolleys, networks of narrow, pedestrian-friendly two-lane streets, and commuter-computer shuttles

A newly refurbished streetcar in New Orleans

can create the necessary positive links for the development of a true small community.

Finally, transportation must be coordinated with the protection of natural resources to assure that sensitive environmental resources are protected. Walking, bicycles, and mass transit are energy efficient and less polluting;they meet the sustainability test. Transit, integrated with a minimum utilization of private automobile provides an enormous potential for more sustainable communities.

## Third Locational Criteria
### Design Characteristics of the Small Community

Location and design must be responsive to the adjacent historic settlement patterns, vernacular architecture, and traditional streetscape scale. Existing historic settlements which typically rate positively in the surveys should be emulated in the planning and design of new small communities . It is critical that these places, which were designed and built before 1938 and are still functioning, be protected and enhanced. Only limited expansion of these historic villages and hamlets is recommended; the choice of preservation enhancement or of compatible historic expansion must be determined by the residents. The widening of roads and additional traffic are serious threats to the character and livability of these places. The ramifications of these alterations must be considered. Alternative strategies of bypasses or significantly lowered speed limits must be considered in evaluating the impact on the community's sense of place.

Walk in the village center of Cranbury, NJ.

The common in New Castle, DE, consistently receives positive ratings.

Existing vernacular architecture can be translated into an appropriate design vocabulary.

A design vocabulary can be established from highly rated images. This semi-attached building has excellent market potential as a home office or an own/rent unit. The treatment of the entrances and roofs are an important feature of this building type.

The existing vernacular architectural character of an area should be employed in its development and/or redevelopment. Maintaining the traditional character of the buildings and landscapes is critical to the balance of building and ground form. The local vernacular provides the appropriate examples to generate a design vocabulary that architects can employ in the drawing of new buildings. The streets, roadways, edges, landscaping, bridges, signs, locations of structures, horse trails, and other recreational facilities must be considered for understanding of the vernacular of an area. Such considerations are most critical when a village has agreed to expand the pattern. This does not mean that the new pattern must be identical to the historic vernacular; the vernacular can be adapted to new materials and needs. Nor does it mean that interiors must be similar. Interiors can provide the widest possible latitude for design interpretation within a vernacular exterior.

The design quality of the streetscape is critical if people are to be encouraged to walk. Sidewalks and other pedestrian amenities must be present. The proportion of the street, the setbacks of buildings, the provision of street trees, and the defining of the pedestrian realm are all critical. All buildings must front directly onto a street; none should be set back with a parking lot in front. These characteristics will be further elaborated in the Ten Design Principles in Chapter Seven.

A design code or design vocabulary should be developed which clearly recognizes the vernacular. The use of existing traditional and positively rated patterns of development combined with the vernacular architecture of various building types can easily be produced as the base of the design code, or design vocabulary. It provides the best potential for positive new development.

## Forth Locational Criteria
### The Location Must Contribute To and Reinforce a Hierarchy of Places

A small community must be designed as a place within a hierarchy of places. Not all the communities need to have an equal number and similar range of facilities. In fact, because of differences in locations, land suitability, size, and development history, no two communities can or should be identical.

Each small community must create a balance of retail, jobs, and civic facilities located within the core based on the number of housing units within the service areas. Each one will, thereby, have some amount of non-residential uses to balance the residential uses. The various communities will become more independent and efficient while being interdependent on other small communities. Several small hamlets should depend on a larger village.

Differentiations can and will occur within the flexibility of the design standards of a small community. Each must define itself as one of the community types; either it is a hamlet, village, or neighborhood within a region. There should be a complementing balance of hamlets, villages, towns, and neighborhoods within towns. Several hamlets should be linked to the village which might contain the grocery store, the post office, or the intermediate or high school. Neighborhoods should be linked to the core of a town which contains regional shopping and services. Each must be identifiable and discrete.

The plan for facilities should be based on the service areas, population, and infrastructure capabilities. A greater number of regional cultural facilities, for example, should be located in the highest order center; only the smallest community facilities should appear in a small hamlet.

An aerial view of Seargentsville, NJ.

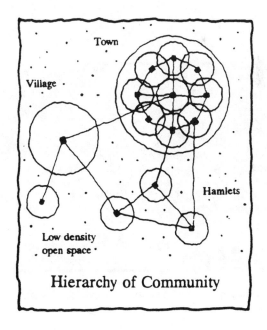

Hierarchy of Community

A positive image for the new main street of Washington Township.

Positive usage of a residential street for the new town center.

Two recent town center plans developed by ANA for Warren Township and Washington Township demonstrate how the various potentials from the VPS ™, community questionnaire, and environmental analysis constitute locational criteria that can be combined in master plan form.

# Washington Township's, Town Center

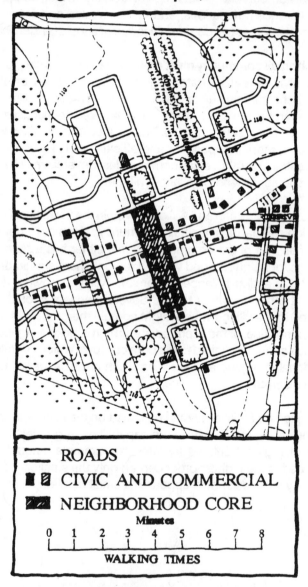

The basic regulatory plan for Washington Township Town Center contains the road layout, public open spaces, and the location of commercial/civic buildings. Lot subdivisions can vary by market demands, provided that streetscape sections are observed.

# Warren Township's, Town Center

The basic regulatory plan shows location of proposed commercial-retail and mixed-use buildings. A new loop road will become the Main Street.

**EXISTING**
**PROPOSED**
**MAIN ROAD**

Desired image of Main Street as generated in the VPS ™ suggests the desired design vocabulary.

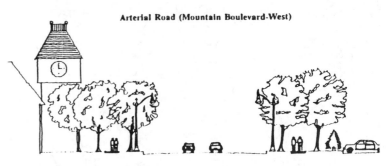

**Arterial Road (Mountain Boulevard-West)**

Street section from the Warren Township plan.

**Community Service ("Main Street") Roads**

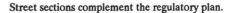

Street sections complement the regulatory plan.

# PROCESS STEP V

## DESIGNING A SMALL COMMUNITY: CREATING THREE-DIMENSIONAL PLANS

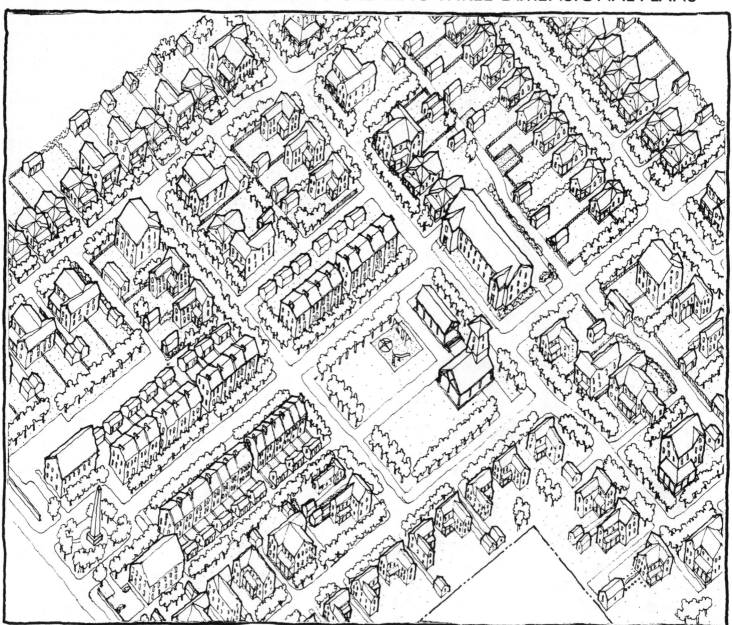

The core of a new neighborhood designed as an infill site.

# DESIGNING A SMALL COMMUNITY USING THE TEN DESIGN PRINCIPLES

CHAPTER
SEVEN

This chapter describes how development can move forward after the biography of the past has been determined, the problems have been defined, the vision has been clarified, the potentials and holding capacity of an area have been determined, and the location factors have been considered. This step refers to generating conceptual plans which can guide master plans as well as site-specific development applications. Development plans must integrate the previous four steps in the planning process and produce plans in three- and four-dimensional form to integrate the design phase of the process. In this step we introduce detailed community design principles that have been developed through observations of traditional settlements and successful small communities and refined through the analysis of many Visual Preference Surveys ™ and Hands-On Model Workshops. These Ten Principles consistently re-emerge. These principles, in a graphic format, are the backbone of the design and planning of small communities .

The most fulfilling and challenging step in the planning and design process is the creation of three- and four-dimensional plans. It is the most difficult step, and that which most planners can not or do typically not do because they lack the training. The case studies, the VPS ™ and the Hands-On Model Workshop have been designed to meet this need by allowing conceptual and pragmatic three-dimensional plans to be visualized by people of all backgrounds and training. The conceptual and pragmatic vision must then be translated into figure-ground regulating plans with accompanying design standards. Concept design must become part of master planning. Master planning must evolve from the amorphous concepts to specific vision and form, within a flexible network that can be market driven. The design principles provide a guide to the specific design of the three- and four- dimensions of small community.

## The Ten Design Principles

These design principles are the fundamental elements of a good plan essential for the creation of small communities. These principles can be used to guide the planning and design of various zones in the master plan as well as the specific design and the resulting three- dimensional form to be used in the development of ordinances. You can also use these as a checklist for applications. The Ten Principles must be present and work together in any small community . They are dependent on one another. Elimination of one of the principles will negatively affect the others.

# Ten Basic Design Principles to Create Small Communities

I.   **Design for the Human Scale**
- design for the human scale and perceptions, creating a sense of neighborhood and community

II.  **Ecological Responsibility**
- design in harmony with nature not against it

III. **Pedestrianism**
- define the primary community by walking dimensions

IV.  **Open Spaces**
- design for internal and peripheral open spaces

V.   **Community Focus**
- design for a neighborhood or community center

VI.  **Streetscapes**
- design for streets internal to the community and highways on the periphery, incorporate complementary movement opportunities

VII. **Variation**
- design for buildings of smaller scale in a pattern of various footprints(figure ground)

VIII. **Mixed Use**
- design for mixed and multiple land uses, also include a mix of housing types, incomes, and a horizontal and vertical mix of uses

IX.  **Design Vocabulary**
- specify an architectural style or styles for the community including facade treatment, walls and fences, streetscapes, materials, and colors

X.   **Maintenance**
- design community materials, and organizations that facilitate short term and long term maintenance and security

Each of these principles must be incorporated into the conceptual design of place which in turn must guide the master plan. The master plan must assume the location and the design intent of small communities. It must be sufficiently prescriptive to assure a municipality that positive small communities will be the end result, but must be flexible enough to encourage design and technological innovation. A more specific application of the principles must be completed as development or redevelopment areas become more clearly defined and as the master plan evolves.

# Principle One

## HUMANISM

*Design for the human, pedestrian scale, to create a sense of community and neighborhood. The community must be a place for people to live, work, play, and interact.*

A small community must be designed for:
- human scale, proportions, and perceptions

- walking and the pedestrian realm on streets in ways that enhance the human experience, and accommodate cars, trucks, and transit

- the facilitation of human interaction by the design of the network of streets, spaces, building uses, and the linkages between them

- private and semi-private areas for all households

- neighborhood/community cores to be a focus for community interaction

- a mix and range of housing types, household compositions, and people of all ages

- participatory community associations

- the fourth-dimension

### Human Scale Proportions and Perceptions

Understanding and respecting the human scale is vital at all levels of design and is critical in the overall design of a small community. The human scale is the relationship between the dimensions of the human body and the proportion of the spaces which people use. This is underscored by surface texture, activity patterns, colors, materials, and details. The measurement of the human scale to the quality of place can be assessed in the values expressed in the VPS $^{TM}$. Those places which respect the human scale offer walks through visually interesting and positive streets and spaces, create opportunities for positive interaction, feel more comfortable to people. The understanding of walking distances and spatial perceptions at a human scale determines the most

An ideal pedestrian realm on a comfortably proportioned street.

Pedestrians move at 2 - 4 miles per hour.

positive placement of buildings and the physical layout of the entire community. Buildings ranging in height from two to six stories, trees and pedestrian-scaled signs and street lights, textured pedestrian paths, and semi-private spaces all enhance this positive scale.

An adult is approximately six feet tall, has an arm span of equal distance, and comfortably walks at about three to four miles per hour (250-350 feet per minute). Our perceptions are more precise at this speed; visual and other sensual input are enhanced. Six decades of reliance on the auto has altered the level of detail and quality of design in most places. Consequently, we must redefine the pedestrian realm, those places where pedestrians feel most comfortable. These basic human dimensions and interactions inside these spaces determine how people perceive a place as they move about, as well as how they can use a place or space. The relationship of building hieght to street width is critical.

The automobile is about 6 feet wide, 12-15 feet long, and it can move at speeds ranging from 10 -100 miles per hour. Most contemporary planning is more in scale with the automobile; the design of our suburbs is a direct result. New suburban developments have a completely different feel and human value than traditional places designed for slower speed vehicles and the limitations of human walking. The more traditional places have been designed with a greater sense of human scale. A sensitivity to human proportions and perceptions throughout the design will assure a more functional community. The creation of streets, not roads or highways, provide the opportunity to create the correct balance of pedestrian and mechanical scale.

A roadway in a new PUD is mechanical in scale; It presents a garagescape.

Human Scale vs. Mechanical Scale

## Walking and the Pedestrian

The walking distance between the home and various facilities must be a fundamental factor in design and layout. The decisions about distances and the design of pedestrian realm must be made early in the design process and must be adhered to throughout; it must be clear that the community is to accommodate people first, and then vehicles. Smaller scaled streets, which can still accommodate cars, are more appropriate and pleasant for pedestrians.

A movement network which supports and encourages pedestrian movement is a design element which creates a sense of place. Pedestrian linkages (sidewalks) between housing and schools, jobs, commercial and social facilities, and recreation areas provide opportunities for people to meet and interact. Greater safety and a feeling of security goes hand-in-hand with a more active street life. In any design plan, the sidewalk must be continuous. It must form a complete network; if there are any breaks it is incomplete and unacceptable.

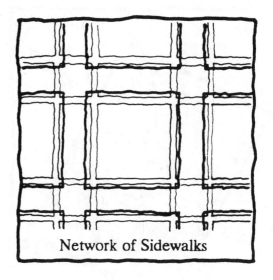

Network of Sidewalks

## Facilitate Interaction Person-to-Person

To reinforce the human scale, the design of a place should facilitate the creation of neighbors, neighborhoods, and a sense of community while insuring privacy. Face-to-face interaction is a fundamental human need and perhaps more important today when the traditional family is waning--the sense of community is the logical substitute. We must design and regulate with this need in mind. The definition of yards, particularly private rear-yards, and semi-public front yards, and neighborhood or community gathering areas is critical. Human elements range from benches and low walls which invite spontaneous gathering to civic spaces and parks which encourage community-wide interaction. All must be provided in each small community.

One of the strongest human experiences is the interaction with the other people.

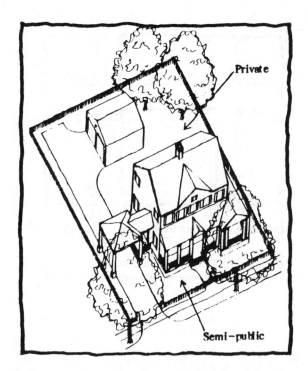

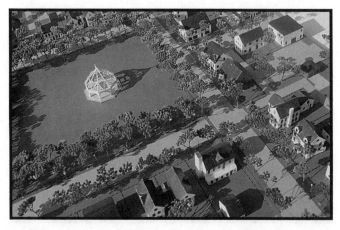

Community space incorporated into a neighborhood plan for Washington Township.

## Semi-Public and Private Spaces

While public life is essential to a livable community, a sense of privacy is also important; "good fences make good neighbors." A private rear yard or other related private space such as a patio or balcony must be provided for each unit. A minimum of 400 square feet for a rear yard or 80 square feet for a balcony or terrace should be provided; these should be screened for privacy.

A semi-public space, the area between the front sidewalk and the building, must also be provided. Semi-private areas, porches which greet the street and front yards defined by short fences or shrubs, create a transitional zone between the public and private domains. Residents can watch the street and greet their neighbors from a front yard or porch while feeling secure in their own environment. Provision of this semi-public space also acts as a crime deterrent particularly for acts at the ground level. Alleys and shared driveways also create semi-private places encouraging neighborly interaction. I have walked down many alleys and am invariably asked, "What are you doing walking down our alley?"

## Community Space

The sense of community is enhanced by the physical characteristics of the common spaces. Small communities need places where people can meet. On the hamlet or village scale, the provision of a green or common area surrounded by civic and/or mixed-use buildings creates the focal point or core of the community and encourages interaction. Country clubs, community centers, cafes, plazas, and even kiosks are places where people can meet in formal or informal situations. The location of such facilities where people can cross paths is a key to a sense of neighborliness. Parks and recreation areas in close association to retail and commercial areas are ideal for facilitating interaction among many groups. The small community has the responsibility to re-create a sense of neighborhood, which can be fostered through the physical layout of the pedestrian realm and the presence of community spaces. In a small community this is the core, green, common, or transit stop. In the larger town or city, community facilities may be oriented toward specific neighborhoods as well as larger focus areas where many neighborhoods meet. The larger the community, the larger the core.

## A Mix of Houses and People
## The Grandpa - Jennifer Test

The sense of a safe, socially healthy, and visually interesting place is enhanced by the provision of a range of housing types and sizes to accommodate households of all ages and sizes. The location of varying housing types within a small community creates physical variation as well as population diversity. The provision of housing for senior citizens allows grandchildren to walk to their grandparents, and for the community to be occupied in the day when most suburbs are devoid of people.

I have a simple test for basic livability; it is called the Grandpa and Jennifer test. Good design requires that you should be able to answer yes to all of the questions.

Question 1: Can Grandpa and Jennifer live in the same community at the same time?

Question 2: Can Grandpa and Jennifer walk downtown safely and comfortably?

Question 3: Will Grandpa find a safe, convenient place to sit down and meet his friends while Jennifer finds something to keep her occupied?

The block with alley provides a maximum opportunity to mix building types and lot sizes.

A range of incomes is desirable and important. Ghettos at either end of the economic spectrum are unacceptable. It is a matter of balance. In New Jersey, based on the litigated Mount Laurel decision, a balance of 80% middle and upper income and 20% low and moderate income households is recommended. In order to achieve this, net densities in the range of 4 to 6 units per acre will be necessary to assure the mix and desired visual character.

## Community Associations

The community decision-making structure has an effect on the sense of community and place. Face-to-face neighborhood associations, town meetings, or homeowners associations allow residents to share in common decisions. The proxy-vote system popular in many such associations does not, however, facilitate community interaction, and township-wide meetings are sometimes too large. Residents and neighbors must be given the opportunity to meet, share, and make common decisions regarding their community or neighborhood. These meetings have the potential to create tremendous citizen participation. Participation is the key to creating a shared sense of community.

## The Fourth Dimension of the Plan

You should be able to plot specific activity patterns, tracing on a plan how people will use the spaces and linkages. Use a colored pencil for each type of person, a three year old, a seventeen year old, a 50 year old and an 85 year old person. Draw how they will use and live in this place. This is the key to understanding the fourth dimension of the plan and the human scale.

Traditional villages, neighborhoods, and small towns display excellent examples of design according to the human scale and sense of community. We have been deprogrammed by many of the characteristics in the current pattern of subdivisions and strip malls. We must focus on incorporating human scaled features and functions into the spatial form of development and redevelopment plans to meet the first and most important principle.

Every regulating plan must plot the activity routes and patterns of persons of various ages.

# Principle Two

## ECOLOGICAL RESPONSIBILITY

*Communities must complement the natural characteristics of the area and respect the environment.*

Small communities must:

- strive for a sustainable balance and mitigate any negative impacts on land, air, water, vegetation, and energy

- be located on land suitable for development

- use transfer mechanisms to protect sensitive and open lands, up-zoning in certain areas and down-zoning in others

- complement the natural environment with indigenous vegetation and colors

- preserve important visual features of the landscape

- preserve and protect open spaces, replacing vegetation destroyed by development

- use conservation measures in site design through solar and wind orientation

- provide environmentally responsive sewer, water and storm drain systems

- be responsive to noise impacts

- make recycling an integral part of the community infrastructure

- provide for walking to jobs, transit, and community facilities

The Association of New Jersey Environmental Commission attracts thousands of concerned citizens.

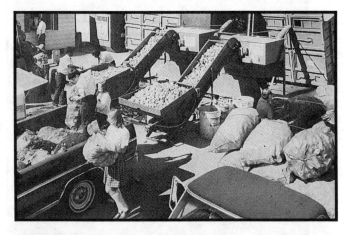

Municipalities and counties have been overwhelmed by the success of the recycling program.

Aerial view of "rural sprawl zoning" of one acre.

## Sustainable Balance

We must minimize our impact on the environment. Ecological responsibility applies not only to the location and siting of the community, but also to the physical design and its effect on the natural landscape, the consumption of energy, and water and air quality. Progress and development can occur without continued long term negative impact on the environment. Today we have better technology and analysis capabilities which can not only chart these negative impacts, but can give us better predictive tools to insure that there is no net deterioration.   Because there has been so much destruction of the natural environment, new development and/or redevelopment must deal both with the problems and costs of clean up and assure that it will not contribute to additional pollution and environmental instability. Clearly the trend is for increased personal and institutional concern about the environment. A large number of Americans now consider themselves environmentalists; recycling has become a huge success.

Environmental protection agencies throughout the country are growing.  They generate regulations and processes to achieve ecological balance.  We will make fewer mistakes in the future, but we are now faced with the almost insurmountable job of cleaning up the past. To survive we must all become more ecologically sensitive. Sustainability will create the new equations for measuring this balance.

The single most important means which we can impose to achieve ecological responsibility would be a revision of the current low density land-use pattern. With its extremely high per capita energy use, high per capita emissions, high storm-water pollution, high physical infrastructure costs, its high social costs, and rapid consumption of agriculturally productive and ecologically important aquifers, forests, and wetlands, It is the very mechanism of environmental degradation.

Small communities must strive for sustainability, an ecological equation in which the negative impact of development and consumption is balanced by responsive land use combined with recycling of resources. This allows for a reduction in the per capita consumption of resources while increasing life quality. It will require a movement away from the trend of personal consumption into more public investment which can be shared by many. This cost balance can be measured and calculated.

## Development Suitability

A development suitability analysis must precede the siting of any development. Communities may only be located on lands that are suitable for development; they may be developed only to the degree that will cause minimum negative environmental impact. Not only will geology, certain soil and topographic conditions, and water supplies limit development, but visual land forms should be considered. Development should not obscure the natural land form. Natural features like ridges, streams, and ponds should be integrated into the design of the public spaces and open spaces of a small community.

A natural resource analysis on unbuilt land must be a part of the development suitability plan. It should include at a minimum, the mapping of the following:
- wetlands
- open water
- seasonal high water table
- flooding potential
- steep slopes
- mature vegetation
- depth to bedrock
- historic sites
- important visual forms and views
- easements and right of ways.
- geology
- endangered species habitats

Certain environmentally sensitive lands or prime agricultural lands in viable farming districts should never be developed, except at very low density ranging from 0 units per acre in the most sensitive lands to one unit per 15 to 50 acres in moderately sensitive lands and/or agricultural areas. It is critical in these areas that Transfer of Development Credits or Transfers of Development Rights be employed.

A ground level view of low density sprawl at ground level.

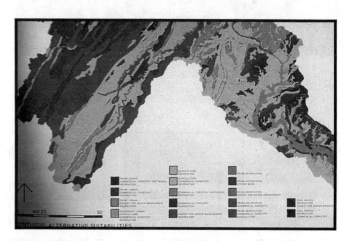

Analysis of national resources is a fundamental component of ecological responsibility. Source <u>Design with Nature</u>.

Many small communities may be created on retrofitted lands which have previously been devoted to other uses. Many of these locations are sites of older industrial areas which may have compromised the environment. Toxic wastes, deteriorated infrastructure, easements, and old foundations will become part of the analysis of the sites and will be impediments, as well as opportunities, for development. These must be located and plotted requiring specific site analysis and mitigation techniques to reclaim these lands.

## Indigenous Vegetation

The small community should strive to complement and enhance the natural environment by using indigenous vegetation. As part of the ecological reconnaissance, specific attention should be given to the types and coloring of vegetation on the site throughout the seasons. Indigenous vegetation should then be used to the fullest extent possible in the landscaping of developments. It will require less maintenance and will complement the other vegetation and natural features of the site.

In many instances smaller trees can be removed from one area and transplanted to another. The "Vermeer" tree scoop can remove trees (four to eight inch caliper trees are the best candidates) below the roots without damage or transplant shock to the tree. Larger scale trees, above eight inch caliper, should be preserved in place. Climax vegetation should be preserved.

## Color

The choice of colors for a development should harmonize with the natural environment, although visual contrasts are both interesting and exciting. Site reconnaissance should document the coloring of soil, rock formations, and vegetation, which is later used in choosing base colors for the community. A minimum of three base colors should be selected to complement or contrast with the site. Three complementing or contrasting colors for each base color should also be selected.

The hydrolic spade move an eight inch caliper tree with little problem.

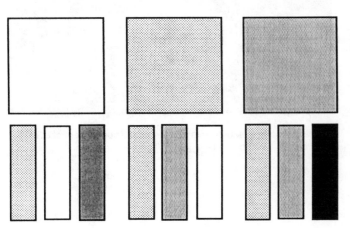

## Views

The siting of buildings and landscape elements is a critical part of ecological responsibility. Communities should be designed so that buildings do not significantly impair, but enhance, the view of important landscape vistas and features. It is not responsible planning to clear-cut a ridge or position houses that block vistas. It is almost impossible to visualize these impacts from a two dimensional plan. Therefore, I recommend the use of either small-scale models or new visual-simulation computer models which can plot the plan over a photograph of the proposed site.

At the master plan level, important vistas should be plotted. These view corridors should be respected by locating development adjacent to this corridor. If this is impossible, the hard edges of buildings must be modified by the soft edge of landscaping; buffers should be planted between the buildings and viewers. In rural small communities, a steeple or narrow clock tower rising above the base landscaping is a positive visual feature which can complement the natural landscape and indicate from afar the center of the community.

Internal views onto green parks or a commons and streets terminated in green spaces are very positive features. The most popular houses have views out the back yard into open spaces whether they be woods, open land, or agricultural fields.

## Solar Power

Solar gain and wind buffering affect energy consumption. These should be considered in street orientation and the siting of buildings. Southern oriented windows and greenhouses with sufficient wall or floor mass to absorb the heat in the winter and nearby trees to shade them in the summer are important features in the reduction of heating and cooling costs. Using coniferous trees on the north and northwest sides of buildings or groups of buildings buffers against the winter winds and can significantly reduce heating costs.

## Documenting View Corridors

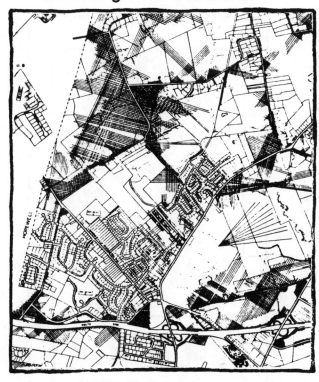

 Unobstructed View Corridor

Ideal solar orientation for housing units

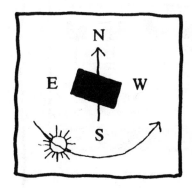

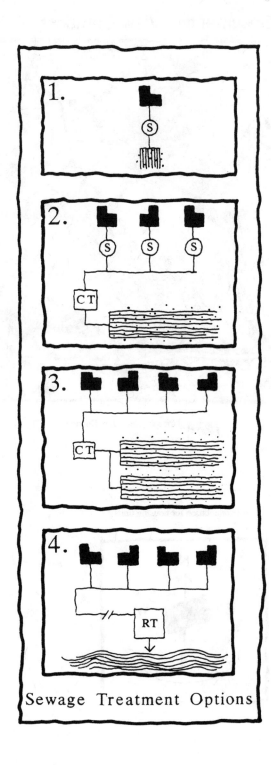

Sewage Treatment Options

## Community Infrastructure

Negative environmental impacts can be eliminated through the use of an appropriate infrastructure technology. Individual lot septic systems must consider soil conditions, have appropriate filtration beds, and utilize alternatives such as low-flow designs. Run-off detention facilities are now required to mitigate the impact of development. Community water and wastewater facilities must be provided when the net density of development prevents the use of individual septic systems.

## Wastewater Systems

The provision of sewers appears to be one of the major impediments to the creation of new small communities.

Wastewater systems can be categorized as follows:
1.- individual septic with individual effluent absorption field
2.- individual septic, community treatment of grey water with a community absorption field
3.- direct connection of unit to a community treatment plant with community absorption field
4.- direct connection of unit to a regional treatment plant with discharge in a stream or river

Locations in close proximity to sewer trunk lines with remaining capacity are prime candidates for the creation of villages and urban villages, assuming they meet other locational criteria. However, the creation of larger small communities may be hampered when connection to existing treatment systems is not possible. Small hamlets may be built using traditional septic systems, if soil and topographic conditions permit.

The open land that remains in many municipalities often presents problems for the use of typical septic wastewater absorption fields. Most townships have zoned areas that do not have public wastewater connections for large lot single family homes. Lot sizes of one- to three- acres per unit are typical of such areas. The resulting pattern is a major contributor to sprawl and is destructive to the rural landscape. When one- to three- acre zoning is used, the creation of the smallest small communities is impossible (unless there is a option that allows all of the density to be concentrated into a hamlet). The availability of new technology and monitoring techniques makes the small treatment plant a viable and ecologically responsible alternative. These alternative treatment systems may be employed to overcome soil and topographic limitations and to generate higher net densities than traditional septic systems would allow. Remember, the most important factor in creating positive small communities is net, not gross, density.

Where limitations are minimal, community design can withstand the use of traditional septic systems. For example, a hamlet or small village may contain narrow lots which are elongated to accommodate on-site absorption fields. Such a design works well in linear communities, but is not practical for larger settlements. For more compact, yet still small, communities, a community absorption field may be utilized. In such a system, each unit has its own septic tank, but wastewater is piped to a small filtration and settlement plant and discharged into a common underground absorption field. The absorption field may lie under community open space. Modifications of the conventional septic tank and leach field system on individual lots can increase the capacity to serve an entire village. These may include pressurization systems which force wastewater through a large network of leach lines allowing one or two absorption fields.

Larger communities provide the economies of scale necessary to allow the efficient use of community treatment facilities. There are a growing number of systems which provide varying degrees of treatment according to specific needs and costs. Small to mid-sized communities also have the option of package treatment. A variety of package plants can provide full treatment and potable water or recycle partially treated water back to toilets. When combined with ultraflow toilets (1-1/2 gallon per flush) recycled effluent systems can reduce the drainfield area by 94% and water needs by 70%. New high-tech systems introduce ever more efficient ways to treat sewage. Some even use a biological process, consuming effluent by use of plants. Since temperature is a critical component, such plants must be located in greenhouses in colder climates like New Jersey's.

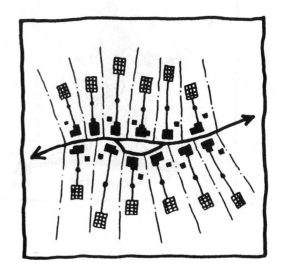

Narrow but elongated lots allow for traditional street scape.

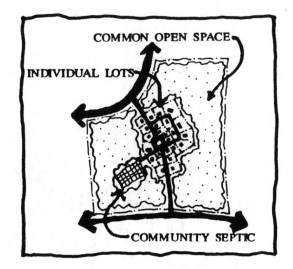

## Individual septic combined with grey water treatment and community absorption fields

### From 30 to several hundred units

This system is highly recommended for hamlets and small villages. It provides treatment and filtration of the grey water. Each lot still has its own septic tank, but rather than connecting to an individual absorption field, the grey water output is sent to a treatment plant, processed, and discharged into a community underground absorption field. Each individual septic tank should be frequently inspected and biologically corrected or pumped of solids, if necessary. The testing of the individual septic tanks, the various processes in the treatment plant, and the final output of the water quality assure biological conformance to standards which are higher than the typical grey water absorption into individual fields.

Regulating plans for a small village.

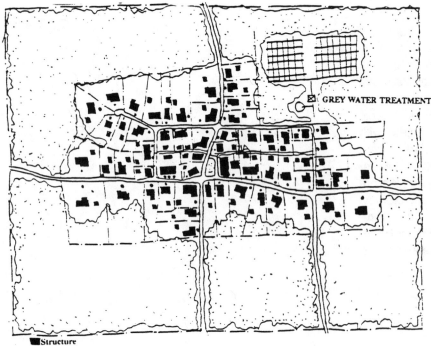

Structure
● Septic Tank
Waste Water Absorption Field

## PROGRAM CHARACTERISTIC
**Small Village**

| | |
|---|---|
| Total Acreage | 192.5 (Base zoning 1du/ 100,000 sq. ft.) |
| Total Number of units | 77 (Average 2.5 A/du) |
| Plotted Area | 107.8 (1.4 A/du) |
| Disturbed Area | 64.4A (33%) |
| Total Septic Tanks | 78 |
| Total Waste Water Fields | 1 |
| Total Conservation Area | 127.6A (66.5%) |
| Image Value | +6.5 |

The piping network that transports the grey water does not require the size of pipes or the expense and engineering requirements, such as manholes, required by gravity sytems that must flush and move solids. Small pipes that move grey water are far less expensive. The treatment plant is computer automated and small, the size of a double garage. It is monitored daily and has built in pumps and warning devices. Home owners in the small community can own and maintain the system.

Two absorption/filtration fields are planned, although only one is built. The second is available if the first one reaches its filtration limit. Variations on this system involve the method of discharge; both underground and overground disposal can be used. Overground land treatment systems can be sprayed or ponded, although both have less public acceptance than underground filtration.

Overground disposal systems can service large numbers of housing units. 10 to 20 acres is required per each 100 housing units. This land can be used as open or recreational space. Lagoons store partially treated odorless water until it is sprayed onto the land for absorption. It is often difficult to assemble a large enough parcel of land to permit the use of this system. Transfer of Development Rights, however, could solve this problem and, at the same time, provide open space.

Communities with populations of 1,500 or more require major treatment facilities; these can be a financial burden on the municipality and its residents who have to finance and build this plant, or expand an existing plant, before assessing hook-up fees and operating costs. To reduce this bond burden, hook-up fees are charged as each unit is attached to the system, or developers can pre-purchase sewer allocation. The result of these measures, however, is that few large regional facilities get built. Growth planned to accommodate a phased system is one answer to the high cost of major treatment facilities. As a community evolves from a small hamlet to a village, it moves from individual septic to community treatment of grey water. Lines can be laid and remain dry until needed; this will save future costs. As the village continues to grow, its small treatment plant can be converted to a pumping station and a larger plant comes online. There are many scenarios to follow when phasing-in a system, but all accommodate growth and make efficient use

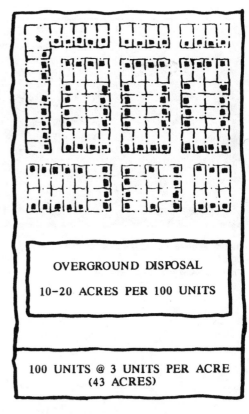

OVERGROUND DISPOSAL

10-20 ACRES PER 100 UNITS

100 UNITS @ 3 UNITS PER ACRE
(43 ACRES)

Overground disposal requires 10 to 20 acres per 100 units. The above example requires 43 to 53 acres.

Small treatment plant serving a village.

of the infrastructure.

Major regional treatment plants call for a hook-up via four inch, or greater, sewer pipes directly to the treatment plants. Most of these systems are gravity systems and/or a combination of gravity and pump station/force main. Careful engineering and field placement of lines is critical. Treatment plants are larger and typically discharge into streams or rivers. Of obvious importance is both the quality and the quantity of the discharge.

## Phasing

Phasing can be a critical factor in the provision of sewer facilities. Many phasing plans are possible starting with individual septic and absorption fields, evolving into a small community treatment and absorption field as the number of units gets larger, and finally hooking up to a larger regional plant.

The phasing of treatment facilities might call for the temporary use of a small treatment plant which is converted into a pumping station when needed. In this case, larger sewer lines are required because the long term plans call for the eventual hook-up to larger regional treatment plants.

## Infrastructure: water

Water service in hamlets can be provided by individual wells, however, a larger community well is most cost efficient and ecologically responsive because it can be monitored and filtered, if necessary. In larger communities, either a community well or a connection to a regional water company is most likely. It is essential that there be sufficient pressure and capacity to provide fire fighting capabilities. Stand pipes boxed into a structure which looks like a bell carillon or clock tower are my favorites. Retention ponds can also be used to store water for fire protection use.

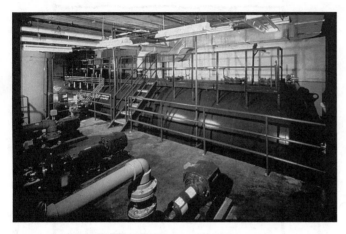

Small community treatment plant is contained in a building the size of a double garage.

*Photo: Advanced Wastewater Technology*

Water tower is built into the clock tower.

## Infrastructure: Electric, Telephone and Gas

All other infrastructure, electric, gas, telephone, and cable must be provided underground as it enters and is distributed throughout the site. These must be provided in the right-of-way or an easement. Electrical magnetic emissions for larger electric cables must be monitored and appropriately located away from housing, pedestrians, and recreation areas.

## Infrastructure: Storm Water Detention

Each site will generate run-off. Most of this must be controlled for quality or the amount of pollution it carries, and for the quantity of water that is generated over and above the current run-off on the site. Most new run-off is directed to a detention basin via ditches, swales, or pipes. Grassy swales are recommended for removing pollutants. Curbing is required where erosion and slope require it.

The size of the detention basin(s) must be provided in relationship to the amount of run-off caused by new impervious surfaces on the site. Too many of these basins are devoid of any ecological or aesthetic relationship to the site. Typically, they are over-engineered holes. My recommendation is that the basin have terraced or gently sloped sides and be planted with wet tolerant vegetation. They should not scar the landscape, but rather be spatially and ecologically integrated into the site so that they look natural.

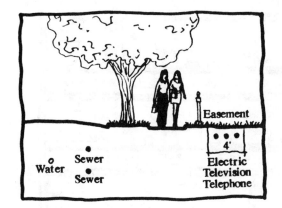

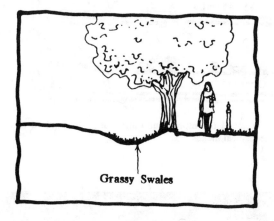

The Storm Water Detention Basin should be intergrated into the landscape.

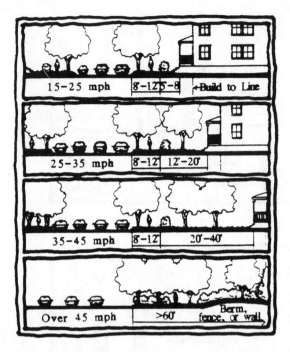

The greater the speed the more sound attenuation is required through distance or mechanical means.

Bicycling is encouraged through the provisions of marked roadways and off street paths.

## Noise

Another aspect of ecological responsibility is the protection of residents from the negative impact of noise. All streets generate some noise. High speed roadways with high traffic volumes can generate levels of noise between 70 and 80 dB; this is unacceptable for residential areas. Speeds in residential areas should be limited to 35 mph or lower to adequately address problems of sound generation. The higher the speed, the further away from the roadway a residence should be sited. If this cannot be done, sound walls or berms are required. Sound should be attenuated to at most 55 dB at the outside walls of residences, a level which has moderate effect on outdoor activity. Normal construction methods reduce indoor noise levels by 15 to 20 dB (with windows closed), and an indoor level between 35 and 40 dB is acceptable. The most useful method of noise attenuation is distance from the source; noise levels drop between 4 dB and 6 dB each time the distance is doubled. Trees do not effectively decrease the necessary distance from the source. The only effective barrier to sound is a solid berm or wall of adequate height. Berms can be appropriately designed to shield homes from noise and are preferable to the sound walls often placed along our highways.

## Recycling

Every small community must have active private and community recycling programs. These must include the design of special recycling facilities and areas within the unit that are easily accessible for pickup. Individual garden composting should be allowed and encouraged. Community recycling of leaves can be composted on site. Creating building materials from recycled materials should be encouraged.

## Walking and Bicycling

The ability to walk, cycle, or use a transit system to reach recreation, retail, office, and job destination can significantly reduce the consumption of energy and the emissions of pollution. These modes also allow for a greater interaction with nature, observation of seasonal and daily changes, and an appreciation of such features as clean air and streets. Facilities and conditions to enable walking and cycling must be incorporated into the site plan.

# Principle Three

## PEDESTRIANISM

*Design for pedestrian dimensions and distances through compact form, layout, and streetscape characteristics.*

Define the size and function of a small community by the following, design in terms of:
- pedestrian precincts

- provide services, facilities, and jobs within walking distance

- locate the highest net density of uses closest to the core

- develop transit expand pedestrianism

- create a network of pedestrian paths

- assure continuity which improves the pedestrian experience

- appropriately size and locate crosswalks and de pressed curbs, with small curb radii

- provide ground texture

- provide appropriate sidewalk widths

- properly proportion the pedestrian realm

- create security in the pedestrian realm

- insure proper treatment of sidewalk edges

- provide pedestrian scaled lighting and other street furniture like benches and trash receptacles

- provide proper signing

- provide bicycle paths

*"We are surrounded by modern inventions designed to keep us from walking. Our environment seems to be telling us that walking is something we should avoid. In fact, walking is good for you. It is an every day activity that you can transform into a regular exercise program to help develop and maintain fitness."*
*American Heart Association*

Some communities are more walkable than others.

## Recommendation of American Heart Association:

**30 to 60 minutes of walking three or four times per week**

Calculation:
250 feet per minute for 45 minutes four times per week = 45,000 feet.

**At a maximum of 1,500 feet from a residential home to the core of your community, you should take this walk 30 times a week as a minimum health requirement, ...that's four times a day.**

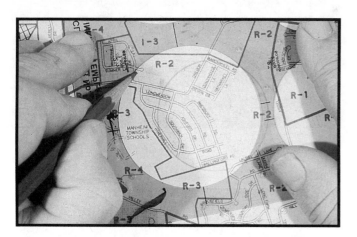

First use the circle template to determine the five minute distance from the core or center of a community.

## Pedestrian Precincts

A pedestrian precinct is defined by walking distances that are acceptable to the average person. For an adult, five minutes seem to be the optimum walking distance between home and the core of a community. Beyond this five minute distance it is most likely that people will use their cars. The following basic pedestrian precincts and corresponding areas must be delineated to define and create places people will walk.

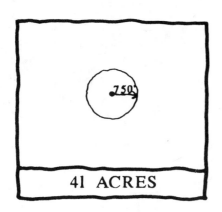

41 ACRES

### The First Pedestrian Precinct

The first precinct is the distance which people will walk from their parked car to the entrance of their destination, the store, a job, etc. This has been generated from questionnaire responses as part of various visual preference surveys. The optimum walk is 750 feet. This defines an area of 41 acres.

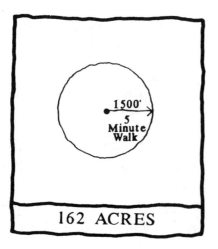

162 ACRES

### The Second Pedestrian Precinct

The second pedestrian precinct is the five minute walk. This defines a neighborhood, a village from the core to the periphery, or an employment area with a center containing a commuter pick-up point. This is an area of approximately 162 acres.

### The Third Pedestrian Precinct

The third pedestrian precinct is a more complete community containing a retail and commercial core. The analysis of the size and length of shopping areas in small towns and shopping centers suggests an optimum walking distance of 1000 feet, providing that the core is interesting and continuous. Pedestrians will easily walk five minutes beyond the core if there is a secure and pleasant pedestrian realm. This defines an area of approximately 230 acres.

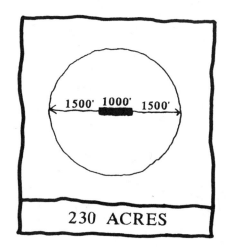

### The Fourth Pedestrian Precinct

The fourth precinct is the area and distance between the home and the neighborhood school. Most municipalities and school boards have a bussing policy which says that children within one-half mile of the school walk when there is a safe and secure pedestrian realm. This distance defines an area of approximately 500 acres.

The acreage generated assumes that there are no ecological or existing land use conflicts. The circles will be transpired into isobars as actual walking paths are plotted.

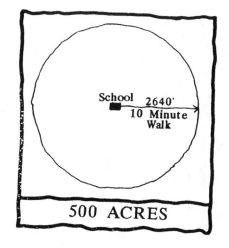

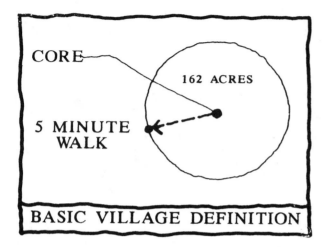

## Defining the Size and Function of a Community by Walking Distance

This is the most important physical design rule. Master plans should be a series of circles and ellipses defining Pedestrian Precincts and small communities. Within each small community there must be a balance of residential and non-residential uses. Residents of a small community must be able to walk to the center of their community, jobs, recreation, community facilities, and transit. In smaller communities, like hamlets and villages, this walk will bring one to a civic business area that also contains a transit-feeder or computer-commuter bus stop. In larger towns composed of linked neighborhoods the walking distance defines the neighborhood. In communities larger than a hamlet, residents should not be dependent on their automobiles for most of their daily trips. They should be able to walk from housing to schools and recreation, to a community and retail center, to places of employment, and to some form of linked transit. If destinations are located at distances of greater than 1,500 feet apart, people will drive.

The following optimum walking distances should be employed in community design:

| | |
|---|---|
| Community core | 1,000 ft. from end to end |
| Between core and community edge | 1,000 - 1,500 ft. |
| Between home and transit | 1,300 - 1,500 ft. |
| Between home and jobs | 1,500 - 2,000 ft. |
| Between home and community facility, school, or recreation | 1,500 - 2,000 ft. |

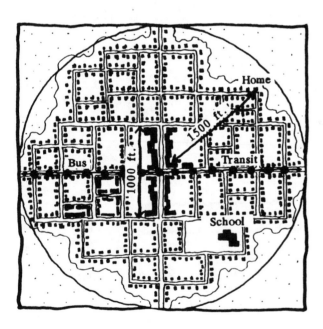

These distances have been verified through field observations, questionnaires used with the VPS ™, and other national and international standards. The case study analyses confirm that these distances held true in pre-automobile era communities. It is crucial for the creation of small communities that these walking distances be respected. While the automobile confers greater freedom in going longer distances, it isolates people. Walking encourages community involvement and promotes a sense of camaraderie. Furthermore, by enabling residents to walk to some or many of their daily needs, car trips can be greatly reduced within and between communities. This has a significant positive impact on air pollution and on the maintenance of paved surfaces. Additionally, when retail shops and services are located within walking distances of homes, the need for parking can be greatly reduced.

## Locating the Intensity of Uses

Community size is influenced by walking distances, but it need not be limited by them. The lower level of small communities (hamlets and villages) has a primary development area extending approximately 1500 feet, or a good five minute walk, with a secondary support area extending 400 feet to a mile from the core. Pedestrianism dominates the primary development area. The secondary support area greatly depends upon bicycles and cars. Hamlets typically extend less than the 1,500 feet. Approximately 80 or 90 percent of the housing units must be located within that 1,500 foot walking distance, or 160 to 230 acre area. By adding the 10-20 percent located outside that area to the primary developed area, we determine the community's size, function, relationship of non-residential to residential buildings and job balance. Units outside the primary development area of a hamlet or village should be very low density (one DU per six to fifteen or more acres) and have access via a continuous network of bicycle paths and streets.

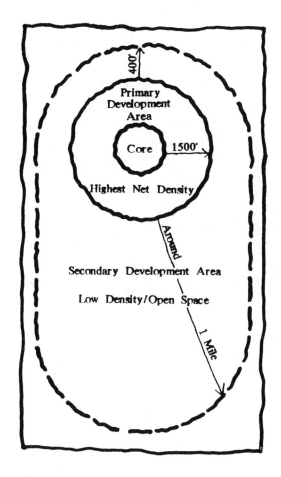

Diagram of core. The primary and secodary development area.

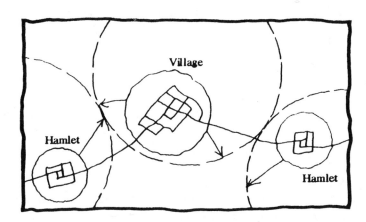

Two hamlets or a village with their secondary support area.

Each hamlet or village has its sphere of influence. Each has a core, a primary developed area, and a secondary/open space area. Hamlets and villages should be sufficiently isolated in order to maintain their own identity.

Larger lots are located on the periphery of the small community.

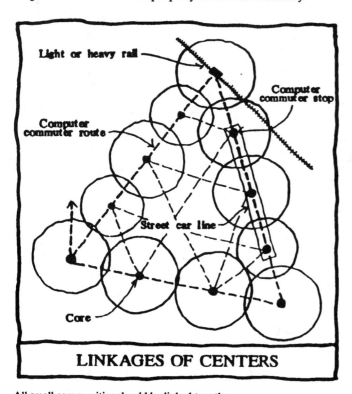

LINKAGES OF CENTERS

All small communities should be linked together.

The highest intensity (scale and highest floor area) of buildings must be in the core, with the highest net residential adjacent to and mixed into the core. Net residential density will decrease as one reaches the edge of the primary development area. The core area should have a minimum net density of one to four dwelling units per acre. Units above shops and offices and multiple use residential units compose this density. The primary developed area, that immediately surrounding the core, should have a net density of four to eight dwelling units per acre. The density then drops radically in the secondary area, except if it is adjacent to a neighborhood. When you have a town with linked neighborhoods, the same low density standard should apply to those edges of neighborhoods which do not interface with another primary core neighborhood. Open spaces, parks, very low density uses, larger boulevards, or natural features can separate neighborhoods.

## Transit Links Expand Pedestrianism

If the pedestrian domain, the walking distance from home to core, is to be extended and auto dependence reduced, pedestrian compatible transit, e.g. the computer commuter should be provided. The provision of transit alternatives can significantly expand the pedestrian range. Streetcars and light rail transit, which move at speeds compatible with pedestrian movement (8-20 miles per hour), are the most favorable alternatives for intra-community transit. They are the most cost effective way to expand the pedestrian range. The area defined by the pedestrian range is measured by a time distance diagram. Most simply, it is a circle of 1000 to 1500 foot radius. The center of this circle should be a transit stop with some open space and mixed-use buildings. In the smaller communities or villages there should be a feeder bus that connects to other centers. If a person can get from his home to any other home, business, open space, civic and social facility, and job location by walking, bus, or transit the system is complete and the pedestrian realm has been optimized.

Every small community must be linked to other small communities by roads, bicycle paths, and transit. Transit options can be provided by a variety of bus types which can function as inter-community and regional transit. Transit connections and bus stops are important design elements of centers; they are important places in the community. A transit stop must have prescribed walking distances and must be linked with other transit stops. They must be thoughtfully designed and located to function at the human scale. The best bus stops are those integrated with a neighborhood retail center, a place to pick up a paper, magazine, or snack. They must be protected from the weather and have clearly posted schedules indicating origin and destinations if they are to be pedestrian friendly. All residences in the primary development area must be within walking distance of these stops because they are excellent traffic mitigation measures. Transit stops can also be used for less formal car and van pools.

## A Network of Walkways

An interlinked network of pedestrian walkways is a basic design feature in the creation of small communities. The network must link housing, schools, retail facilities, community buildings, jobs, recreational fields, open space, and bus stops to one another. Sidewalks must be continuous. The planner must be able to cut out the sidewalk network and lift it off the plan; it should hold together like a lace doily. If it falls apart it is not complete.

The network of sidewalks, alleys, and other pedestrian should be clearly understandable passages. In extremely small communities with very low vehicular volume the road edge may act as this pedestrian way. However, most communities require separate sidewalks. Pedestrian crossings should be clearly delineated and handicapped access curbs are, of course, required. Signs should be posted at the entrance of communities so that the pedestrian has the right-of-way in marked cross walks.

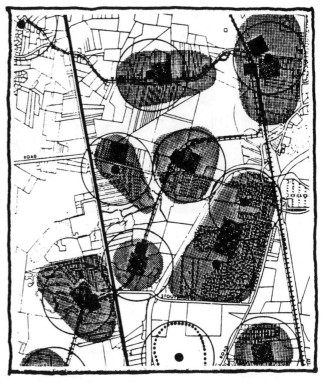

Each small community has a transit or bus stop in the core/center.

The sidewalk network continues across streets and into the surrounding residential units.

The street landscape treatment and building facades create positive visual continuiity.

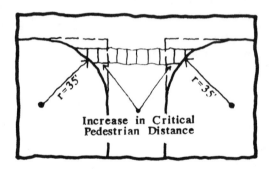

Inappropriate curb radius

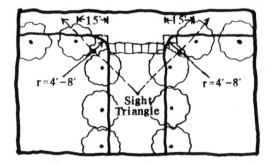

Appropriate curb radius

## Continuity

The walking experience must be pleasurable if people are to choose walking over driving. People are generally willing to walk longer distances if they are provided with a continuous and pleasurable experience. Continuity is created by the placement of trees, the width of the parkway, the treatment of building facades, the treatment of the public and semi-public edge, and the treatment of the vehicular movement edge of the sidewalk. Edge continuity can be destroyed by open edged parking lots, blank walls, and a treeless expanse of sidewalks. Interesting pavement, fences, hedges, and architectural details enhance the experience.

## Curb Radius and Crosswalks

The treatment of sidewalks and streets is especially important at points where they intersect one another. As a rule, the continuity of the sidewalk should continue across the street. In other words, the pedestrian walkway should be defined by a change of texture in the street. A pavement change indicates that at this point drivers must yield the road to pedestrians. Handicapped access must be provided using depressed curbing at all crosswalks. Pedestrians must be provided with the shortest possible route across street intersections; provide small curb radii. It is possible to use a curb radius between four and eight feet while accommodating occasional truck and emergency vehicle access. If parallel-parked cars are prohibited within thiry feet of the intersection, then trucks can use the extra street-width to successfully and easily maneuver. Finally, pedestrians and drivers must be able to see each other. Sight triangles are adequate when trees are kept back fifteen feet from the intersection. These trees should be kept trimmed five to eight feet from the ground, and special species may be used to increase visibility. In areas with projected high volumes of pedestrian traffic crossing intersections, the free right-turn-on red must be eliminated. This movement creates a high incidence of pedestrian accidents.

## Ground Texture

Ground texture is the most important visual surface. Ground texture increases value. It is an important element in creating a pleasurable walking experience. When walking, humans tend to look down at a fifteen degree angle. We pay considerable attention to the ground in front of us. A textured ground surface is more interesting and pleasing to the eye than the usual concrete sidewalk. There are many ways of creating a textured walking surface. One of the classic options is the use of brick or concrete pavers. Pavers come in a wide variety of shapes, sizes, and colors. They allow creativity in their application. It is true that pavers are an expensive option, but, when properly designed and constructed, a brick paver sidewalk is cheaper to repair and will last longer. A less expensive way of creating ground texture involves applying creative techniques in the use of concrete. Concrete sidewalks can be scored in interesting patterns, and they can be colored to simulate natural materials. Concrete can also be used in conjunction with brick accents to create ground texture and define the sidewalk. The more visually interesting and engaging the ground texture and pattern, the more positive the visual experience.

## Sidewalk Width

The width of a sidewalk should be in direct proportion to the projected volume of users. A three foot wide residential sidewalk is comfortable for the lone pedestrian, but two people can walk side by side more comfortably on a four and a half foot wide sidewalk. As the number of pedestrians increases, a wider sidewalk becomes more comfortable.

## Perception of the Ground Plane

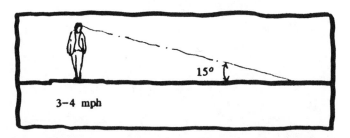

The more ground texture the higher the VPS $^{TM}$ ratings.

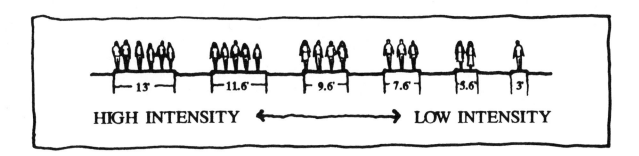

This sidewalk barely accomodates three people. When passing or meeting additional pedestrians someone must step off the sidewalk.

Confortablely proportioned pedestrian realm.

## Proportion of Pedestrian Realm

The proportion of the pedestrian realm is also important to create the positive experience of walking. This proportion is defined as the width of the sidewalk to the height of the edges, walls, and surfaces. The edges of the pedestrian realm can be defined by walls, building facades, overhangs or awnings, street furniture, street lighting, parked cars, and trees. Ideal proportions range from a width to height ratio of 1:1 to 2:1.

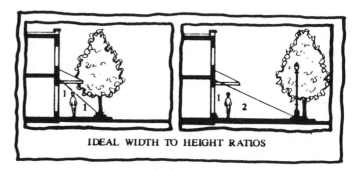

IDEAL WIDTH TO HEIGHT RATIOS

## Security in the Pedestrian Realm

Sidewalks are recommended for streets with a traffic flow of greater than 200 ADT. Pedestrians feel more secure on a sidewalk that is separated from the moving traffic on the street. A parkway in which trees are planted creates a comfortable shield between the pedestrian and the street. Parkways can range in width from four to twenty-five feet, depending on the volume of traffic on the street and on the sidewalk. The heavier the flow of traffic, the greater the need for a wide shield. An even greater shield is created by a lane of parallel parking at the road edge. The presence of parked cars creates a visual and physical shield from moving traffic while reducing road noise as well.

## Edges

The sidewalk edge away from the street may have any number of uses. Its treatment is important. In most cases some sort of boundary should be created to define the pedestrian realm of the sidewalk. In residential areas a low fence or hedge is effective. The relationship of the pedestrian to the front porch or windows of a residence suggests that the ground floor of the house be elevated above the sidewalk level. Privacy is ensured by elevating the ground floor anywhere from two to four feet above the sidewalk. When combined with a fence or hedge, the private and public realms are sufficiently defined and yet integrated. This treatment defines the semi-public edge and acts as a deterrent to crime and intrusion.

Low walls clearly define the pedestrian realm.

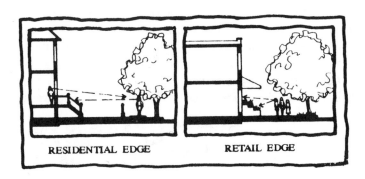

RESIDENTIAL EDGE    RETAIL EDGE

A finished floor that is raised above the sidewalk allows the unit to be pulled closer to the pedestrian realm while respecting interior privacy.

In commercial areas it is preferable to allow buildings to sit directly on the edge of the sidewalk. Not only does the building define the sidewalk, but it indicates that the sidewalk is directly linked to the commercial or public uses inside. A commercial sidewalk is enhanced when the goods sold on the interior are attractively displayed on the exterior. A four foot setback should be required if there will be outdoor displays or other activity. The sidewalk should be on grade with the ground floor along retail frontages, but offices and other civic facilities may be raised above the sidewalk level. Office uses should have a narrow landscaped planting area (foundation plantings) to clearly separate office windows from passersby.

Retail must have direct on-grade access .

Fence or Hedge

When a sidewalk lies adjacent to a park or green edge there may be no need to define the edge of the sidewalk, although such definition produces a more formal linkage to the open space.

## Pedestrian Scale Lighting and Other Street Furniture

Pedestrian amenities will increase the positive experience of walking. Human scale light poles, ranging from nine to twelve feet, should complement the pedestrian realm. The use of lighting varies depending on the land uses adjacent to the sidewalk and the projected amount of sidewalk traffic. Lighting is placed at frequent intervals in busy retail areas, but may be limited to intersections in residential areas. Careful consideration must be given to lighting in small hamlets. The character of these settlements can be drastically altered when too much lighting is provided "for safety's sake." Other pedestrian amenities include benches, flower pots, and low walls for sitting. All of these create a more interesting experience and can provide resting places. Benches should be provided at bus stops and in retail areas. Trash receptacles are required in all pedestrian sitting areas.

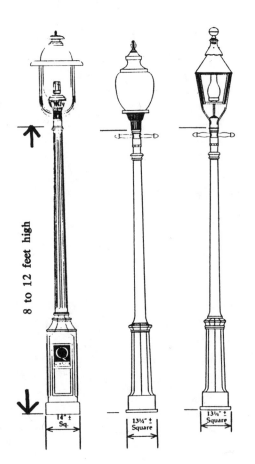

8 to 12 feet high

14" ± Sq.      13¼" ± Square      13¼" ± Square

These are multiple types and styles of poles, fixtures, benches, planters, and trash baskets.

## Signs

The pedestrian experience is enhanced by the quality of signs. Signs can be of a small scale and do not have to shout for the pedestrian's attention. People can absorb much more information when moving slowly; therefore, they do not need the visual clutter or enormous size of competing signage found on highway retail areas. Small signs may be attached to or hang from a facade, painted on the inside of a window, or printed on an awning. They should be limited to approximately two percent of the ground level facade, or if a hanging sign, nine square feet.

Simple attached and hanging signs enhance the character of the building.

Simple projecting sign.

A most creative and playful variation of hanging signs.

A unique, low sign in a planter responds to our natural tendency to look down.

Bike lane in Madison, WI.

## Bicycle Paths

Bicycle paths, although not strictly pedestrian, have a critical role in complementing the pedestrian network. Most local streets have a sufficiently low ADT (less than 500) to allow the bicycle and vehicle mix with little problem. When the ADTs increases, a separate right-of-way should be established. Major arterials and collectors must have bicycle lanes set back from the right-of-way. The minimum one-way lane is 3 (three) feet 4 (four) inches wide per bicycle. Six feet is the recommended width for two-way lanes, but eight feet is still better. Separate designated crossing lanes must be designated at intersections on streets with a high ADT. Specific engineering design must be given to street sewer grates to prevent tire capture.

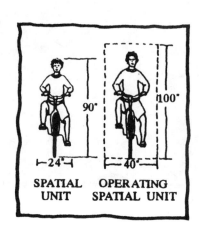

Basic dimensions

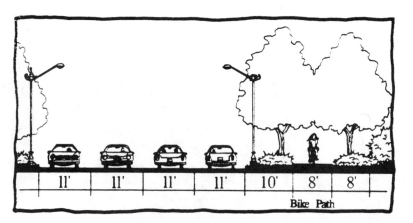

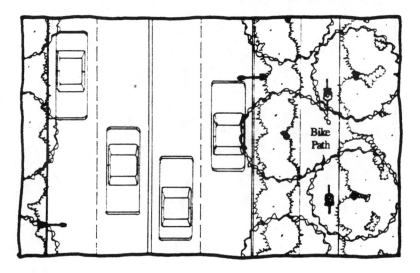

On roads with high ADT separate bicycle paths are required.

# Principle Four

## OPEN SPACE

*Provide for adequate internal and peripheral open spaces*

Open space is one of the most valuable commodities, not only for its visual and aesthetic qualities, but also for its recreational, ecological, agricultural, and economic functions. Open spaces, both peripheral and internal, provide recreational and civic areas. They can serve as a buffer against incompatible uses, an ecological resource, and a boundary for development.

There are several types of open spaces that are integral to a small community, and they serve many functions:

    private spaces
        -private rear yards
        -semi-private front yards

    public spaces
        -parkways
        -active and passive recreation parks
        -community greens and commons

    peripheral spaces
        -open space management
        -peripheral buffers of parks, agricultural lands, very low density developments, or land trust preserves
    TDR, TDC
        -open space generated through transfer mechanisms including TDC on site, adjacent site, and TDR

A highly rated community green. Every small community wants to have a small green or common center.

Peripheral open space is preserved by Hands-On Model workshop participants.

Every single family unit is required to have a small private yard.

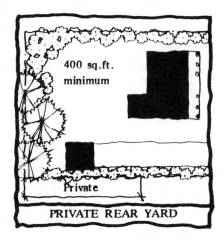

400 sq.ft. minimum

Private

PRIVATE REAR YARD

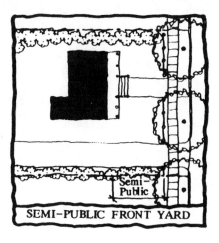

Semi-Public

SEMI-PUBLIC FRONT YARD

## Private Spaces

Private spaces are critical to the basic function of any household. Outdoor privacy is also important to all households, but is especially important for smaller units. While larger units achieve privacy through large yards and greater distances from the public realm, smaller units must rely upon screening or fencing to achieve the same effect.

## Rear Yard

A modest, yet private, landscaped rear yard is necessary open space required for most housing types in a small community . These yards should be at least 400 square feet in size, and should be defined by a hedge or fence about five feet high. The yard can also be defined by rear-yard garages including a storage shed for garden tools, recreation equipment, etc. These can be integrated into the fence. Yard sizes and layouts will vary with housing types and should reflect the use which such a household would normally require of a yard. Small rear yards are ideal spaces for small children and mature adults. The yard will become too small for children eight years old. These children must be able to walk on a sidewalk to a park, playfield,or other open space.

## Front Yard/Semi-Public

A second type of private space is the front yard. This space lies between the public sidewalk and the entrance to the private house; it should function as a transition zone. The semi-public front yard should be physically defined by a low fence or hedge along the sidewalk, and the house should be placed from five to twenty feet further back. The space is thus physically defined as a private area, but is open to view from the street. To reinforce the transitional quality of the front yard, the porch and ground floor of the house should be elevated by two to four feet above the sidewalk. The front porch is a place from which residents can keep an eye on the street and interact with their neighbors. Even the smallest front yard acts as a filter. It is a defined space through which any visitor or intruder must pass in order to enter the private realm of the house. The semi-private space is destroyed when more than twenty-five percent of the front yard is open and devoted to a driveway.

## Public Spaces

Public open spaces are critical to the function of the community. They can take many forms and serve various functions. They provide opportunities for green spaces within the community, formal and informal gatherings, as well as active and passive recreation. Public open spaces must serve all age groups of the community and should be integrated into the pedestrian framework of the community. This public space should include parkways, community greens, commons, and active/passive recreation. They become critical components of the plan as the lot sizes become smaller. Small yards are compensated for by adjacent parks.

## Active and Passive Recreation

Public open spaces should include active and passive recreational uses. These spaces must be geared specifically to the number and age of residents who will occupy the community over time. Active recreation should focus on field sports and games; they should be within walking distance for all children. One field can serve multiple purposes. The size of recreation areas should be larger where older children are likely to participate in organized sports. These are most likely located in the peripheral open spaces. The more passive recreation uses should be encouraged in the commons and in the peripheral open spaces that surround or separate small communities.

Large recreation fields are ideally located on peripheral open space. Golf courses are possible uses for peripheral open spaces if potential non-point pollution is strictly controlled. Larger field recreational facilities will require facilities such as toilets and storage areas.

## The Parkway

One of the most overlooked forms of internal public open space is the parkway. Commonly called a planting strip, this vital open space lies between the sidewalk and the street. The parkway extends internal and peripheral parks and open spaces into the network of streets. Parkways are also used to create boulevards by separating two-lane streets. Besides extending and linking open spaces, parkways serve to separate and define roadways and sidewalks. Parkways vary in width from four to fifteen feet, depending on the street type and intensity of adjacent uses. Street trees should be planted at eighteen to twenty-five foot intervals within the

Small public open space compensates for the lack of a large front yard.

A public common or green in the center of the community accomodate informal as well as community wide activity.

Parkway

parkway. The types of street trees will vary by regional location but should be of a type that will form a canopy over the street.

## Community Greens and Commons

A central green or commons acts as a foundation for the social life of the community and should be an integral element of every small community. Open spaces provide areas for community picnics, bazaars, holiday displays and activities, as well as a place for children to play, and people of all ages to meet and gather. The optimal size of a community green is related to the population of the village; 200 square feet per housing unit is recommended. The green is best located where it is accessible to the highest possible number of residents and adjacent to any mixed-use core. Thus, the commons will be surrounded by buildings which should enclose and define the central space. The relationship of the height of surrounding buildings to the width of the green should fall between 1:1 and 1:5 to assure a spatial definition. The actual size (dimension) can vary, based on the heights of adjacent towers, steeples, or roofridges.

A common green in the center of a small community becomes part of its image of place.

Public space in downtown Lititz, PA..

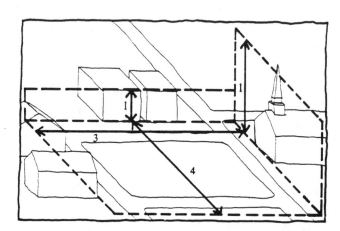

The above example shows a community green which has a proportion of 1:3 in one direction and 1:4 in the other. The proportion is based on the perceived average height of the adjacent structures which form each side of the green.

## Peripheral Spaces

Peripheral open spaces should define the edge of the community. They enhance the sense of place by making the settlement identifiable in the landscape, and they create a sense of entry and exit. Peripheral open spaces also prevent the intrusion of sprawl by establishing a clear development boundary and buffers agricultural lands from developed areas. More importantly, peripheral open space protects and preserves valuable land whether it is environmentally sensitive or used for agriculture.

When working in suburban retrofit situations, it may not be feasible or desirable to surround new development with open space. In such situations, edge definition should occur through changes in density and the reservation of park and recreation areas to help set off one neighborhood from another. Edges of neighborhoods should be defined by the lowest density within each community. As communities become larger, like a neighborhood in a town or city, neighborhood edges are often defined by hard seams, or roads. These seams are typically wider roads with non-residential uses at street level.

## Open Space Management

The provision of peripheral open spaces can result in a number of preservation and management options based on the development policies and design strategies. These include:

- dedication to a home owners association
- dedication to the municipality or quasi-public agency, e.g. watershed association
- conservation easements
- very large lots ownership with conservation easement
- requirement that the land be held, maintained and managed by a home owners association made up of all households within the Community. The state of New Jersey has set forth clear regulations for the penalties upon default of obligation. Each homeowner is required to pay a monthly or yearly maintenance fee. The land can be rented or leased for agricultural use or can be kept natural.

Golf courses are ideal peripheral open space, but care must be taken to control the quality of run-off.

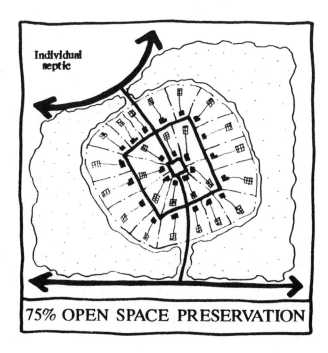

The hamlet in a rural setting has the maximum opportunity for open space preservation. The open space can be managed by a home owners association.

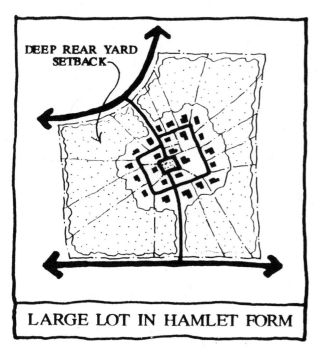

DEEP REAR YARD SETBACK

## LARGE LOT IN HAMLET FORM

Every lot in the hamlet is subdivided to include the entire property. Conservation easements can be incorporated on each peripheral lot

The black areas illustrate the continuous open space network in West Windsor, NJ.

- requirement that land ownership be held by public or private not-for-profit organizations. The ownership can be placed in a nature conservancy or be deeded back to the township as permanent open space.

Under all of these alternatives the land can be deed-restricted against development, although agricultural uses and low intensity recreational uses should be allowed.

In rural situations where development is taking place on a single, large site peripheral open space can be created by the on-site transfer of units into a hamlet. If the existing base zoning is large, over one and a half acres per unit, fifty percent open space preservation is the minimum. A small community, except at the very highest density, can easily result in over fifty to seventy-five percent open space on the site. If a small community is not allowed in the zone, then an overlay district must be created. (See Chapter 8.)

The preserved open space around a small community may also be managed by permitting subdivision into very large pie shaped lots ranging from six to fifty acres per unit. These estate lots cannot be further subdivided, thus preserving the open space. Under this method, however, the open space may not be accessible to the public. Peripheral open space held in private hands may be opened up to the public through deed restrictions or by dedicating some portion of the land as a public conservation easement. Open space easements could also be dedicated for walking and equestrian paths where residents and land owners agree. By placing houses at the front of these very large lots adjacent to woods or hedge lines and off ridge lines and hills, a majority of the land can be fully preserved for open space in perpetuity.

## Contiguous Open Spaces

The peripheral open space will contain environmentally sensitive land as well as land without constraints. All of this land can be placed in an easement with restrictions. To the extent possible, this land should be joined with other peripheral open spaces and environmentally sensitive lands to form a continuous open space. Stream corridors are typically those land forms which naturally join various parcels together. The creation of contiguous easements makes good environmental sense as well as economic sense since houses located adjacent to these easements are typically more valuable. A very controversial issue is the linking of these openspaces with paths for jogging, walking, and/or equestrian uses. These should be encouraged, but only when individual adjacent property owners or home owner associations which have granted the easements agree.

## Transfer Mechanisms

Transfer of Development Rights (TDR) on a municipal or regional scale, or Transfer of Development Credits (TDC) on large and adjacent sites, offer other methods of preserving open space. The Pine Barren Community in New Jersey has the longest history of effectively using this technique.

## Transfer of Development Rights

Where specific property is planned to be preserved in low density uses or for agriculture, TDR mechanisms should be used. Although TDR is complex in application, and limited in its locational application here in New Jersey because of enabling legislation, the concept is simple. In short, the number of units allowed on a parcel of outlying land under base zoning is transferred to a receiving zone which has been planned for a small community at higher net densities. The owners of the land get paid for each unit they sell, these rights are transferred while the owner of the land retains the right to keep it as farmland. Using this method, the ownership of land remains in private hands. All sending area property owners thus receive just compensation for their land provided that the market is driving sales. Unfortunately, this typically only works in boom times. The limitation is clearly determined when a farmer wishes to sell and there is no market for the potential development rights. A bank, using bonded money, can be approached to buy and hold these rights. A municipality can create its goal of achieving a community and prevent sprawl without ecological, social, and economic deterrents.

The other large potential advantage is that the people in the sending area retain valuable production lands close to their market. These agricultural lands are likely to become increasingly more valuable over time. The difficulty today is that many farmers have been conditioned to base the value of land on the developmental potential. There are only three municipalities in Burlington County and the Pinelands that have the legislated right to use TDR. In order to preserve open space and agriculture, and to maintain the economic

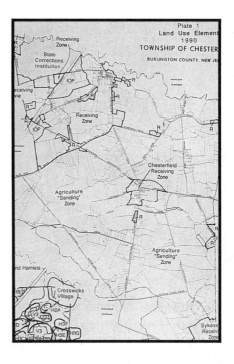

The Transfer of Development Rights (TDR) Master Plan for Chesterfield, NJ.

Farm area to be preserved in Burlington County, Chesterfield Township TDR plan.

## 11 units at 1DU/3 acres in the sprawled pattern divides all of the land and discourages a sense of community.

16 dwelling units and other non-residential uses have a variety of lot sizes, including some very large lots on the periphery. 70% of the land is open. Its design creates the positive benefits of a small community and its diversity provides a broad market potential.

viability of farming, every municipality should be given that right. We should particularly try to preserve Class I, other productive agricultural lands and ecologically sensitive lands

## Transfer of Development Credit (TDC)

Until there is municipal wide TDR legislation, municipalities must allow and encourage Transfer of Development Credits (TDC) on large parcels and in joint venture agreements between owners of contiguous properties. Assuming that the land meets the locational criteria, these joint ventures will ultimately be able to create small communities. The base zoning should be low (one to five units per acre) and equitable across all parcels. Incentives for land preservation must be present.

Such a situation might have the following scenario. In the rural, suburban fringe, or an ecologically sensitive area, we have a 60 acre parcel of land. The previous zoning was for one unit on three acres, if all septic criteria could be met. At best, a development density of 20 units could be achieved. The owner would now have the right to subdivide the property at the base density (in this example 20 units) if, and when, all of the infrastructure criteria (roads and septic) were met.

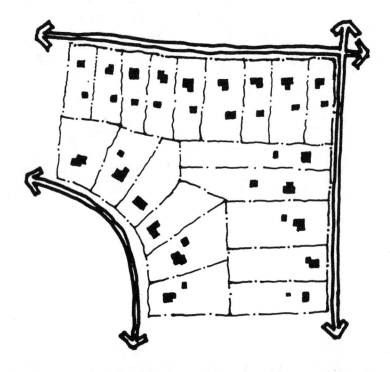

**Conventional 3 acre zoning**

---

**60 acres - 20 acres**
(assumes no environmental constraints and ability for each lot to perk).

---

| | |
|---|---|
| Open Space Preservation | 0 |
| Non Residential Uses | 0 |
| Civic Uses | 0 |

The new master plan has specified development areas with specific recommendations for layout, number of units, etc, on various parcels. The option to create a community could be either a principle permitted use or a conditional use in the zoning.

In this case the owner has opted for the right to develop in a small community. They use the same number of units plus a 20% increase to determine the total number of units, allowed on the parcel. (This bonus may be necessary because developers argue that smaller homes will not achieve as high a profit margin as larger single family homes which can be built at slightly lower square foot costs, and there is a slight increase in the length of roadways or other such issues.) In addition, to create a small community other non-residential uses, civic, job related recreation etc. are required based on the total number of units in the community. This provides an additional incentive. There could be an additional 10% increase in the number of units, if 5% affordable housing were provided.

## Small Community Zoning

| | |
|---|---|
| Allowable number of units | 20 |
| 20% bonus for smaller lots | 4 |
| 10% bonus for 5% low and mod. | 2 |
| Total units | 26 |
| Non Residential Uses - | 9,100 sq. ft. |
| •26 units x (1 job per household) | |
| x 300 sq. ft. per job = | 7,800 sq. ft. |
| •26 units x 50 sq. ft. retail = | 1,300 sq. ft. |
| Civic Uses 26 x 300 = | 7,800 sq. ft. |
| Open Space Preservation | 65% |

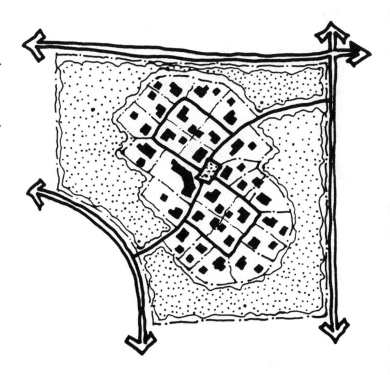

The market advantages to a hamlet include a greater market diversity in unit sizes, and greater appeal to people who want a sense of community and land responsibility. Agricultural or horticultural use of the remaining open space means the ability to live adjacent to permanently preserved open space.

The concept of development credits can be used by several property owners. They can negotiate with adjacent property owners to purchase credits. or owners can create a joint venture and place the development in a specified area. If an owner agrees to the transfer, he or she should also be allowed the 20% dividend. When owners of peripheral adjacent property transfer, they still have the right to develop at the peripheral density of one unit on fifteen to fifty acres of land.

In rural areas the peripheral open space should be dedicated to agricultural or horticultural uses. For example, home owners and members of the association should be allowed to graze animals and keep one horse per unit. Planting Christmas trees is another option.

The opportunity for non-residential uses, permanent preservation of open space, and a larger number of lots should provide the necessary incentives for development profit.

# Principle Five

## CORE

*Every community must have a core or community focus.*

There must be a core that contains commercial, residential, and civic buildings, a green or commons, and that provides a focal point for the community. The size of the core is dependent on the number of homes. The core should be the central point for transit.

The core requires:
- a central and integrated location for equal access
- a balance of residential and non - residential uses
- retail uses in proportion to housing
- job space in proportion to housing
- civic and social facilities
- specific design standards for streetscapes and facades
- vertical element(s) that render it immediately identifiable in the landscape
- the core must be the central point for transit

Core of a small hamlet as seen from the common.

The community focus is the most identifiable aspect of a hamlet, village, or neighborhood for residents and visitors alike. It is an activity center which unifies the community, and its character often becomes the image of the community as a whole. The core allows residents to perform most of their retail, commercial, civic, and social activities in a central place. It is the central pick-up and drop-off point for transit.

The community focus provides potential places of employment, and it provides places for people to interact or congregate. There are three major elements of discussion for the community focus: location, building/land uses, and design.

The highest concentration of pedestrian activity should be in the core.

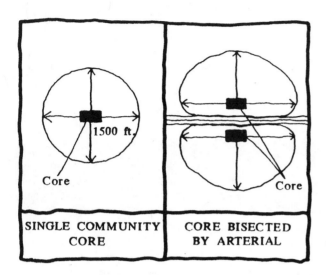

SINGLE COMMUNITY CORE | CORE BISECTED BY ARTERIAL

The parallel parking spaces in the core are the most desirable as demonstrated here in Palmer Square, Princeton, NJ.

## Location

The core should be designed to provide a central place such as a square, green, plaza, or crossroad. Although the linear core is more common in New Jersey, when the core is a square it becomes more memorable. If it is designed as a linear core, the higher buildings are typically located on a curve. The core symbolizes the center of the community, as most activities flow through it, and, to the extent possible, it is surrounded by the community. The core must front on to a street, or streets, within the primary movement network. Where possible, buildings within the core should define the space or spaces. In the case of a small village or hamlet, where a large core cannot be supported by the adjacent residential units, the retail area should occur on one or more sides of the civic space. Head-in and parallel parking around the green or square can absorb large numbers of parked vehicles to reduce off-street parking lots. This will enhance the pedestrian activity pattern on the street.

As the size of the core increases, access becomes more important. The core must be accessible by car, foot, and public transit. Its location will be influenced by existing roads, rail lines, bus stops, and the surrounding residential pattern. If a major arterial or rail line bisects the core it usually bisects the sense of place into two communities.

The size of the core must be in direct proportion to the number of units in the community. A small hamlet will have a small core, while a larger village will have a larger commercial element. A neighborhood within a town will probably have a smaller core than that in a village. However, there should be a balance where all the neighborhoods are connected to one larger downtown main street, or central business district.

## A Balance of Building and Land Uses

If the community is expected to create a true core or community focus, then it must have an appropriate balance of housing to other uses such as retail and services, civic and social, offices and job-generating, light industrial, open spaces, and greens.

The amount of retail and office space should be compatible with the number of housing units and potential users within the primary walking and secondary support areas. This should apply to the construction of new hamlets, villages, or neighborhoods, and also to the redevelopment of older strip malls and residential subdivisions. In suburban retrofit sites, existing sprawled commercial areas should be integrated with residential, civic, and recreational elements to create mixed- and multiple-use cores.

## Retail Uses

Each small community must have a minimum amount of local or neighborhood retail facilities. Generally, between 22.5 and 56 square feet per unit will be required to create an appropriate balance with the provided housing; the minimum must be provided. It is likely that in a hamlet, with a small amount of retail space, only the most basic services will exist. Typical uses found in villages might include a general store, deli, restaurant, hardware store, attorney's office, travel agent, beauty salon, card store/gift shop, video rental, or antique shop. Greater numbers of specialty shops are found in larger villages; small community shops are focused on the daily needs of residents. A village of at approximately 700 housing units may be able to support a small grocery store.

## Jobs

A small community must provide jobs in proportion to the number of housing units in the community. Previously discussed retail uses create a small number of jobs which may adequately meet the recommended job-to-housing ratio for the smallest communities. In larger communities additional space must be allocated for offices, services, and light industrial uses. Most of this should be in the core, but some, particularly light industry, can be allocated to other areas. The following table outlines the recommended ratio of jobs-to-housing units in various communities. The optimal ratio is indicated by the high end of the listed range.

The village of Basking Ridge contains a balance of residential to non-residential uses.

## RETAIL TO HOUSING RATIO

### MINIMUM AND MAXIMUM SQ. FT. OF LOCAL/ CONVENIENCE RETAIL

Minimum: 22.5 sq. ft. per residential unit within primary and secondary community radius

Maximum: 56 sq. ft. per residential unit within primary and secondary community radius

Viable retail uses dominate Main Street in this town center.

To maintain a community focus, it is critical that the appropriate balance between jobs, retail, and housing be maintained within the 90 percent primary community development area. If a new retail use group is created beyond the primary neighborhood/community area, another community neighborhood focus should be designed. Should the amount of retail on a square foot ratio increase, it will become more regional in character; if this happens it will become more auto oriented, unless linked by transit.

The jobs-to-housing ratio can be used as a tool in several ways. It must be used when planning a new small community. In this capacity, the ratio is used to help determine the size of the community from the standpoint of both jobs and housing. In retrofit situations, the jobs-to-housing ratio can be used to determine the number of jobs to be created in an existing residential area, or the number of housing units to be created in conjunction with an existing commercial development.

Downtown jobs in mixed use buildings - retail below, offices above.

## JOBS-TO-HOUSING RATIO

### MINIMUM AND MAXIMUM JOBS TO HOUSING RATIOS

**MINIMUM**

| | |
|---|---|
| Hamlet: | .25 to 1 |
| Village: | 0.5 to 1 |
| Neighborhood with Town: | 0.5 to 1 |

**MAXIMUM**

| | |
|---|---|
| Hamlet: | 1 to 1 |
| Village | 1 to 1 |
| Neighborhood with Town | 1 to 1 |

1991 ULI study for general office space
1 Job equals from 150 to 350 square foot of building space. .

Job generating uses are based on an average of 150 to 350 square feet per employee. Using this figure as a multiplier, the total building floor area can be determined. Once the figure ground is determined, parking needs must be calculated. In a small community the parking ratios are half of the normal suburban standards, or one space per 350 to 600 square feet of building area.

Most job opportunities should be created at the core, although light industrial uses are often better located at the periphery of the community. Within the core, offices should be located in the midst of retail uses. They can be accommodated above retail stores or in adjacent buildings. Office buildings should not differ significantly from their retail neighbors. The proportion of jobs-to-housing should stay at 1:1. If it exceeds this number, the amount of outside traffic will negatively impact the small community.

## Civic and Social Facilities

The third component of the core includes civic and social spaces such as places of worship, libraries, post offices, police and fire stations, and community and recreation centers. As these uses will be major focal points of the community, specific sites should be set aside to accommodate them. The size of these sites is calculated at a minimum of 450 square feet of building lot per housing unit. Day-care and educational space requirements are calculated independently of other civic spaces according to the following basic requirements:

> 1 day care/nursery school per 300 units
> 1 elementary school per 1,400 units
> 1 junior high school per 3,000 units

Educational calculations are dependent upon current regional capacities in existing schools. The local board of education is a source of local information and space requirements. School buildings should be integrated into the fabric of the community. Large recreational fields are best suited in the peripheral open space.

The church along one edge of the town green locates an important civic and social facility in the center of the community.

Successful retail requires good visibility. Well designed outside displays are always a positive addition.

Model of a mixed-use core for a new village.

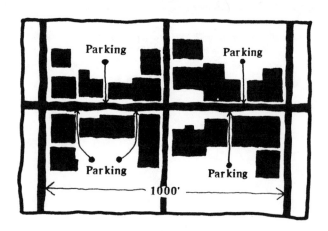

Conceptual figure-ground plan of large village core.

## The Design of the Community Core

Design elements should be used to ensure the retail viability of a core. The core should have buildings of a greater scale and at a higher density than the rest of the settlement. Buildings should have a range of footprints from a minimum of 2,000 square feet to a maximum of 15,000 square feet.

Retail uses need visibility. Retail must front onto a street providing vehicular and pedestrian access. Retail requires a seamlessness or continuous frontage of shops, entrances, and shop windows. These frontage design features are critical to maintain the pedestrian interest. People must not pass in front of blank walls or parking lots as they walk between stores. A greater intensity of activity occurs when retail uses are concentrated. Therefore, buildings at the core should be closely spaced, and the street level should, where possible, be reserved for personal services and retail uses. Cores should have an optimum length of 1000 feet or less. This number has been derived from measurements of existing shopping malls, and working main streets. This 1,000 feet can be extended if the retail frontage is continuous.

Buildings in the core should range from two to four stories. One story buildings should be avoided. Mixed-use buildings with retail on the ground floor and offices or housing above are preferred. Offices and/or apartments should be located on upper floors to enhance the economic, visual, and operational vitality of the core.

Parking must never be allowed in the front of buildings, unless it is on-street, parallel, or head-in. Larger, well landscaped parking areas must be confined to the rear of buildings and connected to the front sidewalk by well designed pedestrian alleys. Rear entrances are encouraged. Rear lot trash receptacles should be well integrated into the architecture or well screened.

The core should have a traditional main street look with architectural details like large display windows, awnings, decorative street furniture, small hanging and attached signs, transoms, and cornices. New buildings should have a sense of being grounded in history and should seek to establish a design dialogue with the underlying historic vernacular of the township in which they are located.

Design the streets so that primary views terminate at larger buildings, distinctive architectural elements, natural features, parks, or open spaces. Pedestrian presence is critical; it signals the vitality of the community. The streetscape should be alive with architectural and human interest.

VPS ™ results and hundreds of model workshops have indicated that a core must have a high point; a core should be identifiable from a distance. This vertical landmark, a steeple, cupola, or bell tower will serve as that focal point. It should also form the visual termination of a street or the common/square.

## Transit in the core

Bus, van pool, school bus, and light rail stops in larger neighborhoods must be integrated into the core of a small community. These are critical pedestrian locations and require specific design treatment to make them work effectively. The location must be central for the majority of the walking patrons in the community. It follows the same 1,500 foot rule. It must be accessible to all residents within a 1,500 radius or approximately a five minute walk. The stop location(s) must contain, at a minimum, a place to sit which is covered and comfortable, newspaper and bicycle racks, a place to purchase a cup of coffee or snack, a trash receptacle, a clock, a telephone, and a bulletin board.

This streetscape in a community core contains many of the desired design features.

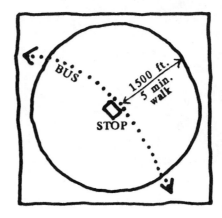

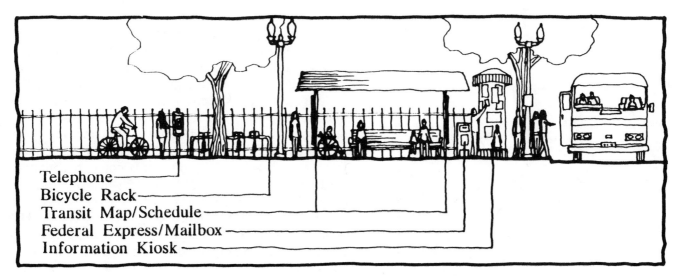

Telephone
Bicycle Rack
Transit Map/Schedule
Federal Express/Mailbox
Information Kiosk

# Principle Six

## STREETSCAPE

*Streetscapes create the form and scale of the community and must accomodate the pedestrian and the vehicle.*

As the foundation of settlement patterns, streets are our most important public spaces and, therefore, require thoughtful design.

There are several basic street and streetscape elements that are critical to the creation of a positive community image.

- the layout of the street in a hierarchical network
- the form of streets
- the sense of focus and enclosure
- the proportions and dimensions
- a response to the natural features
- street furniture

We experience most places from the street, from the public viewshed. The first impression, positive or negative, that a visitor has of a community is that provided by the street. Even long-time residents see their hometown primarily from the street. Since the streetscape plays such an important role in the community image, its design should be considered a major element of the community planning process.

This viewshed is our primary cone of vision. The width of this cone of vision is narrow when traveling at high speeds and expands as speeds lower. At slower speeds we can more fully experience the visual details of the street. The average pedestrian moves at approximately 3 miles per hour. At 3 mph the quality of the space in which you are moving must be continuously rich in details and visual interest. At 50 mph a driver's cone of vision is about 30 degrees. The faster one drives, the smaller the cone of vision becomes and requires more concentration. To read signs at 50 mph, they must be large. At 20 mph, the cone of vision is about 90 degrees. Building edges are important and signs can be smaller. The most negative images occur in strip commercial areas when traffic on a roadway designed for 55 mph actually moves at 20 mph. You feel out of scale. Conversely, when a street originally designed for 20 mph traffic is widened to accom-

A new, high-density residential streetscape in Harbortown, TN, by RTKL.

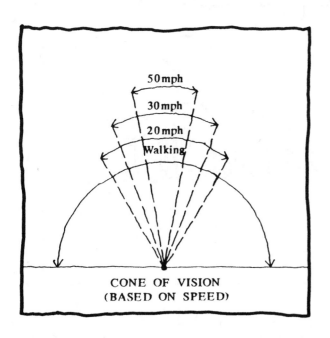

CONE OF VISION
(BASED ON SPEED)

50 mph

30 mph

20 mph

Walking

modate 45 mph traffic the positive value is seriously eroded. Our Visual Preference Surveys [TM] consistently indicate a negative response to most sprawl-related, high speed roads and a positive response to more traditional, lower speed roadways.

### The Layout of Streets in a Network

Streets create the basic form of the community; they define the pattern of development by lot distribution, width, and depth. The layout of streets will influence pedestrian and vehicular movement. Streets should function as a network to provide order and legibility. Two types of layouts are currently typical. The first is the dense network of streets. The second is the omnipresent, curvilinear suburban pattern.

A positively rated an older main street in the center of Tewksbury, NJ.

## Comparison of Two Street Networks

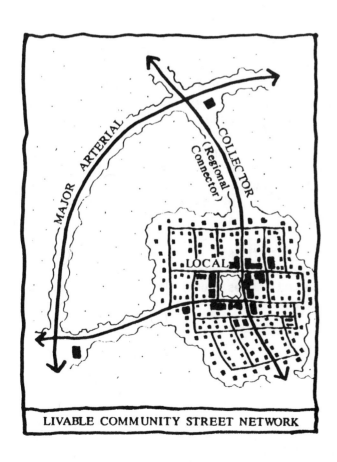

LIVABLE COMMUNITY STREET NETWORK

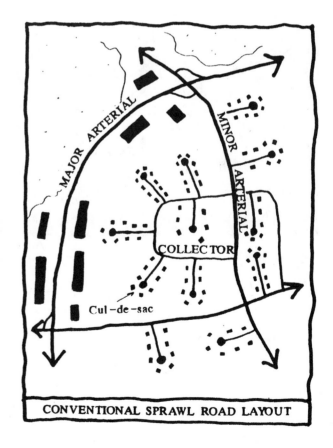

CONVENTIONAL SPRAWL ROAD LAYOUT

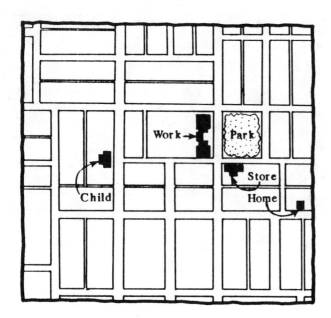

A network of streets.

## The Dense Network of Streets

A dense network of interconnecting, narrow streets laid out in a modified grid is the best way to provide a sense of where you are and to appropriately distribute the flow of traffic. The street network should integrate the community focus and the surrounding residential uses. The main focus area should be served by two principal streets. All other streets should be secondary.

The network relies on freeways, divided highways, multi-lane parkways, and major arterials to provide road types which interconnect small communities. These major through-roads should be routed around a small community. If they go through a community at high speed, they will divide the community, particularly a hamlet or village, and never let the community achieve the potential of its core. Streets inside a small community must be limited to one- or two-way two-lane roads with adequate on-street parking. No other types should be permitted.

Persuasive new arguments and model analysis indicate that a dense network of streets, in combination with the other design principles, provides the maximum ability to create a positive small community. Furthermore, they have the ability to move an equal number of cars more safely and pleasantly than the conventional hierarchy of roads serving an equal population. The network requires that every street connect to at least two other streets. Cul-de-sacs should be employed only when environmental constraints preclude a connection to at least two other streets. The dense network of streets has many advantages over a conventional layout of roads and provides a more positive visual experience. (1)

## Compact land use

The dense street network promotes a tight mix of land uses and lot sizes where buildings are required to front onto streets.

---

1. See Walter Kulash, "Will Traffic Work".

**Narrow roadways** (typically two lanes with parallel parking) The network recommends more interconnected two-lane roadways rather than the conventional, sprawl hierarchy of two, four, six or more lanes. The conventional hierarchy relies on greater use of four- to six-lane arterials and collectors to move traffic. The network relies on freeways and parkways but substitutes the continually wider suburban arterials with a greater number of narrow, local roadways.

**Buildings front directly onto streets**

The most positive streets are those where buildings front directly onto the street accommodating both pedestrians and vehicles at slower speeds.

**Parallel parking on one or both sides**

Parallel parking acts as a buffer between the pedestrian and moving traffic. It accommodates a significant amount of parking. Parallel parking directly in front of stores and shops provide the most sought after spaces.

**Street trees in a parallel parkway**

Street trees must be present in all positive streets.

**Small reduced curb radius**

Slower speeds allow for a smaller curb radius (4 to 8 feet) and help to accommodate pedestrianism.

**Short two phase signals**

The network requires only two phase signals at major intersections as opposed to three phase signals which are less efficient and unfriendly to pedestrians.

**Shorter but more frequent intersection delays**

There are more intersections in the network.

**Trips are shorter**

Because of compact mixed land use in the core and the interconnection of all roads, the typical trip is shorter. The small community requires that there be a balance of housing to jobs in the community and that retail and recreational facilities be within walking distance. These are the significant factors in reducing trip length.

Main Street as part of a dense network of interconnecting streets.

A narrow residential street that is part of a dense network of streets.

Another narrow residential street in a dense network of streets.

New residential street.

Commercial street in the core of a village.

## Lower maximum speed

Because the roads are laid out in a network, the typical high speed/low speed hierarchy is modified to more narrower streets of lower speed. Traffic moving above 25mph negatively impacts the pedestrian function of a street.

## More multiple purpose trips

Because of the compact nature of the building pattern, many trips can be combined into a single auto trip, and many destinations are accessible by walking.

## Multiple alternative routes

The network eliminates dead ends, cul-de-sacs, and wide, traffic-jammed arterials.

## Less aggressive driving (more routes at lower speeds)

Most aggressive driving occurs on wider roads which typically have higher posted speeds (although lower actual speeds) and where the driver is attempting to save a few seconds of time. The network can eliminate much of this.

## Pedestrian friendly

The two lane roadways must provide a parallel network of sidewalks. Tree parkways and parallel parked cars provide a buffer between moving traffic and pedestrians. Street traffic must move at speeds between 25 to 35 mph, thereby allowing pedestrians to feel and hear each other comfortably.

## Provision of bicycle paths

Attractive, well-maintained bike routes can lead to significant non-auto mode splits and to a healthier community.

## More positive visual experience

The narrower streets of the traditional neighborhood have consistently rated higher on Visual Preference Surveys TM.

## Pedestrian scaled lighting

The network of streets with its narrow width lends itself to pedestrian scaled lighting.

## Traffic calming

Traffic moves faster along streets with wide lane widths and long straight cartways than it does along streets with narrower cartways. Lower vehicular speeds increase pedestrian and vehicular safety and decrease noise. Wider streets can be calmed through devices such as planted islands, curb bump outs and traffic circles.

## Levels of service

Standard engineering practice mandates that traffic move at designated speeds in order to accommodate a specified numbers of vehicles with reasonable safety at all times. This is evaluated in engineering language as levels of service ranging from A to F. The A level of service is free flow. Level F is stopped and jammed. Optimally, one wants to maintain a level of service at C, but frequently we settle for D. However, this ranking system does not evaluate the visual quality of the trip, the ability to attract and accommodate pedestrians and bicycles, or the ability to accomplish more trips using fewer vehicles. Communities can actually reduce trips through the proximity of land uses, and the provision of pedestrian linkages to related land uses and public transit.

A village street with a common traffic calming element.

The neighborhood thinks that this traffic calming devise is an ideal technique to reclaim the streets.

Level of service A to B.

Level of service D to F.

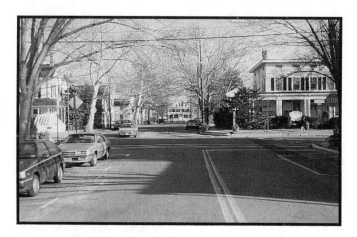

Modified grid in Cranbury, NJ.

## The Form of Streets

A street network does not necessarily require that the layout be in a strict grid. There are several basic patterns that can be employed; these are based on parcel configuration, projected size and on such environmental constraints as topography, wetlands, water, steep slopes, archaeological sites, and easements. All will contribute to the shape and the form of the network. In traditional villages and hamlets these forms have been widely used to create a wonderful sense of enclosure, vista, and sequence. These forms should be studied when laying out a new hamlet or village.

# 6   Basic   Street   Types

We have found that there are six basic street forms in traditional settlements. These include the Curve, the T, the Crossroads, the Commons, the Modified Grid and the Composite. When employing one or more of these forms in the design of a new hamlet, village, town, or retrofit, specific design requirements regarding the placement and size of buildings must be considered.

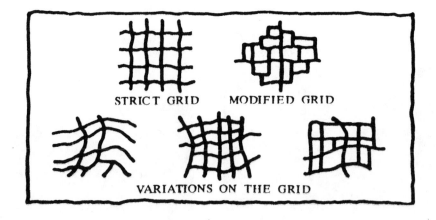

## 1. The Curve Street Form

The linear curve is valued as one of the most positive street forms. Buildings sited along a subtle or irregular curve create an enclosed space. Both the front and the side facades are visually critical. Avoid blank walls! Taller or more distinguished civic or mixed-use buildings should be located on the bend in the roads to give them visual prominence. Horizontal curves created by the layout of streets combine well with vertical curves created by the topography of the land and can create a wonderful sense of enclosure and a continually interesting spatial sequence.

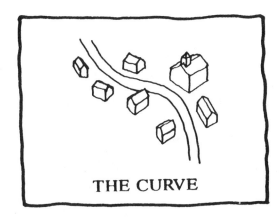

THE CURVE

## 2. The T Street Form

The T can create a dramatic sense of visual termination and space enclosure. A tall and visually predominant building should be located as the visual termination of the T.

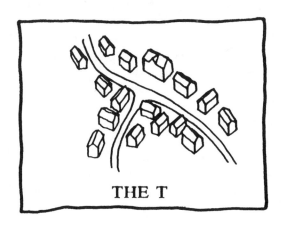

THE T

The tower terminates the curve.

The church forms the perfect visual termination for the T.

A modified grid is created by multiple use of T intersections.

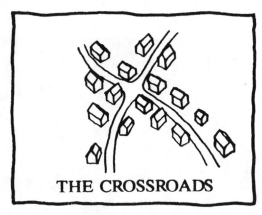

THE CROSSROADS

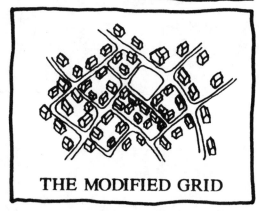

THE COMMON

THE MODIFIED GRID

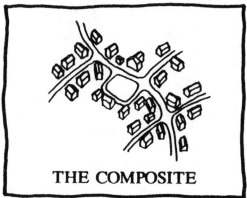

THE COMPOSITE

### 3. The Crossroads Street Form

The crossing of two roadways in an essentially perpendicular relationship requires that traffic stop in all four directions. There are many ways to treat these intersections. The most interesting is to create a planted island or circle with perhaps a monument, or flagpole. These features are common in older villages, and they are in current use as traffic calming devices in rectangular grid cities in the northwest. If the crossroads meet at less than right angles, a larger or architecturally more imposing building should be located at the visual termination.

### 4. The Common Street Form

The form that is the most popular with design teams in the Hands-On Model Workshops is a series of roadways that create a common or community green. When teams are given model kits and asked to create a small community, almost all will place the larger, mixed-use and civic buildings around a commons forming the community center and focus. The specific layout of adjacent access roads to the common will dictate where larger community and commercial buildings are located. These buildings surround the common, and one or two larger buildings are used for visual termination. The common becomes the focus of the community; it cries out to be enclosed by buildings.

### 5. The Modified Grid Street Form

The modified grid relies on the use of the T and the crossroad intersection. The irregular grid is the richest in positive visual and spatial characteristics. The modified grid responds well to incorporating topographic features and creating a road form where the community is surrounded by open space. Streets can be visually terminated by larger buildings or green vistas. The modified grid allows ideal street enclosure from both ends and provides for multiple alternative routes. Sidewalks in a modified grid can be formed into continuously linked networks.

### 6. The Composite-Street Form

The composite-street form is a type of modified grid which incorporates most, if not all, the road forms indicated above. It can be the richest visual and spatial experiences, while providing legibility and order.

## Visual Termination

A design feature critical to all street forms is visual termination and the enclosure of space. Visual termination focuses the emphasis, or long view, on the visual end of the streets. Streets should be visually terminated with important buildings, vistas of open space, water, or distant topographic features. The T and the Curve, as illustrated above, are ideal for locating buildings that result in visual termination. Terminating buildings should be grander and more civic in scale than their neighbors. For example, churches, community buildings, larger commercial structures, or perhaps smaller buildings with architectural embellishments, such as towers, create focal points that are appropriate for these significant locations.

The four diagrams below illustrate the relationship between the road layout, building size, mass, and location to enhance visual termination and the sense of enclosure.

The municipal building in Cranbury terminates street.

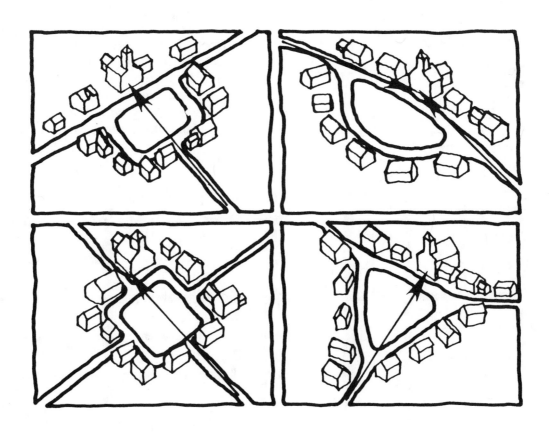

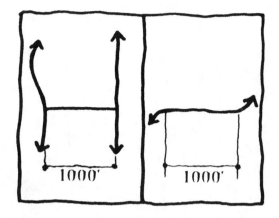

## Visual Length of Streets

The spaces created by straight and curved streets should range in length from 500 to 1000 feet. Subtle reverse curves or terminations at 600 to 1,000 foot intervals provide the greatest visual interest and spatial enclosure. This can also be achieved by vertical changes in topography. The 1000 foot rule is visually critical!

## The Block

The modified grid block length ranges from 200 to 400 feet. The block is the basic structuring element of the network. It provides an understandable and legible structure to community space and provides order to the placement of buildings. It allows a multitude of positive visual and spatial occurrences. The block is generally a rectangle, a modified rectangle, or another distinct geometric shape. To the extent possible, blocks should be designed to have a length which allows the pedestrian to traverse comfortably at a diagonal. The most comfortable is 220 feet by 220 feet from right-of-way line to right-of-way line. This can be expanded but seems to have a limit of approximately 400 feet. The depth of the block is dependent upon the proposed use and/or the employment of an alley. Typical residential lot depths range from 100 to 120 feet deep. Blocks sizes should allow a variety of lot widths and depths. Blocks can accommodate a full variety of uses along the right-of-way edge with parking arranged in the interior of the block behind the buildings.

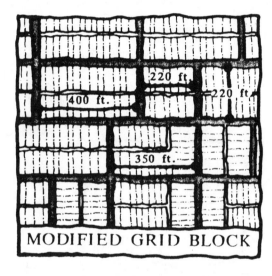

MODIFIED GRID BLOCK

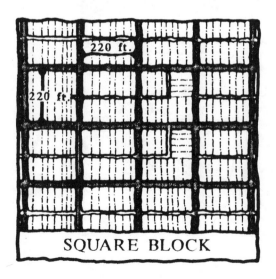

SQUARE BLOCK

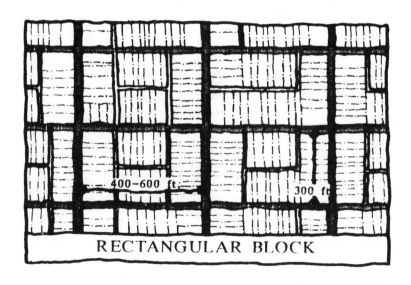

RECTANGULAR BLOCK

## The Alley

The use of the alley is recommended, where possible, in large hamlets, villages, and neighborhoods. The alley can contribute positively to the form of the street, and it has many advantages. First, it allows the most positive streetscape because it eliminates the need for driveways and the visual intrusion of garages. The front garage is the most negative feature of suburban housing. Furthermore, narrower lots engender a more positive sense of community. When the garage is on the side of the house, a wider lot is needed to encompass the driveway. Garage doors at the end of the driveway predominate the view of those who drive by. This feature is particularly detrimental when garages are larger than a single car width.

Secondly, the alley can create a positive neighborhood space. Older children can play more safely here than on the front street; for example, basketball hoops are frequently located here. Alleys are where firewood is piled, gardens and compost piles are located, and where residents work on their cars and recreation vehicles. In addition to safety and storage, residents become possessive of their alleys. As I photograph alleys around the country, it is not uncommon for people to ask, "What are you doing in our alley?" Recommended rights-of-way for alleys are 20 feet with an eight- to twelve-foot pavement. Garage entrances can be perpendicular or parallel to the alley. They should be set back three feet from the right-of-way of the alley.

Third, when the garage is located in rear yards off the alley, interesting opportunities arise for creating inviting exterior rooms using the garage as a privacy wall and divider of space. Garages off alleys can be directly attached to the house for those who want to walk directly from the garage to the inside of the house.

New alley in Laguna West, Sacramento, CA. The positive quality of the streetscape and the narrowness of the lots occurs because of the alley.

An older subdivision with a popular alley where residents have elected to keep the rear yards open. A positive sense of neighborhood happens in the rear yards.

A classic old street with low ADT. The pavement width is overly wide because there is little need for parallel parking on both sides.

## Streetscape Elements

There are many elements of streets and streetscapes which must be combined to create a positive, human scale environment, a streetscape with charm and character.

They include the following features:

1. the proportions and dimensions of the streetscape, the relationship of building height to street width

2. buildings which define a built-to-line

3. the semi-public space, the front yard, porch, and entrance

4. the delineation of the pedestrian realm including sidewalk widths, fences and edges, and parkway

5. the parkway width including spacing and type of street trees, and of street lights

6. the street furniture including street signs, benches, light fixtures, etc.

7. screening of parking lots

8. curbs

9. a low travel speed (10 to 30 mph)

10. the location and placement of the garage

11. parallel parking

In addition to these design features, the street includes a right-of-way, the wire-utility easements, curbs or swales, sewer and water pipe locations, turning radii, sight triangles, as well as specific engineering and construction material specifications. The correct combination of these features with the appropriate pavement widths and visual termination can create a valuable and positive sense of place.

# 1. The Proportions of the Streetscape

The proportions and lenght of the street are critical to the image of place. The spatial enclosure is a major determinate of whether a person feels comfortable in the space and whether it can be defined as a positive place.

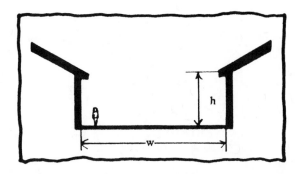

The relationship of building height to street width defines the proportion of the street space. The extent to which the street can define space is determined by the relationship of wall **height (h)** (generally defined as to the cornice or overhang line) to the **width (w)** between the walls (generally defined as the primary facade surface). It includes the pavement width plus the building setback. This proportion defines two surfaces of this spatial enclosure. We view this relationship in terms of a ratio.

There are certain ratios in which people feel more comfortable. This has come from analysis of VPS $^{TM}$ results and measurements taken from models after completion of workshops and case studies. A ratios from 1:1 to 1:2 (building wall height: street width) is considered ideal and most often used. Those streets falling between 1:4 and 3:1 are acceptable although wonderful small pedestrian passages have measured at 4:1. Beyond 1:5 the space will not be well defined--there is little sense of enclosure. Where this occurs, large street trees are critical to reconstruct and correct the proportions. Street trees can enhance any streetscape, but they are particularly critical when the proportion of the street exceeds 1:4. Trees and understory plantings, as well as topographic walls and hillsides, can modify the proportional relationship creating extremely positive urban and rural streets. Above 4:1 the street begins to resemble a canyon; it is dark with little sunlight. The proportion of 1: infinity is very important; this proportion defines the long view. Places where buildings are built on one side of a street with a long view of a water area or open field on the other are considered very positive.

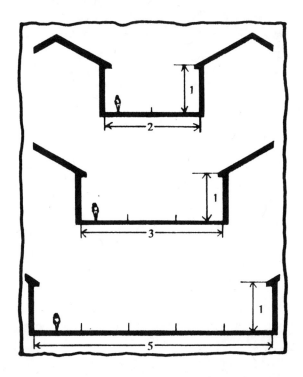

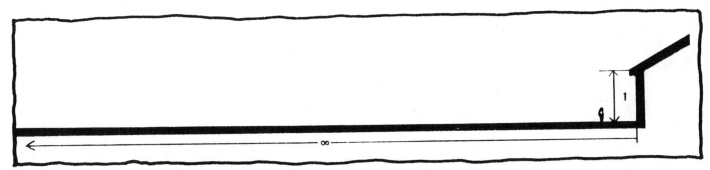

A new street in Harbor Town illustrates the strict use of the Build-to line. The facades help define the public space across the street.

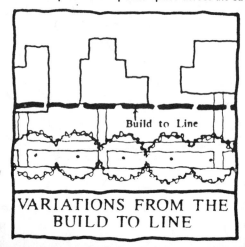

VARIATIONS FROM THE BUILD TO LINE

The picket fence defines the front yard as a semi-public space seen from the sidewalk and a semi-private as seen from the house.

## 2. Setback, Build-to Line

The structures that line the street will also determine how well the streetscape is defined. Height, width, and massing of the structures plays a role in defining the spatial qualities of the streetscape, as do the building setbacks. Streets should have a build-to line. This is a line which determines where the majority of the primary facades should be located. A variation of this would allow a more flexible front yard setback. Front yard setbacks should vary according to uses, street types, and the speed of traffic. However, they should be set at a depth which creates a positive proportion. The setbacks of the primary facades should remain fairly uniform along each street except for retail and civic uses. In a retail or commercial setting, the building should normally be placed against the edge of the sidewalk, as these uses depend upon direct pedestrian access. In other words, a 12-14 foot setback from the curb is appropriate. Civic uses such as a church or community building can be set further back than the build-to line.

Residential uses at the street level should have a build-to-line that makes a small front yard possible. Some buildings should be allowed to deviate 10 to 25% from this standard by being in front of or behind the build-to line. As an example, if the build-to line is established as ten feet on a certain type of street, the front facade could be on this line or between 1 foot and 2 feet 6 inches in front or in back of this line. Porches can intrude into this setback line. Setbacks in residential areas vary from 10 to 35 feet, depending on the street type and passing traffic. The placement of structures in a hamlet, village, or town must attempt to create a sense of visual continuity and enclosure.

## 3. Front Yard and Entrances
### The Front Yard

The front yard is the area between the house and the public sidewalk. The more defined it is, the more it becomes classified as semi-public, which means that this area is partially enclosed to form a space. The enclosure is typically a low fence, hedge, or wall three to four feet tall. The front porch may form one edge of this enclosed space. The enclosure of the front yard, complete with entrance gateway, gives guests and strangers the feeling of entering into the private domain of the house. Porches, stairs, and stoops elevated above the front yard and sidewalk reinforce the sense of the semi-public space. There is evidence that the provision of this semi-public space as part of the front yard is a deterrent to crime and provides a greater sense of security for residents. Porches, stairs, and stoops can intrude into the front yard. Some porches can consume the entire front yard with the railings acting as the semi-public edge. Yard edges are an important part of the streetscape. The most highly rated typically contain a low picket-type fence, low hedges, a low masonry wall, or some combination of these elements. Entrances are articulated by decorative posts and sometimes a gate. Fences range from three to four feet high. Chain link fences should only be allowed if combined with a hedge.

In commercial and mixed-use areas with retail facilities on the ground floor the front yard should consist of wider sidewalks, creating opportunities for sidewalk cafes or some other use (fruit stand, sidewalk displays, etc.) Mixed-use buildings with offices on the ground floor should be set slightly further back, with the opportunity for a small semi-public space or a planting area; these uses do not have display windows, typically. Civic uses can and should have larger front yards.

Commercial Main Street in Clinton, NJ.

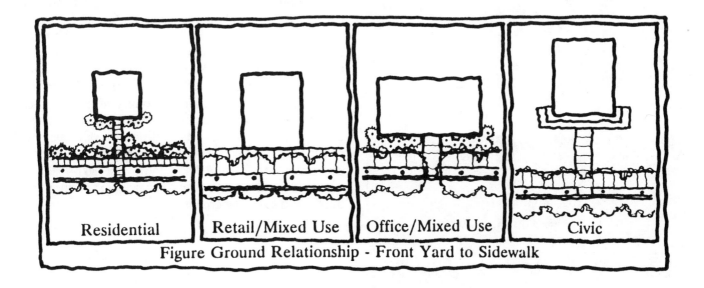

Residential      Retail/Mixed Use      Office/Mixed Use      Civic

Figure Ground Relationship - Front Yard to Sidewalk

Well defined entrances.

A well defined pedestrian realm.

Sidewalk enhanced with plants and flowers.

### Entrances

Entrances to buildings should be clearly defined. The level of the entrance above the sidewalk creates a relationship between the structure and the street. On residential buildings, the entrances should be elevated at least 18 inches above the sidewalk. As residential buildings are located nearer to the sidewalk, the ground floor elevation must be increased so that a person standing on the ground floor can see over the top of the pedestrian while the pedestrian cannot see directly into the unit. In commercial or mixed-use areas, the front entrance is usually flush with the sidewalk. Multi-family units require handicapped access.

## 4. The Pedestrian Realm

The elements which define the pedestrian realm include sidewalk widths, fences, hedges, building edges, parkways, street trees, street lights, and parked cars.

### Sidewalks

According to Jane Jacobs, " Lowly, unpurposeful and random as they may appear, sidewalk contacts are the small change from which a city's wealth of public life may grow."

Throughout the community, the sidewalk is a critical element that allows and encourages free pedestrian movement. Sidewalks should connect the front and side doors of all units to the core retail area, civic and social buildings, and major recreational facilities. The sidewalk should be considered as a separate network, paralleling the roadways but also diverging between buildings to provide access to areas like parking lots or interior shopping courts. Sidewalks should be continuous. The width of the sidewalk should change from the edge of the community to the center or core depending on utilization. The sidewalk should be allowed to wander around large trees and outcroppings without being overly rigid in its placement.

Generally the sidewalk should start on the periphery of the hamlet or village where the lot widths begin to narrow; less than 200 feet is the general rule. In these locations the sidewalk can be narrow, but not less than three feet. As the potential intensity of pedestrians increases, the sidewalk must be widened. A four foot sidewalk is the most comfortable for two people to walk side by side or to pass a person pushing a baby carriage or one in a wheel chair.

Sidewalk widths must become broader in the commercial core. The sidewalk should extend from the edge of the building to the edge of the pavement. A minimum width of eight feet is required although ten to sixteen is more adequate since sidewalks in the commercial core may contain trees, lights, outside displays, awnings, and auto overhangs.

To the extent possible the sidewalk should be textured, scored, inlaid, stamped, or constructed of material that will produce textural variety in the ground form. Brushed concrete and blacktop must be avoided unless used for a bicycle path. Concrete can be scored into small rectangles, stamped to look like brick or slate or inlaid with brick as edges or dividers. Alternative, sidewalks can be constructed from brick or pavers, or created from small gravel edged in wood or metal. Gravel can be used for park walkways and for those near the periphery of the community. No sidewalks are appropriate on narrow roads of ten to eighteen feet in width, with slow speeds and an ADT of less than 250. Sidewalks should be placed to accommodate changes in topography, or the presence of large trees.

**Chart of sidewalks width relative to lot widths.**

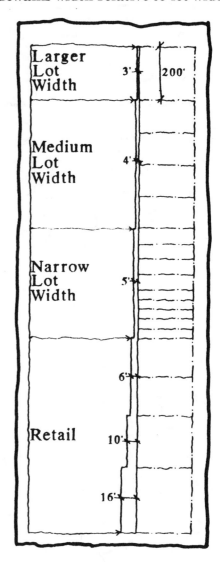

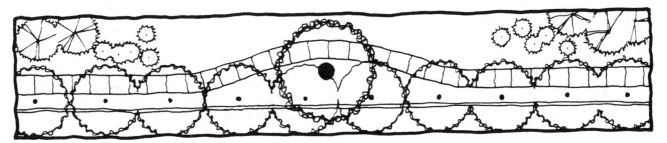

Curve sidewalks to preserve large trees.

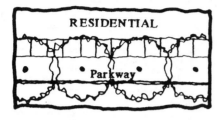

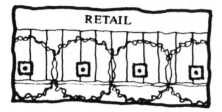

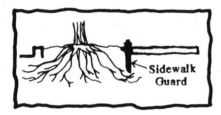

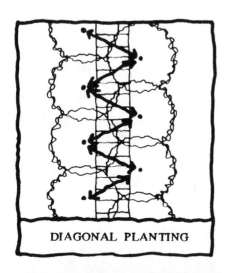

DIAGONAL PLANTING

## 5. Parkway/ Street Tree Planting Area

We call the street tree planting area the "parkway" because it is the extension of the park system into the small community. It is placed between the roadway edge and the sidewalk. Typically it is planted with grass and has trees planted at 18 to 30 foot intervals, depending on the tree species. In commercial areas the grass-planted parkway is substituted replaced by continuous pavement and trees in grates or in pavement openings. One of the most important functions of the parkway is its definition of the pedestrian realm, separating it from the street.

The existence of trees on the street side of the pedestrian realm is critical; to have them on both sides of the sidewalk is a real joy. When this occurs, the trees should be staggered in rows in order to create a wonderful pedestrian canopy. Street trees serve many functions: spatial enclosure, air filters, shade, and so on. The spacing of the trees should be as tight as possible. Close planting allows them to have some immediate and short term (five to ten years) impact on the street. Unfortunately too many street tree ordinances specify that trees be planted at extremely small caliper (one to two inches) and at large spacing 35 to 50 feet; at that rate it requires at least fifty years for these trees to reach maturity and fill in the space. If street trees are planted with a minimum size of three inch caliper or twelve feet tall then they will provide pleasant shade in only a few years.

Tree species should be indigenous to the area and capable of growing to a height of at least fifty feet. Of particular interest are types which will create a street canopy and will do little harm to the sidewalks. Sidewalk root guards can be installed to direct root growth away from sidewalks and utility lines.

Wherever possible, existing small trees should be Vermeered out and replanted as street or yard trees. The Vermeer mechanical spade can move trees up to six or eight inches economically. This is an ideal way to save site trees and provide larger new trees without huge nursery purchases The Vermeer process uses the mechanical spade to first dig holes, prune root, and move trees which are temporarily replanted into a pre-dug hole. The trees are then trimmed and fertilized. When the street construction is nearly finished, the trees can be moved into permanent positions. If there is an insufficient number of trees to meet the recommended spacings, the Vermeered trees should be interspaced with smaller new trees.

## Street Furniture and Street Lights

Street furniture complements the function and form of the street. The street furniture typically found in smaller small communities includes benches, planting tubs, trash baskets, street lamps, hitching posts, etc. This furniture must complement the architectural style selected for the community, and it must be scaled to the speed and dimension of the pedestrian. Such furniture gives the street an additional human dimension, helps to keep streets cleaner, and provides places for people to sit. Most of this street furniture should be confined to the core. Furniture must occur in the community green or common in proportion to the population served.

## Street lights

The style and height of street lamps, including the pole and fixture, are particularly important. (Several examples of these were given in Principle One.) Most older, smaller communities are minimally lit, new ones should follow the same pattern. One should try to avoid high level footcandles (fc) of light and not use typical roadway lighting standards. Cobra headed light fixtures on wooden poles are to be avoided. They make streets look like highways! Heights should be limited from eight to twelve feet and should only be placed on critical corners, along sidewalks which are heavily used, and in the retail core. A 60 to 80 foot spacing is recommended in these areas, creating a diagonal pattern with lights located across the street. Off-street parking lots should utilize a similar fixture. Porch lights can supplement or replace street lights on very low use streets.

A simple bench adds to the comfort and character of the street.

Street lights and the pedestrian scale enhance the character of the street.

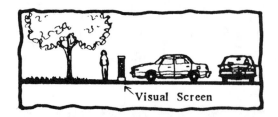

Visual Screen

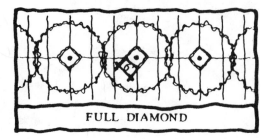

FULL DIAMOND

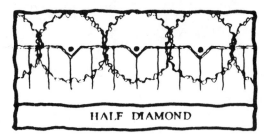

HALF DIAMOND

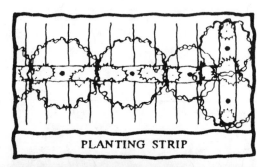

PLANTING STRIP

## 7. Screening of Parking Lots

Parking lots consistently receive negative ratings in the VPS ™. It is critical to the streetscape that these lots be visually buffered from the vehicle and the pedestrian viewshed. Parking lots should be small or divided into small sections of approximately 20 to 25 cars. Off-street parking must not be placed in the front yard setback but placed behind the build-to line. Driveways should be kept as narrow as possible, approximately twelve feet wide.

Parking lots must be screened from the street. This can be accomplished with fencing, hedging, or walls. The material must be a minimum of three to four feet high at the time of planting. A car is approximately five and one half feet tall; the design goal is to completely conceal them.

The interior of the parking lot must also contain landscaping. There are several basic rules. Ten to fifteen percent of the parking lot interior should be landscaped with screening materials. There should be one deciduous tree for every six to eight spaces, planted in a geometric pattern. One very successful technique is a planting diamond that is six feet per side. It can be incorporated into a parking lot without losing any parking spaces. The curbs are five inches high and open on the sides to accept water which runs off of the parking lot. Half diamonds can be used along the parking lot edge.

Planting strips or islands with a minimum width of six feet provide good planting beds that visually break up a lot into smaller increments. This size can contain a great variety of trees and shrubs.

A parking lot with a small planting diamond.

A well screened corner parking lot.

## 8. Curbs

Curbs are not generally recommended except in traffic areas above 500 ADT. Areas with high potential run off and edge erosion should also have curbs. Curbs should be limited to the following materials and positions:

> concrete with a six inch square edged and a six inch step from pavement
> belgian block laid vertically with a six inch exposed face
> belgian block laid at a forty five degree angle with six inches of exposed surface.
> granite blocks typically four to six feet long

Curb Block Position

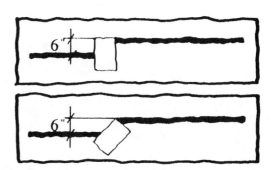

## 9. Street Speeds

**There is a direct relationship between the positive quality of a street, pavement width, the setback of the buildings, and the speed of the roadway.** Speed generates noise . Speeds over 30 mph are incompatible with pedestrian edges and buildings with entrances set close to the street. Speeds should never be posted over 30 mph on local collector streets lined with housing. Local residential streets should be limited to 25 mph. As speeds increase to over 40 mph, significant setbacks should be required in addition to walls and hedging. Berms and sound walls should only be used as a last resort on collectors, but might be required on arterials that serve larger communities .

The narrower and the more visually constricted the street, the lower speeds will be.

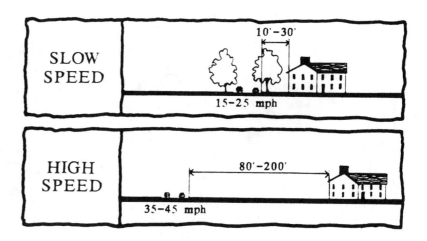

A negatively rated garagescape.

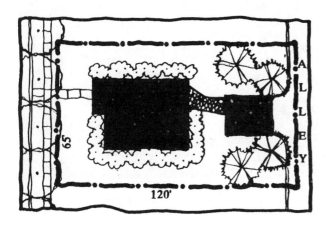

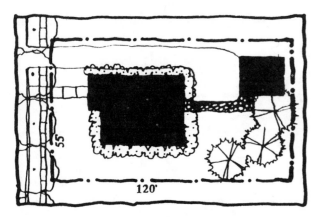

Garages located in the rear yard, off an alley, behind the front yard set back, or screened from primary views enhance the positive character of the street.

## 10. The Location and Placement of the Garage

The location of the garage, and particularly of the garage door, is an important site-location decision for achieving positive streetscapes. To the extent possible, garages should be located in the rear yard, set-back a few feet from the property lines, and they should look like traditional out-buildings. A two foot side yard provides access for mainte-nance and four to six feet allows for some planting. This location provides the opportunity to screen the rear yard and create interesting rear-yard spaces. Ideally, vehicular ac-cess to the garage is available from an alley and secondarily from a narrow driveway (eight feet) which can be shared by more than one property. The garage door can be directly perpendicular to or parallel with the alley. Garages should never be located in the front yard and should <u>never be the dominant visual element of the viewshed on the streetscape.</u>

There is some criticism of this design feature from those who believe that you cannot sell a house without an integrated garage. To meet this criticism we recommend that the garages be oversized with the opportunity for an additional room or work space/shop, that the pedestrian exit of the garage be tied to the house with a pergola, and, if a driveway is used, a traditional "portcochere" or a porch roof be extended over the driveway to allow covered access to the house in rain or snow. Remember, the majority of garages in this country are detached and these properties continue to sell.

The portico provides an ideal answer to cover parking close to the house. Most houses in the United States still have garages in the rear yard.

Classic rear yard  carriage house  and parking

New residential unit with garage plus second story studio in the rear yard.

## 10. Parallel Parking

Parallel parking should be encouraged and allowed, particularly in front of retail, mixed-use, and multi-family buildings and along collectors. Parallel parking is recommended as guest parking and should count as part of the total parking requirements. The size of the parking spaces should be seven to eight feet wide with an effective length of twenty feet. Several specific design details should be present.

Good Layout for Parallel Parking:

> 1. Spaces should be designated, and curb bump outs particularly at corners are recommended.
>
> 2. Parallel spaces should provide for a four foot maneuvering area between spaces to allow for easy entry and exit.

Narrow street with parallel parking.

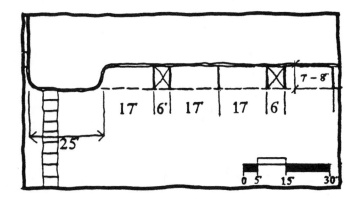

Classic narrow residential street.

## Street Types

Each community will have a number of street types determined by the edge uses, location in the community, carrying capacity, and speed. They must be codified to contain all the elements as listed in this principle.

There are literally hundreds of street types, thousands if you include the various types of building, setbacks, and variations on features such as pavement width, shoulders, traffic direction, pedestrian realm etc. When one looks at the street types in the traditional community, it becomes apparent that part of the richness of such a place is the variation on pavement widths, and sidewalk and building locations in contrast to the rigid standards imposed by contemporary engineering standards. In older hamlets and villages which have not grown significantly in the immediate past, but which nontheless accommodate modern trucks and fire engines, many of the most positive streetscape conditions exist.

The street hierarchy for the small community begins with the lowest order of street, the alley. A street is defined as a path which accommodates both the vehicle and the pedestrian. The following is a listing of the eight most commonly recommended street types and three access road types, with a discussion of their purposes. This hierarchy does not include narrow and/or unpaved roads which can serve the rural areas outside of the community development boundaries.

**Type 1.** the lowest order is the alley, the backbone of a block

**Type 2.** the narrow residential one-way street with parking on one side

**Type 3.** the narrow two-way residential street with parking on one side

**Type 4.** the two-way residential street with parking on two sides

**Type 5.** the commercial/mixed-use street with parking on two sides

**Type 6.** the commercial/mixed-use street with transit and parking on both sides

**Type 7.** the commercial/mixed-use street with head-in parking

**Type 8.** the boulevard with parking on both sides and a bike lane

**Type 9.** the two lane arterial with optional shoulders, breakdown lane and bike lane

**Type 10.** the three lane arterial with optional shoulders (green setback), breakdown lane, and bike lane

**Type 11.** the major access, high speed freeway, with high occupancy vehicle lanes designated

The following matrix indicates those types of streets and roads most appropriate to serve the various small community types. All of these streets and roads are in use and have been positively evaluated. They meet the required dimensions to accommodate cars, trucks, and emergency vehicles.

STREET
TYPES     ROAD AND COMMUNITY TYPES

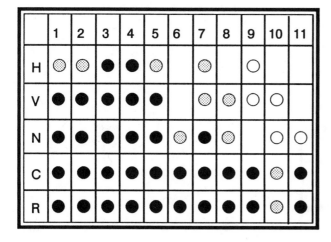

●   Very high utilization in the interior of a community

◉   Low utilization

○   Regional access

H - Hamlet
V - Village
N - Neighborhood
C - Core Town
R - Regional Center

Numbers, 1-11, refer to list on this and the previous page

# TYPE 1

**THE ALLEY/LANE: THE LOWEST ORDER OF STREETS**
20 foot right-of-way
3 foot build-to line
15 mph

The alley is the backbone of a block, a semi-public neighborhood space. The alley provides access to the rear of the property and eliminates the need for front yard driveways. The alley provides the opportunity for a more positive front yard streetscape. It can decrease the cost of the lot through the opportunity for narrower lots. Utility easements are easily accommodated in the alley. A three foot build-to line is recommended. Alley lighting should be provided at intersections and by fixtures attached to garages.

**ADJACENT LAND USES**
Garages
Parking Lots
Accessory units above garages
Accessory residential units

**STORY HEIGHT**
1 to 2 stories

Section

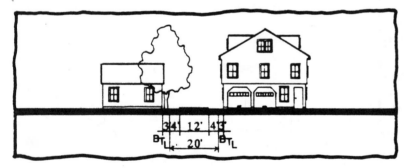

Figure Ground

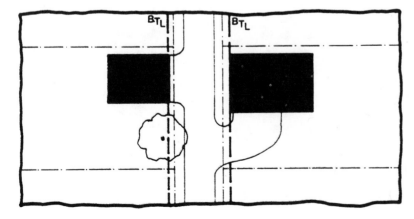

# TYPE 2

## THE NARROW RESIDENTIAL ONE-WAY STREET, PARKING ON ONE SIDE
38 foot right-of-way
10 to 15 foot build-to line
15 - 20 mph

This residential street accommodates a small number of vehicular trips, 200 to 1,000 ADT. Pavement width varies from sixteen to twenty feet. Parallel parking is allowed on one side. Each unit has vehicular access from an alley. Bicycle riding is safe and easy on this type of road. Street lighting should be scaled to pedestrians and located primarily at intersections. Porch or gate lights are recommended, as are fences or hedges. If the utility easement is not provided in the alley, a three foot easement is recommended adjacent to the sidewalk. Electric, telephone, and cable television lines are located in this easement. Water, sewer, and gas lines, and storm drains are located in the street.

## ADJACENT LAND USES
Small lot single family
Duplex units
Townhouses
Multi-family

## STORY HEIGHT
2 to 2 1/2 stories

## ENTRANCES:
Finished floor 2 to 4 feet above sidewalk grade

Section

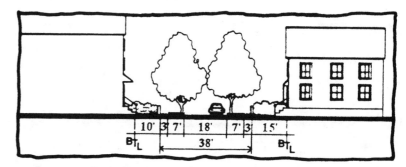

Figure Ground

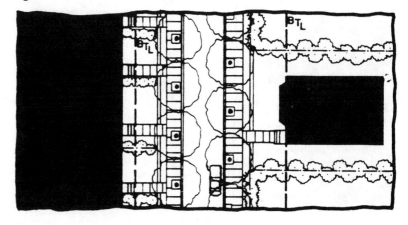

## TYPE 3

**THE NARROW TWO-WAY RESIDENTIAL STREET, PARKING ON ONE SIDE**
50 foot right-of-way
10 to 15 foot build-to line
15 - 20 mph

This residential street will accomodate a small number of vehicular trips ranging from 500 to 1,800 ADT. Pavement width ranges from 20 to 27 feet. Parallel parking is provided on one side. Each unit has vehicular access from an alley. Bicycle riding is safe and easy on this type of road. Street lighting should be located in the parkway and be pedestrian scaled. Fences or hedges should be set back three to four feet from the sidewalk. A three foot utility easement can be located adjacent to the sidewalk, if it is not provided in the rear alley. Electric, telephone, and cable television lines are located in this easement. Water, sewer, and gas lines, and storm drains are located in the street.

**ADJACENT LAND USES**
Small and medium width lot single family
Duplex units
Townhouses
Multi-family
Large lot single family houses with large setbacks

**STORY HEIGHT**
2 to 3 stories

**ENTRANCE:**
Finished floor 2 to 4 feet above sidewalk grade

Section

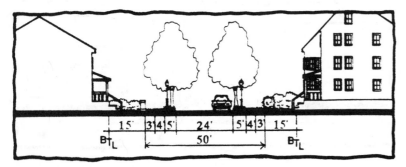

Figure Ground

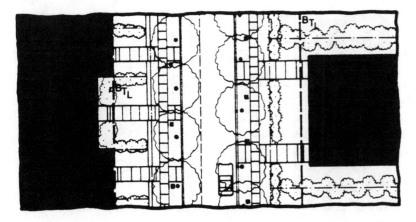

# TYPE 4

## THE TWO-WAY RESIDENTIAL STREET, WITH PARKING ON BOTH SIDES
60 foot right-of-way
15 foot build-to line
20 - 25 mph

This residential street will accomodate a moderate number of vehicular trips ranging from 500 to 3,000 ADT. Pavement width ranges from 30 to 36 feet. Parallel parking is provided on both sides. Each unit can have vehicular access from a driveway or an alley. Bicycle riding is more difficult on this type of road. Street lighting should be located in the parkway and be pedestrian scaled. Fences or hedges should be set back three to four feet from a five foot sidewalk. A three foot cable utility easement can be located adjacent to the sidewalk, if it is not provided in the rear alley. Water, sewer, and gas lines, as well as storm drains are located in the street.

## ADJACENT LAND USES
Small, medium and large lot single family
Duplex units
Townhouses
Multi-family
Home offices

## STORY HEIGHT
2 - 3 stories

## ENTRANCE:
Finished floor 2 to 4 feet above finished grade

Section

Figure Ground

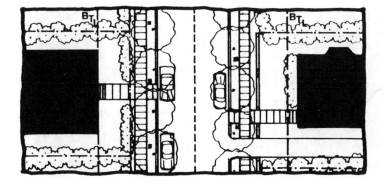

# TYPE 5

## MAIN STREET: THE COMMERCIAL/MIXED-USE STREET, PARKING ON TWO SIDES
64 foot right-of-way
34 to 36 feet of pavement
0 - 4 foot build-to line

This commercial/mixed-use street accomodates a moderate number of vehicular trips, from 2,500 to 6,000 ADT. Pavement width ranges from 34 to 36 feet. Parallel parking is provided on both sides. There should be a continuous building frontage with small pedestrian paths between buildings that lead to rear parking lots. Vehicular access to parking is from an alley. A minimum of a fifteen foot wide sidewalk must be provided which includes space for street lighting and street trees. Commercial buildings can be set back an additional four feet if an outdoor display or cafe. is

## ADJACENT LAND USES
Community Commercial -Offices or Retail
(of limited footprint)
Mixed-use
(retail on ground offices or housing above)

## STORY HEIGHT
2 - 3 stories

## ENTRANCE:
On grade level with the sidewalk.

anticipated. All utility easements are located to the rear of the building in the parking lot or alley.

Section

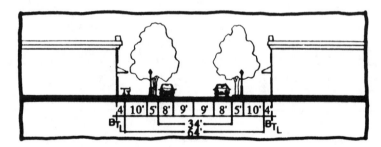

Figure Ground

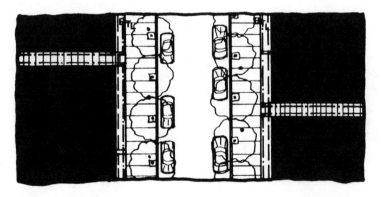

# TYPE 6

## THE COMMERCIAL/MIXED-USE STREET, WITH TRANSIT AND PARKING ON TWO SIDES
76 foot right-of-way
46- 48 foot pavement
0-4 foot build-to line
25 mph

This commercial/mixed-use street provides an opportunity for low tech (street car type) transit located in the center of the street while accommodating two moving lanes of traffic and parallel parking on both sides. There should be a continuous building frontage with small pedestrian paths between buildings that lead to rear lot parking. Vehicular access to rear parking is by an alley. Sidewalks a minimum of fifteen feet wide must be provided; these shall provide space for street lighting and street trees. Street trees should be spaced 35 feet on center and street lights at 80 feet. Commercial buildings can be set back an additional four

## ADJACENT LAND USES
Commercial--Offices or Retail
    (of limited footprint)
Mixed-use
    (retail on ground offices or housing above)
Civic Uses

## STORY HEIGHT
2 - 3 stories

## ENTRANCE:
On grade level with the sidewalk

feet if an outdoor display cafe is anticipated. All utility easements are located to the rear of the building in the parking lot or alley.

**Section**

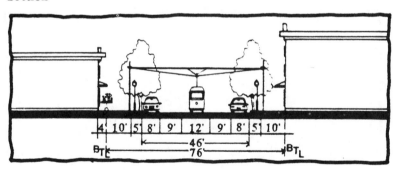

**Figure Ground**

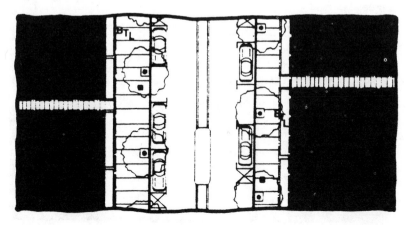

# TYPE 7

**THE COMMERCIAL/MIXED- USE STREET WITH HEAD-IN PARKING**
82 foot right-of-way
52 foot pavement
0-4 foot build-to line
25 mph

This commercial/mixed-use street provides opportunity for head-in parking, thereby doubling the parking capacity of the commercial street, while accommodating two moving lanes of traffic. There should be a continuous building frontage with small pedestrian paths between buildings that lead to additional rear lot parking. Vehicular access to rear parking is from an alley. Sidewalks a minimum of 15 feet wide, which includes space for street trees 35 feet on center and street lights 80 feet on center, must be provided. Commercial buildings can be set back an additional four feet

**ADJACENT LAND USES**
Commercial--Offices or Retail
　(of limited footprint)
Mixed-use
　(retail on ground offices or housing above)
Civic Uses

**STORY HEIGHT**
2 - 3 stories

**ENTRANCE:**
On sidewalk grade

if an outdoor display or cafe is anticipated. All utility easements are located in the rear of the building in parking lots or the alley.

Section

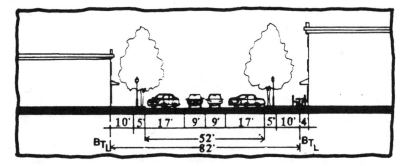

Figure Ground

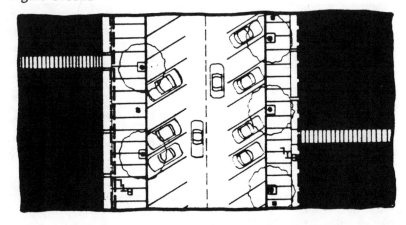

# TYPE 8

## THE BOULEVARD WITH PARKING ON BOTH SIDES AND A BIKE LANE

86 foot right-of-way
25 to 35 foot build-to line (residential)
10 to 15 foot build-to line (regional commercial)
25 - 35 mph

This residential street provides for a moderate number of vehicular trips, ranging from 3000 to 5,000 ADT. Pavement width ranges from 17 to 18 feet on either side of a 16 to 20 foot landscaped median. Parallel parking is provided on both sides. Each unit can have vehicular access from a driveway or an alley. Bicycle riding is more difficult on this type of road. Street lighting should be located in the parkway and be pedestrian scaled. Fences or hedges should be set back three to four feet from a five foot sidewalk. A three foot cable utility easement can be located adjacent to the sidewalk if it is not provided in the rear alley. Water, sewer, and gas lines, and storm drains are located in the street.

## ADJACENT LAND USES

Small, medium and large lot single family
Duplex units
Townhouses
Multi-family
Home offices
Civic uses
Regional Commercial

## STORY HEIGHT

2 - 3 stories

## ENTRANCE:

Finished floor 2 to 4 feet above sidewalk grade.

Section

Figure Ground

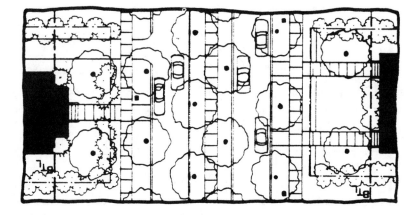

## TYPE 9

**THE TWO LANE ARTERIAL WITH OPTIONAL SHOULDERS OR BREAKDOWN LANE AND OPTIONAL BIKE LANE**
52 to 70 foot right-of-way
22 foot cartway
45 - 50 mph

This road connects the lower level communities. Pavement width is recommended at 18 to 22 feet with a compacted grassy shoulder on either side. Each side of the roadway should be framed with additional landscaping, twelve feet on one side and eighteen on the other. The wider side should provide a six foot wide bicycle path flanked by rows of trees. Water, sewer, and gas lines, and storm drains are located in the street or under the shoulder. Curbing is used only where erosion by storm water would occur. Edges should be extensively landscaped with low shrubs close to the road

**ADJACENT LAND USES**
Agricultural/rural
Open spaces/environmentally sensitive
Large lot single family
 (recommended minimum 6 to 15 acres)

**STORY HEIGHT**
2 - 3 stories

edge and trees located further back. Residential buildings should be set back 100 to 250 feet unless the roadway is scenic or historic and has very low ADT. In this case buildings can be fronted within 20 feet of the right-of-way.

Section

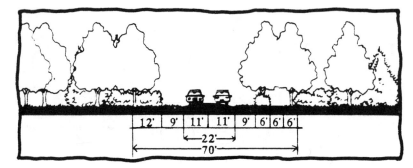

Figure Ground

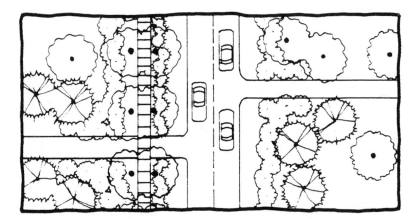

## TYPE 10

### THE THREE LANE ARTERIAL WITH OPTIONAL SHOULDERS OR BREAKDOWN LANE AND OPTIONAL BIKE LANE

78 foot right-of-way        45 - 50 mph
32 foot cartway        Signalized intersections

This road provides major connections between larger communities. 32 foot pavement width is recommended with a center lane that functions as a turning lane or a grassy median. This road type has a compacted grassy shoulder on either side. These shoulders can be paved to become the fourth lane with a turning lane, if required. An additional twelve feet is recommended on one side for landscaping. The other side contains a six foot bicycle path framed on either side with rows of trees. Water, sewer, and gas lines, as well as storm drains are located in the street or under the shoulder. Curbing is used only where erosion by located storm water would occur.  Edges should be extensively land-

### ADJACENT LAND USES
Agricultural/rural
Open spaces/environmentally sensitive
Large lot single family
 (recommended minimum 6 to 15 acres)
Regional commercial or industrial

### STORY HEIGHT
1 - 3 stories

scaped with low shrubs close to the road edge and trees further back. Residential buildings should be set back 100 to 250 feet unless the roadway sounds are buffered. Regional commercial uses including offices, retail, or other employment centers can have frontage on this road provided that they are set back and screened. No front yards parking lots should be allowed.

Section

Figure Ground

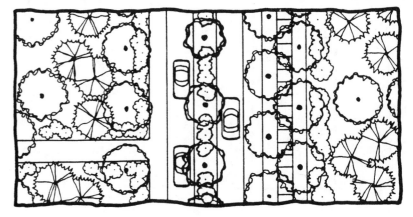

## TYPE 11

**THE MAJOR ACCESS, HIGH SPEED FREEWAY, WITH DESIGNATED HIGH OCCUPANCY VEHICLE LANES**
206 to 254 foot right-of-way
52.5 foot cart way on either side of a median
55 mph
Grade separated intersections

This road is the major regional connection between larger communities. Pavement width of 52.5 feet consists of three moving lanes and a paved shoulder on both sides. The outside lanes are recommended for High Occupancy Vehicles (HOV); these lanes are reserved for vehicles carrying more than 2 persons. A grassy, shrubed median is recommended with a minimum width of 12 feet and a maximum width of 60 feet. This area should be landscaped with low shrubs and hedges. Future mass transit could use this median area. An additional 50 feet is recommended on both sides for landscaping. Edges should be extensively land-

**ADJACENT LAND USES**
Agricultural/rural
Open spaces/environmentally sensitive
Large lot single family
  (recommended minimum 6 to 15 acres)
Regional commercial or industrial
  (reverse frontage)

**STORY HEIGHT**
1 - 3 stories

scaped with low shrubs close to the road edge and trees further back. Residential buildings should be set back 200 to 500 feet unless the roadway is sound buffered. Regional commercial uses including offices, retail, or other employment centers can have reverse frontage on this road providing that they are set back and have a 100 percent visually impervious screen.

Section

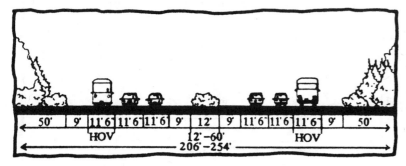

Figure Ground

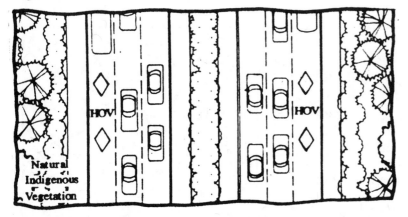

## Connections between various road types

How do the different prototypes relate to each other within the context of the overall circulation network, and which prototypes intersect? For ease of reference, this information has been compiled here on a map and in a matrix.

Both the entry and access road types 9 and 10, and the boulevard type 8, can be used to provide access from an arterial or highway in the existing public road system. Road type 9 shall, whenever possible, be used to connect the development, through the peripheral open space to other adjacent developments. The boulevard can be used both to provide primary access and entry type 8 or act as a principal organizational and visual character street within the community network.

THE ADJACENT GRAPHICS SET FORTH THE CONNECTIONS BETWEEN THE VARIOUS STREET TYPES.

The main street type 5 shall be used for the primary commercial and civic streets within the small community. The residential street type 4 is a collector street, while the residential street types 3 and 2 are local streets; a combination of these residential street types may be treated as private streets and any lot having access from a lane may additionally front upon one of the other types of streets.

| | Type 1 Alley | Type 2 One-Way Residential | Type 3 Two-Way Residential | Type 4 Two-Way Residential | Type 5 Commercial/Mixed-Use | Type 6 Commercial/Mixed-Use with Transit | Type 7 Commercial/Mixed-Use Head in Parking | Type 8 Boulevard | Type 9 Arterial (Narrow) | Type 10 Arterial (Wide) | Type 11 Limited Access Highway |
|---|---|---|---|---|---|---|---|---|---|---|---|
| Type 1 Alley | ● | | ● | ● | ● | ● | ● | ● | | | |
| Type 2 One-Way Residential | | ● | | ● | ● | ● | ● | ● | | | |
| Type 3 Two-Way Residential | | | ● | ● | ● | ● | ● | ● | | | |
| Type 4 Two-Way Residential | ● | ● | ● | ● | ● | ● | ● | ● | ● | ● | |
| Type 5 Commercial/Mixed-Use | ● | ● | ● | ● | ● | ● | ● | ● | ● | ● | |
| Type 6 Commercial/Mixed-Use with Transit | ● | ● | ● | ● | ● | ● | ● | ● | ● | ● | |
| Type 7 Commercial/Mixed-Use Head in Parking | ● | ● | ● | ● | ● | ● | ● | ● | ● | ● | |
| Type 8 Boulevard | ● | ● | ● | ● | ● | ● | ● | ● | ● | ● | ● |
| Type 9 Arterial (Narrow) | | | ● | ● | ● | ● | ● | ● | ● | ● | ● |
| Type 10 Arterial (Wide) | | | ● | ● | ● | ● | ● | ● | ● | ● | ● |
| Type 11 Limited Access Highway | | | | | | | | ● | ● | ● | ● |

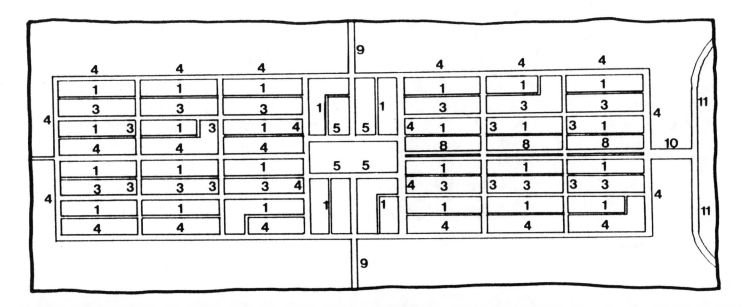

# Principle Seven

## VARIATION

*Variation within the design conformity creates the most visually positive communities.*

The community is unique because individuality is encouraged through a fabric of diverse elements within a defined compact and varying framework of streets. A building pattern of varying sizes, shapes, and forms is required.

This can be best achieved by utilizing the following:

- variation of lot widths and depths, block sizes, and alley configurations
- variation of building footprints illustrated in figure ground plans
- build-to lines
- a mix of building and housing types
- variations on the third dimension of height and mass (build-up line)
- street elements
- details
- the creation of more architectural design types

Variations on basic patterns must be encouraged in order to prevent a dull sameness. If a particular building or up to three buildings are simply repeated, the result will be boring and mass produced.

One of the elements of traditional hamlets and villages is the individuality of each building, individuality that exists within a commonality of design. Although neighboring structures must respect one another and the selected design vocabulary (which can be modeled upon a vernacular form), there must be some differences in building, mass, facade treatment, and details.

Model of a section of a small hamlet.

This new commercial core exhibits variation within a consistency.

## Lot Width

Varied lot widths are a tool that will help to ensure variation in structures. Using a standard lot width is one of the surest guarantees of a dull streetscape and the chief characteristic of suburban sprawl. Lot widths of different sizes encourage variation among building masses. A wide lot placed on an important corner or bend in the road can dictate that a dominant structure will anchor that strategic location. Narrow lots interspersed along block lengths help to break the monotony that occurs with uniform lots.

Lots of different widths should be dispersed, but lot size generally increase from the center of the community to the edge. Lot widths should vary, with no more than two contiguous lots of the same width. The lot widths should use a basic measurement of five foot increments, starting with 20 foot wide lots for small row houses. Recommended lot widths range between 20 and 200 feet.

Wider lots must be located on the periphery of the community. The wider the lot, the larger the building footprint should be. Wider lots limited to 80 feet will be required to accommodate the retail and mixed-use buildings in the core. Further variation can be achieved through the use of multiple small buildings rather than one large building.

Variation of residential lot widths creates unusual interest and modulation in the appearance of the street.

Variation of lot width in these mixed-use buildings contributes to their visual character.

# Lot width recommendations for various building types.

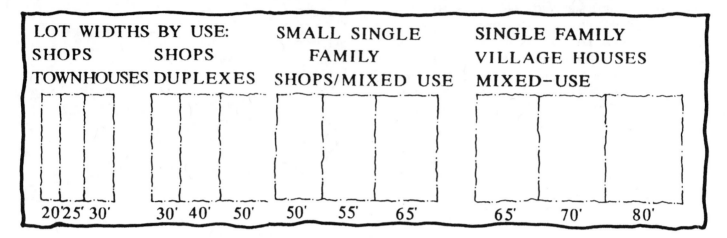

LOT WIDTHS BY USE:
SHOPS     SHOPS
TOWNHOUSES   DUPLEXES

20' 25' 30'    30' 40' 50'

SMALL SINGLE
FAMILY
SHOPS/MIXED USE

50'   55'   65'

SINGLE FAMILY
VILLAGE HOUSES
MIXED-USE

65'   70'   80'

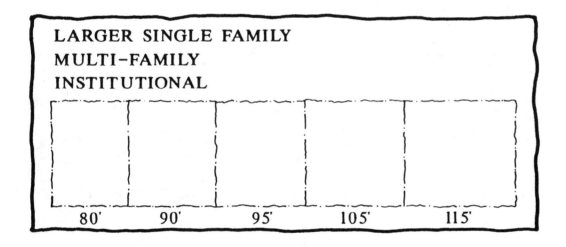

LARGER SINGLE FAMILY
MULTI-FAMILY
INSTITUTIONAL

80'   90'   95'   105'   115'

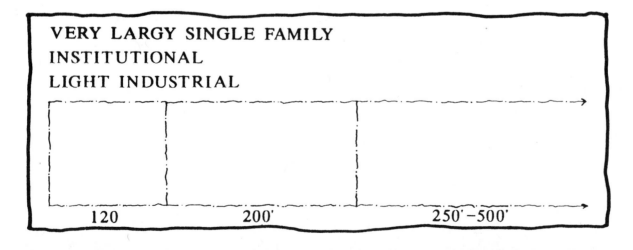

VERY LARGY SINGLE FAMILY
INSTITUTIONAL
LIGHT INDUSTRIAL

120   200'   250'-500'

## Lot Depth

The lot depth is critical to the configuration of a street network which is laid out as a series of blocks. Lots of equal depth can be used to create the traditional block configuration. I have found that a 120 foot deep lot is ideal. This lot depth can be used to create a 240 foot by 240 foot block with varying lot widths. Such a block is pedestrian compatible, offering a one minute walk per side. Variation is encouraged among block configurations, and different blocks can be created using lots of the same depth. Some blocks can accommodate alleys.

If a block or back-to-back layout of lots is not created, lots can be extraordinarily deep. It is critical, however, to maintain a small width to assure the positive streetscape. Lots do not necessarily need to be rectangular. Much of the rear of the lot can be dedicated to a conservation easement or in smaller hamlets can contain the waste water absorption fields.

Ideal Lot Depth

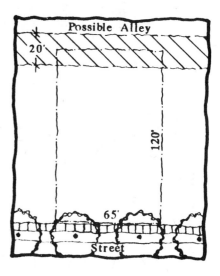

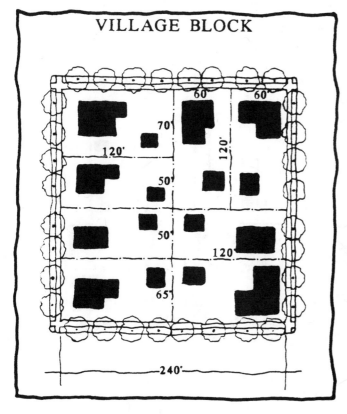

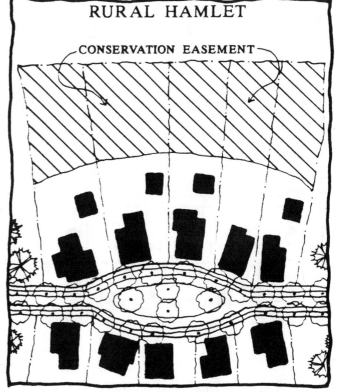

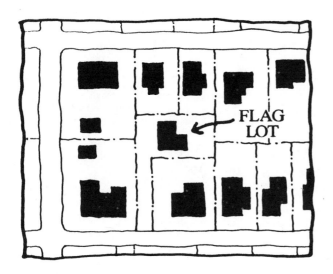

## Flag Lots

A small number of flag lots are encouraged in order to create variety, providing that the lane leading to the lot is at least 24 feet wide and that the lot is at least one half acre.

## Block

A variety of block layouts and configurations is recommended, while respecting the basic depth of 120 feet. The variety should include blocks ranging from square to rectangular in order to reinforce the modified grid. To the extent possible, block length should be kept shorter than 480 feet.

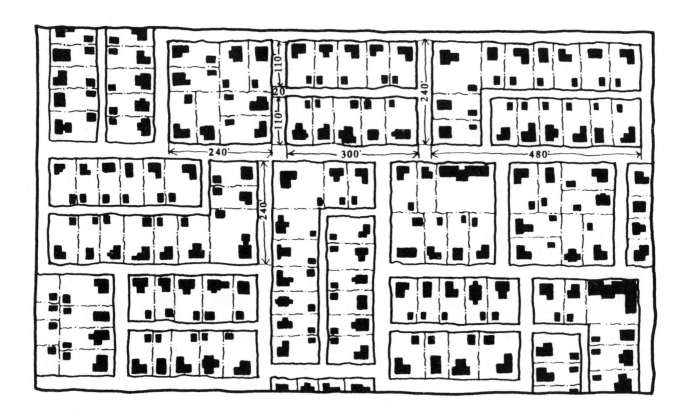

Modified grid using the basic 240 ft. block.

## Alleys

Alleys are recommended for all block types, but particularly those containing attached, multi-family, mixed-use retail, commercial, and small or narrow lot single family units. There are several variations including straight, L, and Z configurations. Alleys should be contiguous and provide garage access. Care must be exercised in lot and alley configuration so that turns in alleys allow easy access to every garage. Remember that a wider lot is required for side-access garages.

## Figure-Ground Plans

The two dimensional expression of the individuality of a building is the footprint and space surrounding it. The figure is the footprint of the building, typically shown in black. The space surrounding the building is typically left white. A figure-ground plan shows the location of the building(s) on the lot or space in which it is located. A diversity of footprints creates a more interesting street. There should be a range of figure-ground plans and sizes, with the aim of encouraging a greater percentage of smaller structures.

Building footprints should range from 400 to 2,500 square feet for residential structures and from 2,000 to 10,000 square feet for mixed-use office and multi-family structures in hamlets and small villages, but a few may be as large as 35,000 square feet in a larger village or town. Larger buildings violate the basic scale of a place, and should be allowed only by variance; 75 percent of the footprints should be under 2,500 square feet.

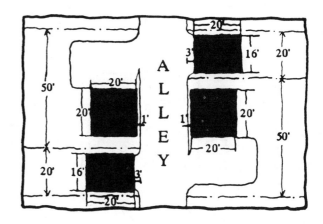

Garages can be located parallel or perpendicular to the alley. Parallel access requires greater width.

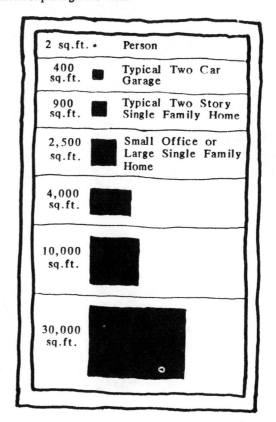

|  | |  |
|---|---|---|
| 2 sq.ft. • | | Person |
| 400 sq.ft. | ■ | Typical Two Car Garage |
| 900 sq.ft. | ■ | Typical Two Story Single Family Home |
| 2,500 sq.ft. | ■ | Small Office or Large Single Family Home |
| 4,000 sq.ft. | ■ | |
| 10,000 sq.ft. | ■ | |
| 30,000 sq.ft. | ■ | |

Comparison of footprint areas.

## Impervious Surfaces

The size of buildings can be modulated by the amount of impervious coverage. The impervious coverage of residential lots should be maximized at 50 percent; one half of the lot may be covered over with paving, sidewalks, buildings, and exterior features such as pools and decks. Based on the lot dimensions and the mix of lot widths, sizes can lead to appropriate variations and density. Impervious coverage is typically increased to 80-90 % in commercial/mixed-use core.

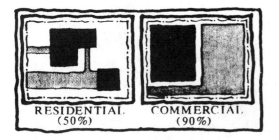

Recommended impervious surface coverage.

## Build-to line

Variation is also encouraged through the use of the build-to line. The build-to line, which is typically set back 5 to 35 feet from the curb, is necessary to define the proportions of the street. However, the build-to line allows for the variation which is necessary for an interesting streetscape. A percentage of buildings along a street (10-30%) should deviate from this line, by approximately 25 percent of the distance between the set back/build-to line and the right of way line. Public and religious buildings are exempted from the build-to line. These buildings are usually greater in mass and should be setback farther. Additionally, the build-to line only defines the location of the primary building mass. Porches, stoops, bay windows, and other minor building masses can and should project over or be recessed from the build-to line. The result is a streetscape with well-defined edges into which various masses protrude to give dimension and rhythm to the space, creating visual interest.

Variation on build-to line creates visual interest on the street.

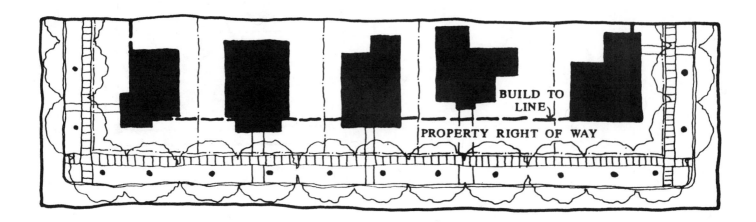

## Build-up line

Building individuality is also expressed in the third dimension with height and mass. The third dimension defines the relationship of buildings to other structures and to the street. Axonometric drawings should be used to illustrate mass, height, and roof variation in the third dimension adding the facade and roof to the figure-ground plan.

Structures can vary in height, with taller buildings placed at points of visual termination and corners. Roof pitches and ridge lines can also vary; some ridges may be perpendicular to the street, some parallel. The majority of the ridgelines should be parallel to the street. Too many perpendicular ridge lines make lots appear narrow to many people. Ridge line heights can create excellent variation. The same building can vary with the addition of porches, windows, roof projections, chimneys, garage locations, fencing, and landscaping. The height of buildings in a small community should be an average of two stories, with or without attics. Many ordinances specify heights by the distance between the average ground elevation and the height of the roof. In reality, the cornice or edge of the building is the predominant visual dimension. Like a horizontal build-to line, which specifies a setback, a build-up line specifies a cornice height which defines the street proportion. The height of the cornice will vary depending on the height of the various floors, street types, uses and whether or not the building is elevated above ground level. A two-story building build-up line can range from **20 to 25 feet above average ground level.** Similar to the variations suggested in the build-to line, build-up lines should also vary. There should be no more than three buildings in a row with a similar cornice or roof line. Fifty percent of the units should vary from the build-up line. Cornice lines should vary between one story and two and a half stories. Ridge line orientation to the street can also vary. Exceptions to this are institutional and civic buildings, if interspersed within a residential street.

Axonometric shows build-up line.

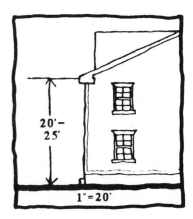

20'–25'

1" = 20'

BUILD UP LINE

This image of mixed building types in Crosswicks, NJ, always receives a high, positive rating.

## Housing Types

There are several basic housing types that should be included in the hamlet, village, and neighborhood types. These include:

- single family detached houses with private yards

- a semi-attached unit which can be two units or a unit and professional office

- duplex or two-family houses with private yards

- single family attached townhouses with private yards, limited to four units

- condominiums or apartments, with six or fewer units, that look like large single family units

- apartments in a house (granny flat)

- apartments or condominiums above commercial units

- accessory units (less than 600 Sq. ft.) in rear yards

Approximately 80 percent of the units in a hamlet or village should be the traditional single family detached house with a yard.

## Non-residential

There are several business, civic, and mixed-use building types that should be included in the small community. These include:

- retail stores

- retail stores at ground level with offices or residential above

- offices

- religious buildings

- social service buildings, like day and elder care

- fire/police stations (on periphery)

Commercial/Mixed-Use in Cranbury, NJ, receives a very positive VPS ™ rating.

- light manufacturing (on periphery)

- research facilities (on periphery)

Analysis of existing hamlets, villages, and neighborhoods reveals that large variations are present. Road pavement widths vary, curbs vary, the width of the parkway varies, the spacing of trees varies, the type of semi-public front edge treatment varies, building  lots vary, building mix varies. Careful consideration must be given to design for these variations. A repetitive consistency is boring and dull. Unfortunately, most street standards and bulk standards call for total uniformity. Yet, the only consistent element in the analysis of older places, places that receive positive ratings, is the incredible variation of spacing, size, mass, and pattern within a consistent design vocabulary. The art of site planning is the art of variation.

A mix of residential and non-residential uses in the core of Oldwick, NJ.

Retail, mixed-use, and civic buildings define the character of this village.

# Principle Eight

## MIXED AND MULTIPLE USES

A mix of land uses, housing, jobs, and incomes creates a more balanced community, reduces traffic, costs and creates better fiscal balance.

A small community must have:
- mixed and multiple use
- a mix of housing types and costs
- affordable housing
- the add-on houses
- criteria for locating large square foot uses
- a proper jobs-to-housing balance
- a fiscal balance
- a transit balance

### Mixed and multiple uses

The lower order small communities differ substantially from Euclidean subdivisions in form, function, and particularly in land use. Hamlets, villages, and neighborhoods should contain mixed and multiple uses. It is desirable to provide a mixture of compatible, indeed interrelated, uses within a community, similar, in fact, to many traditional communities. A mixture of uses paves the way for the provision of daily services, goods, and jobs for the residents. A small communities requires a greater opportunity for mixed and multiple uses.

There is a difference between mixed-use and multiple-use. Multiple use refers to uses adjacent to each other, typically in separate buildings. Mixed-use, requires that the uses be in the same or interconnected buildings. A mixed-use building can occur both horizontally and vertically. For example, small offices, particularly home offices, are compatible in the same building as housing (horizontal mixed-use). Housing can also be provided above shops and offices (vertical mixed-use). Offices can be located above shops. Even some light industrial uses can be located above shops.

Because offices and retail uses will be utilized by residents on a daily basis, they are interrelated with housing. They should not only be in close proximity to each other, but should be adjacent to each other in the core of a community where most people are within walking distance and will pass by in the course of a typical day.

There are any number of uses that are compatible within the hamlet, village, or neighborhood core; it is not necessary to compile a list of desired uses. There are, however, some uses which are clearly unacceptable. A list of obnoxious or unacceptable uses should be prepared. Some but not all of these include industry, automobile painting shops, and drive-in restaurants. These uses should be separated from the community proper, perhaps into a separate industrial zone. There are other uses which might not be acceptable in the core of a lower order community because the buildings are too large, like warehousing or large supermarkets.

The core should be where the largest number of jobs occur. The number of jobs in the community must be in proportion to the number of housing units established through the jobs-to-housing ratios. Mixed and multiple-use buildings provide job locations. Offices above retail or in separate smaller office buildings in the core are ideal. Non-industrial jobs such as those that are information and process oriented are compatible within a core.

Offices within housing units must be allowed on larger lots located on streets that allow parallel parking. Home offices should also be allowed in separate ancillary structures on the lot. The lot should have a minimum size of one half acre, to have a separate accessary office; offices can be located above the garage.

Mixed-uses come in a number of attractive combinations:
- retail on ground level with housing above
- retail on ground level with offices above
- retail on ground level with parking above
- retail, parking, and housing
- retail, parking, offices, and housing

Mixed- and multiple-use in the core of Allentown, NJ. Housing is located above and adjacent to retail.

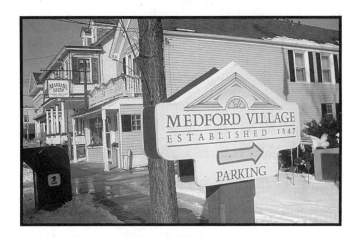

A classic mixed- and multiple-use downtown.

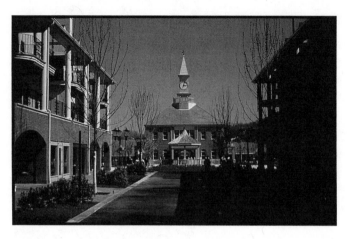

The housing units above the commercial were the first to be sold in this new Main Street in Vorhees, NJ.

Two levels of parking above retail.

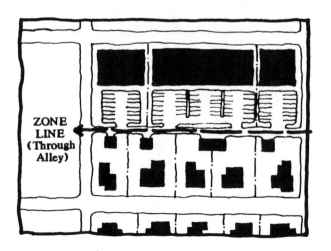

ZONE
LINE
(Through
Alley)

### Housing Above Retail

Of all the mixed-use types, housing above retail is the most appropriate for the hamlet, village, and the urban neighborhood. Housing should, in fact, be encouraged above retail in the mixed-use core. To accomplish this a unit above a retail or commercial use should only be assigned .5 unit. These units should be designed for singles, younger couples, and elderly people without children. Each unit above this retail must have a minimum of 36 square feet of exterior patio or balcony space. These should be apartments with big rooms (more loft-like), with higher ceilings and good light. Exterior entrances separated from the commercial uses should be provided.

### Retail on Ground Level of Parking Structures

In larger communities, and particularity in retrofitting situations, there will be a growing need to introduce parking structures. Of all the mixed- and multiple-use the most important is the requirement of retail on the ground level of parking structures.

### Mixed-Use Zoning Boundaries

Mixed-use zoning lines should run at the rear of property lines rather than down the middle of the street. Both sides will be coded the same and create a more harmonious streetscape.

## Housing Mix

A mix of housing types should be provided to help achieve the necessary visual quality and the market and economic mix. With the changes in demographics and the aging of the baby boomers, new housing types are required. New households will have a greater variation of bedroom and bathroom configurations required by the growing numbers of singles, elderly females, and single persons with children. These must be included to achieve a balanced community.

The community should also offer housing in a range of prices. Rather than marketing to a single socio-economic category, providing a range of housing sizes, types, and prices, creates market diversity and better opportunities to capture a greater percentage of the market. Diversity in the housing stock will generate a more balanced community.

Affordable housing interspersed with market rate housing.

## Affordable Housing

Affordable housing is becoming ever more important and needed. The neo-traditional pattern can readily provide opportunities for low- and middle- cost housing to be mixed with other residential and non-residential uses. Housing types that can accommodate low and moderate income families should be dispersed throughout the community, not be relegated to one area. They are typically of high net densities.

Larger more expensive homes, which occupy more land, typically occur on the periphery of the community. The mix of housing in a community should include a 20 percent mix for low and moderate incomes. The now famous New Jersey Supreme Court Mt. Laurel decisions have mandated that every municipality must accept its fair share of such housing to meet the regional needs. These units should be divided into ten percent low and ten percent moderate income units. Low is defined as a household income below 50% of median with moderate between 50 and 80 percent of median. The minimum density required to achieve such a mix is approximately five dwelling units per net acre. Some communities have set lower density standards and also have reduced the total number of low or moderate unite to five or ten percent of the total. No matter what the actual percentage, communities must include housing and jobs for low and moderate income households.

It is critical that affordable housing be fully integrated into the fabric of the community. Affordable housing should be indistinguishable from other units.

Most houses have been remodelled and expanded over time.

## The Add-on House

The analysis of traditional small communities clearly shows that most, if not all, houses have grown over time. Greater affordability could be achieved for many families if a small house, e.g. 1,200 to 1,600 square feet, could grow into a larger house as income and family size increase. The small house illustrated below has a combination kitchen/dining room, a half bath, and small living room on the ground floor with two bedrooms and a full bath above. This can be expanded with a larger family room on the lower level and a master bedroom above. Garages can also be optional, expandable, or add-on. This is a practical and time honored technique of providing a mix of housing.

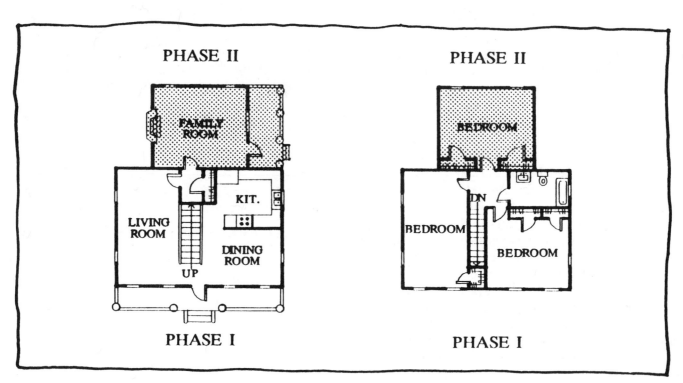

Design lots for small houses that can expand over time.

## Locating Large Uses

Many people have asked where they should locate the uses with large footprints like warehouse supermarkets, home-improvement stores, and discount groceries, etc.. Most of these uses have footprints of 60,000 to 120,000 sq. ft. These establishments usually insist on being in a single use, flat-roof, one-story building, and they demand large, at grade parking lots. They do not fit within the core of a small community . The only conceivable answer is to locate these in a separate, industrial warehouse area within a reasonable commute, from the outside boundary of the community. They are typically a single destination stop. The most negative aspects of these areas are the large parking lots, large truck service areas, the flat-roofed one-story buildings, and the blank-wall facades. To make these visually and spatially acceptable, they must be screened from the view of residential areas and, to the extent possible, from passing motorists. Low signs along the arterial are recommended to direct the motorist to the stores. Extensive landscaping must be used to screen the parking lots on the exterior and to soften the negative impact of the parking lot on the interior.

Buildings with large square footage and high parking requirements (above 3/1000) are difficult to intergrate into a core.

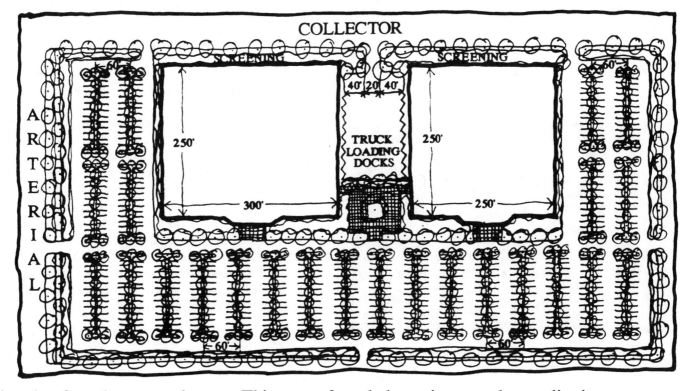

Site plan for a large warehouse. This type of use belongs in a warehouse district.

**JOBS TO HOUSING RATIOS FOR DIFFERENT COMMUNITY TYPES**

| | |
|---|---|
| HAMLET | .25:1 to 1:1 |
| VILLAGE | .5:1 to 1:1 |
| NEIGHBORHOOD | .5:1 to 1:1 |
| CORE OF A TOWN | 1:1 to 2:1 |

Many new jobs are office/service type jobs requiring from 150 to 350 square feet per employee.

Small businesses are ideal tenants in mixed-use buildings. Many buildings can share one elevation.

## Jobs-to-Housing

Each of the small community types has a recommended jobs-to-housing ratio. Such a ratio provides an optimum mix of jobs within the community. Today, based on the US Census, the average job is a 25 minute commute from where people live. There is little choice. Most land uses are still Euclidian, and very little multiple or mixed-use is allowed. Office parks don't have housing and housing developments don't have offices. When people select housing, they will typically choose a location between where they work and where they live. Most will try to get as close as possible to where they work . Day care and schools are also powerful determinantes of housing location. The more jobs, school, day care, and recreation that can be located within a community, the greater the probability that people who work there will also be able to live there.

National trends indicate that in the future an increasing number of individuals will work at home. New communications technology will facilitate this. The closer jobs are to home the greater the savings to the individual, community, and municipality. Instead of driving thirty minutes you can walk fifteen minutes. More jobs in the community will encourage more face-to-face contact. If jobs were within walking distance in our communities and neighborhoods, neighborhoods would be safer, time and energy would be saved, and the sense of community would be heightened.

The bulk of American businesses are small businesses. Many small businesses start out in the home and then expand, absorbing small office spaces ranging from 500 to 2,000 or 3,000 square feet. What better place for these businesses to expand than into the community where employees live?  Several buildings which contain multiple, smaller offices can be easily incorporated into the community core. Office building figure ground plans should be limited to the 7,500 square foot range.  Buildings larger than this should be placed in the core of a large regional center, in specific pedestrian based employment centers, or within an easy computer commuter bus ride.

Once the number of housing units has been determined, the number of jobs can be projected. Conversely, if the jobs exist, the number of housing units within the precinct can be determined. For each job, I have assigned a range of between 150 to 350 square feet of building space. This is based on current space-occupancy statistics per person. The optimal minimum and maximum square footage of job generating space should be mandated for each community. To the extent possible, job generating building space should be constructed in the core. Hamlets which have lower jobs-to-housing ratios will have fewer jobs, whereas the core of a larger town, comprising several neighborhoods, will have the highest. The ability to provide jobs within the community has the advantage of achieving transit and fiscal balance.

## Fiscal Balance

Most people feel that they pay too much in taxes relative to what they get in return. Most tax jurisdictions attempt to balance the expenses inccurred against the taxes collected. Knowing that the school tax and county tax are the majority of the tax burden (60 to 90 percent), single family homes that generate a large number of children and a large number of trips are fiscally negative, unless the home is very expensive (above $300,000) in some municipalities. A subdivision of only large expensive houses is anti-small community. High end housing should be mixed within a small community so that it can play role in image making and land stewardship. All types can be accommodated within a community while maintaining and giving value. The more positive the small community the greater the value.

A small community must have a balance of housing types for both young families and older persons without children. A small community with a mix of incomes, housing types, and non-residential uses has the opportunity to achieve a fiscal balance.

**DETERMINING SQUARE FOOTAGE OF JOB SPACE BASED ON NUMBER OF HOUSING UNITS.**

(Number of units) x (Ratio of jobs) x (square footage per job) = Total square footage of building

The goal is to achieve a commercial-to-residential balance which contributes to fiscal balance. The model illustrates a balance of non - residential and residential building types.

Municipal short falls in revenues are partially relieved by aid given by the federal and state governments through road improvements, school aid, etc., but it seldom seems like enough. The municipality, through taxes paid by non-residential uses or residential uses that generate few school aged children, attempts to achieve a fiscal balance. Most municipalities over-zone for non-residential or large lot residential. Municipalities compete with each other for these non-residential ratables, creating the ratable chase.

To create a fiscal balance each small community should attempt to achieve a balanced ratio of residential to non-residential uses; the greater the balance of housing to jobs, non-residential to residential uses, the greater opportunity there is for balance in the tax equation. Balancing housing costs with non-residential surpluses in each separate small community can help to achieve this balance. Therefore, a balance of residential and non-residential tax generating uses within every small community is required.

**Multiple transportation modes must exist in a small community. Higher order modes must not hinder the functioning of the lower order.**

## THE ORDER
- Light Rail
- Computer Commuter
- Van and Car Pooling
- Automobiles and Trucks
- Bicycles
- Pedestrians

## Transit Balance

A multiple- and mixed-use community designed in accordance with the principles has the potential of a balance between walkers, bicycle riders, van and bus users, and auto users. A significant reduction in the number of auto trips generated by conventional suburban development can be achieved particularly when the core of the community has the balance of jobs to housing, the correct ratios of recreation facilities within walking distance or a short bicycle riding distance, local retail is within walking distance of most homes. This is an obvious advantages of mixed use, particularly when the mixed-use core is within walking distance or short transit distance. The jobs-to-housing ratio will not only provide the opportunity for a large number of jobs within the community, but will reduce the number of trips taken outside the community. Small communities will make basic transit more viable because of the layout and positive spatial and visual characteristics.

# BASIC TRANSPORTATION MODES APPLICABLE TO THE SMALL COMMUNITY.

Walking is the lowest order transportation mode. It is the most critical mode for creating a safe and successful small community.

Bicycling is an excellent means of transportation, particularly for the young.

The bus is the most flexible transit option but lacks legibility unless it is well organized around specific, identifiable stops.

The private automobile has the greatest flexibility, speed, and cost. To the extent possible small communities should strive for only one car per unit.

# Principle Nine

## DESIGN VOCABULARY

*A small community is physically unified by common design features which include building mass and style, facade treatment, materials, colors, landscape, and streetscape details.*

A basic design vocabulary should include the following:
- vernacular architectural style recommendations
- building detail guidelines for windows, doors, and roofs
- a listing of acceptable materials and colors
- streetscape elements
- a diversity of these components within a defined framework

A distinctive unity must be created in a small community where all buildings share a thematic character. All buildings should share basic design elements which complement each other; this is called a design vocabulary. New communities and retrofitted places can and should strive for such a positive unity by adopting a design vocabulary which sets forth guidelines for buildings and landscape features including: mass, roof types, wall materials, eaves, canopies, arcades, entry doors, windows, corner details, decorative elements, fences, edges, paving materials, textures, and colors. This should be illustrated for both residential, retail, commercial, mixed-use, and community buildings. A matrix of the recommended design features in sketch or photographic form should created. The design vocabulary matrix will have the design features down the edge with the building types across the top. Each space is filled with a colored photograph or sketch which best characterizes the forms and details desired. Planning boards then scan the photographs and compare these to the elevations, sketches and perspectives presented by applicants. Conversely, applicants clearly know what board will accept.

Every place has a defined design vocabulary. It is easiest to see the design vocabulary in a small historic community. Many features of the design vocabulary can be taken from a positively rated image.

The VPS$^{TM}$ performed for a community will aid in the preparation of the design vocabulary by indicating those architectural styles, details, colors, materials, etc. which are appropriate and acceptable. Typically the positively rated images reflect the more traditional scale, thematic character, details, and street scale elements. Photographs of the more positively rated images can be the basics of the design vocabulary. The

## Good architects look for a context into which they place their design.

design vocabulary matrix should become part of the ordinance code of a community. If a community does not want to prepare a design voabulary, the developer can be asked to prepare it. Images can be taken from builders catalogues, architectural supplies (like doors, windows, siding, etc.), or photographers from a field trip of the latest completed projects.

Many times there might not be a specific style clearly apparent in an area, particularly if that area has experienced high suburban growth levels in the past years. You might have to reach into the region to determine the vernacular character, which can be tested through visual preference. In some instances you might not want the community to be only one style, but want a mix of styles as is typical in most older villages which have grown over time. A compatible mix of styles is acceptable providing that other basic design features which create a unity within this diversity are present. This should not prevent a developer from creating a group of homes or entire streetscapes with a thematic character.

The design vocabulary is not intended to create monotonous repetition. It provides some required and some optional features of the local vernacular architectural style and serves to create a framework in which diversity and originality are encouraged. It is a pallet from which the architect, engineer, builder, developer, or purchasers can design. The compatible use of materials, colors, and facade treatment will result in visually positive buildings for the community. The greatest diversity is to be encouraged using a variety of these design elements. As a general rule, no two detached buildings within a viewshed should be exactly the same.

Using a design vocabulary generated through the VPS $^{TM,}$ the residents of a municipality have helped to establish the consensus vision of place. Many municipalities and developers do not want a design review board. Many planning boards have expressed a desire to have greater control over the actual design but do not know how to implement this. Many planning board members and elected officials are disappointed with the final look of the buildings they approved, and wish there was an easy way to help direct the design of buildings. The design vocabulary generated through the VPS$^{TM}$ is such a technique. The design vocabulary primarily uses photographs and sketches to make recommendations and set forth guidelines.

Communities which have withstood the test of time typically embody a regional vernacular architectural form which can be applied in contemporary buildings.

Positively rated images provide many acceptable design features.

## DESIGN VOCABULARY MATRIX  (Each rectangle needs to be infilled with a sketch,

### Residential Building Types

| | | | | | | | | | | |
|---|---|---|---|---|---|---|---|---|---|---|
| 1. Building Massing and Style | | | | | | | | | | |
| 2. Roof Types & Materials | | | | | | | | | | |
| 3. Facade Treatment & Materials | | | | | | | | | | |
| 4. Entry and Doors | | | | | | | | | | |
| 5. Windows | | | | | | | | | | |
| 6. Eaves, Porches & Arcades | | | | | | | | | | |
| 7. Trim | | | | | | | | | | |
| 8. Towers | | | | | | | | | | |
| 9. Cross Gables and Dormers | | | | | | | | | | |
| 10. Gutters | | | | | | | | | | |
| 11. Chimneys | | | | | | | | | | |
| 12. Walls, Fences, and Hedges Front Yard | | | | | | | | | | |
| 13. Walls - Fences and Hedges (Side and Rear Yards) | | | | | | | | | | |
| 14. Colors | | | | | | | | | | |
| 15. Driveway | | | | | | | | | | |
| 16. Pavement Materials and Textures | | | | | | | | | | |
| 17. Curb Treatment | | | | | | | | | | |
| 18. Streetlights | | | | | | | | | | |
| 19. Street signs | | | | | | | | | | |
| 20. Street furniture | | | | | | | | | | |

a photograph of existing buildings, or from manufacturer catalogues)

**Commercial Building Types**

**Civic Building Types**

**Outbuilding Types**

Examples of massing, style, and roof treatment for single residential building. This photograph is typical of images to be included in the matrix.

This image illustrates the facade treatment, door material, and window treatment. The illustration of these features do not have to be taken from older buildings and facades but can be taken from manufacturers specifications.

## 1. Building Massing and Style

The building mass is the volumetric shape of a structure including sides, and roofs, and the size of the base, or footprint. It will show the expected range of base size. Massing will also reflect the style of the structures.

## 2. Roof types and materials

The variation of roof types should show the various pitches, shapes, and forms. Acceptable materials should be specified.

## 3. Facade treatments and materials

The facade is the primary element that defines the character of a building. There are various facade elements which must be shown, including window and door openings and proportions.

Most facades should have a defined base or foundation, a middle or modulated wall, and a top formed by a pitched roof or articulated cornice. These divisions create a more positive relationship to the human scale. All buildings, except retail, should be raised above sidewalk grade. A range of acceptable materials should also be specified in the design vocabulary. Wall materials within the community should be based upon the traditional use of materials in the area. An analysis of existing positively rated buildings can produce a checklist of materials in common use. Those which have aged without excessive deterioration will prove to be the best for the local climate. New materials may be introduced if they closely emulate the look and feel of traditional materials.

## 4. Doors

Doors are perhaps, the most important facade feature because they are the entry, the physical transition between the inside and the outside. The location, orientation, and proportion of entries and doors should be illustrated. Door types and edge treatments should be illustrated including sidelights, trim, and transoms.

## 5. Windows

Windows are the visual transition from the inside to the outside and vice versa. From the outside they enhance the human scale of the facade. The use of window openings should vary between buildings while respecting a common model, for example, the consistent use of punched windows as opposed to the occasional interruption of continuous horizontal strip windows. A common window vocabulary can be used in various ways to create an infinite variety of facades. Very important window feature includes the number of panes, the way it opens, the trim around it and whether it should be embellished with shutters or a wing.

Illustration of window treatment

## 6. Porches, Covered Patios, and Arcades

This category should illustrate the style, mass, roof form, overhangs, columns, balustrades and stair types.

Illustration of porch types.

## 7. Trim

The trim adds detail and character to the facade. It should include the eaves, corner boards, gable and eave boards, pediments, friezes, lintels, sills, quoins, belt courses, balustrades, etc.

Illustration of trim.

Detail photograph of a roof dormer which can be inserted on the design vocabulary matrix.

Picket fence types.

## 8. Bays, Towers, Cross Gables, and Dormers

Cross gables and dormers can transform a stylistically simple building into one with a unique character and thereby distinguish it from its neighbors. This architectural embellishment adds articulation and rhythm to the entire neighborhood.

## 9. Other decorative elements

Decorative building elements can include belvederes, copulas, and pergolas.

## 10. Gutters

Roof gutters and down spouts should be specified. This indicates whether they are a "U", "K" or halfrounded. Indicate how they are attached or built-in, or integrated with the trim.

## 11. Chimneys

All units should have a chimney. Various types of chimney exposures and locations should be indicated. Chimney caps should be indicated where appropriate. Materials and colors should be shown.

## 12. Front Yard, Walls, Fences, and Hedges

The treatment of the front yard should be defined using landscaping, hedging, fencing, stone walls, or a combination of those elements. This defines the transition from the public, semi -public, and private space. Size, height, materials, and character should be illustrated. Front yards should be defined by a three foot high fence (not chain link) or hedge. Walls are recommended in situations where the yard is at a higher elevation than the sidewalk. The entranceway and corners of the front yard can be articulated with high posts or other embellishments. A listing of acceptable fence and gate types should be prepared. Again, there should be variety within a harmony. If a wall is required, flat or board-form poured concrete should be avoided. There are many patterns that can be used as framework. The wall surface should be textured. Stone or stone facing is desirable. Brick and textured patterned concrete is also acceptable. If and when concrete is used, it should be base planted with ivy. If retaining blocks are used, a variety of sizes are recommended. Pressure treated six by six boards should be avoided.

## 13. Side and Rear Yard, Walls, Fences, and Hedges

The smaller the lot the greater the need to assure privacy. As lot widths decrease, the side and rear property lines defining the backyard should be enclosed. The height, size, material, and design character needs to be illustrated.

Example of wall types.

## 14. Colors

A harmonious range of colors should be used within a small community. The use of too many colors in a community creates visual clutter, but the use of only a few is boring. Most traditional settlements have used a range of colors which may have changed with the various architectural periods, yet they remain compatible. These colors can be matched, and compatible colors may be added. Color choices for a new community may also be derived from the natural setting. Color clues can be taken from the soil and vegetation on the site. Acceptable colors will enhance the natural characteristics of the area. A palette of these colors must be prepared and made available. A minimum of two base colors and four to six accent colors is recommended for smaller hamlets, with up to four base colors and an equivalent number of complementary and contrasting colors for larger communities. The VPS ™ can be an excellent source for creating a color balance.

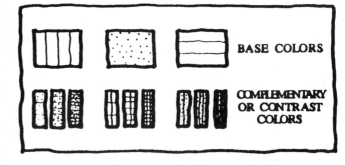

## 15. Driveways

The size, location, relationship to building surface materials, and edging of the driveway should be specified. The treatment of shared driveways is very important.

Illustration of one driveway treatment in a residential area

Pavements materials.

## 16. Streetscape pavement materials and textures

Pavement materials, textures, and colors must be included for pedestrian areas. Concrete is the basic sidewalk material, but alternatives should be pursued to replace or highlight concrete. Concrete can be colored and scored to replicate traditional paving materials. Brick pavers may replace concrete or define the edges of a sidewalk. The more surface texture, the more positive the area appears. The patterns, colors, and materials that will be accepted should be specified.

Pavement color and texture can be specified for cartways, driveways, and areas that mix the pedestrian and vehicle at low speeds. Asphalt can be colored by use of the aggregate or dye. A combination of concrete paving and asphalt can be designed for low speed mixed pedestrian and vehicle areas.

## 17. Curb Treatment

Granite slabs are the most durable and can be temporarily removed when necessary for repairs. Another common curbing with a positive visual impact, is granite block, often called Belgian block. When concrete curbing is used it should have a square profile and be gray, not white, in color. All curbing should step six inches from the pavement. Rolled asphalt curbing is unacceptable. No curbing is an alternative in areas with very low traffic volumes below 250 ADT.

## 18. Streetlight

Streetlight should be scaled to the pedestrian between ten and fourteen feet high. The style of light posts and fixtures which complement the architectural characteristic of the community and other streetscape elements should be shown. The base, port and fixtures should be illustrated. Lighting standards should maintain visibility at intersections, but residential areas must not be over lighted. Footcandles should be specified. Most specified footcandle (fc.) levels for residential areas are too high. Most small communities only need light in the core and intersection areas. The use of cobra head and highway style lighting is to be avoided. Lights provided by gate posts and porch lights are sufficient for most residential streets. Night sky glow from these lights should be restricted by use of cutoffs and caps. Light should be as close to incandescent as possible. Multi-halide is the best, color corrected sodium the second.

An illustration of streetlight pole and fixture.

### 19. Street signs

Signs include street signs with street names, traffic signs, bus stop signs, signs and numbers on buildings. It should be easy to find street names and house numbers in a small community. Many municipalities in New Jersey use a reflector type sign on a pole for street signing. Most of the time they only designate one street and not cross-streets. These signs have been rated as neutral or negative. The more positively rated signs are those on vertical posts within clear sight distance at the intersection. Letters are attached to either wooden or masonry posts.

Photographs of the various sign types, sizes, and locations should be shown.

Hanging street sign

### 20. Street Furniture

The specific character and design of benches, trash baskets, planters, bicycle racks, kiosk, etc. should be selected to complement the architectural style and pavement characteristic.

### Conclusion

All the above elements of the design vocabulary should be coded into a matrix to become the guidelines for development. These are best illustrated in photographic form. If the municipality has not predetermined a design vocabulary, then the developer must establish one for each small community. It must be approved at the time of preliminary application. Refinements can be made through final approval.

Benches complement the streetscape

Use of a design vocabulary does not represent a standardization of design. It is a guide for the architects and builders who will be designing the buildings. The greatest diversity of buildings and edges is to be encouraged and can happen with the use of the design vocabulary. My experience has been that a good designer will review the vocabulary and then improve upon it. However, the design guidelines ensure the use of similar elements that respect the character and vision of the community. Communities which share a common design vocabulary typically have more overall community pride and greater sustaining value.

Creating a design vocabulary using photographic prints is easy and effective.

Land with low density uses on the periphery of a rural village or hamlet.

Pride in a community is expressed in everyone's desire to maintain it.

# Principle Ten

## MAINTENANCE

*A small community must have a commitment to maintaining its character and quality of place.*

Community maintenance must consider the following:

peripheral open space maintenance
- land stewardship
- large lot zoning
- Transfer of Development Credit T.D.C.
- Transfer of Development Rights T.D.R.
- property associations
- conservancy and stewardship
- public land
- agricultural zoning

internal open space maintenance
- maintaining streetscapes in the public viewshed
- litter and trash pickup
- street maintenance
- street furniture maintenance
- street landscaping and landscape maintenance

property maintenance
- commercial and industrial property
- multi-family residential

historic preservation

building with low maintenance materials

maintaining a sense of security

Designing and building a beautiful small community can be achieved by employing the first nine principles. Once a place worth living has been built it must be maintained. The importance of this cannot be overstated. Maintenance does not only mean keeping the streets clean, and maintaining order and safety, though certainly these are very important. Maintenance involves caring for all aspects of the community, its buildings, its streets, its open spaces, and, last but not least, its ecological systems. Maintenance is the one overriding principle to ensure the continued viability of the other design features generated through the principles. We plan and design not only for the benefit of the current inhabitants but also for future generations. And surely one of the important lessons to pass on to our successors is the importance of caring for and preserving our environment.

A well maintained and preserved small community rates very high.

## Peripheral Open Space

Peripheral open space maintenance among the smaller communities is most cost effective if simply left to its natural succession. This will require some inevitable litter pick-up, and the area must be guarded from illegal dumping. Natural access and walking trails are recommended for such recreational uses as cross country skiing or hiking. Planting the land in forest products such as Christmas trees or other nursery stock is a good alternative. Open spaces can be farmed or leased to farmers for crop production or grazing land. This provides some funding for continued maintenance. Golf courses are recommended for peripheral open space, although serious controls must be implemented to avoid environmental pollution. Cemeteries provide open space maintenance possibilities.

Peripheral open space can have several functions, including agriculture.

## Land Stewardship

Smaller community, on an individual owner parcel, requires a minimum of 50 percent of open space be preserved. The peripheral open space may be maintained by allowing subdivision into very large lots that range from 10 to 50 acres per unit. These estate lots must be deed restricted so they cannot be further subdivided. Land stewardship in private holdings is one technique by which open space can be preserved. Under this method, however, the open space may not be accessible to the public. Peripheral open space held in private hands may be opened up to the public through dedication of some portion of the land into a conservation easement. By placing houses at the front of these very large lots, a majority of the land can be dedicated to open space in perpetuity.

Very large lot parcels encourage land stewardship.

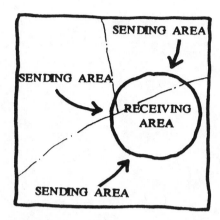

Transfer of density from a single or a joint venture ownership of adjacent parcels to a single village or hamlet.

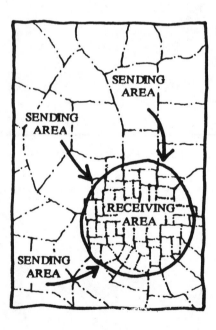

TDR can apply to a township or a region.

## Transfer of Development Credits (TDC)

Transfer of Development Credits (TDC) is a technique by which the development potential generated in one area of a site can be transferred to another area of the site. This can be applied to one or more immediately adjacent parcels. In this case they can form a joint venture and transfer the base number of units to a more appropriate location which meets the criteria as a potential location for a small community. This allows great amounts of open space to be maintained while assuring benefits to the land owner.

Because TDR is not allowed in most municipalities in New Jersey, the TDC technique is the most viable option. Municipalities should actively encourage adjacent land owners to participate in this process.

## Transfer of Development Rights (TDR)

Transfer of Development Rights (TDR) offers another method of preserving open space. Although TDR is complex in application, the concept is simple. In short, the number of units allowed on a sending zone is transferred to a receiving zone which has been planned for a small community. The number of units in the sending zone is based on the building capacity and natural resources of the land. The receiving zone, which has similar low base zoning, is assigned a density increase in order to make the economic equation of purchasing the development rights from an owner in the sending zone. Using this method, the ownership and main-tenance of land in the sending zone remains in private hands, while open space and agricultural uses are preserved.

The New Jersey Legislature permitted this to occur in three townships in Burlington County, where prime agricultural land needs to be preserved. My recommendation would be to allow TDR as a matter of right in all municipalities that wish to preserve agricultural lands, large tracts of environmen-tally sensitive land, or woodlands. Specific areas in a munici-pality should be designated as receiving zones--areas where development is to be designed as a small community.
One of the great difficulties of this application is when an owner in the sending zone needs or desires to sell his property's development rights and there isn't a buyer for such rights. The property owner would then apply to a T.D.R. bank to purchase the rights. The establishment and funding of the bank and establishing the value of a development right is one of the largest impediments to the implementation of T.D.R.

## Property Associations
### Home Owners Association

Other methods to preserve peripheral and internal open space require the land ownership and maintenance by public or private not-for-profit organizations. In one alternative, a homeowners association can own, manage, and maintain the open space with a fee assessed to each unit.

### Conservancy and Stewardship

A second alternative places the land ownership and maintenance in a nature conservancy, such as a watershed association or a hunting club.

### Public Lands

Another alternative involves actually deeding the land to the township as permanent open space to be owned and maintained by the municipality as a park or nature preserve.

Under all of these alternatives the land can be deed-restricted against development, although agricultural uses and low intensity recreational uses on the periphery of a hamlet or village should be allowed. If the township assumes ownership the maintenance is paid for out of tax dollars through property assessment.

### Agricultural Zoning

The land can be zoned for agricultural uses at very low density. The right-to-farm provisions must be applied to these areas to prevent complaints from land owners on the periphery of the agricultural zone.

The open space in Radburn has been maintained by a homeowners association since 1930.

New small machinery can improve street maintenance.

This image received extremely low ratings. Low ratings impact negatively adjacent uses. Very low ratings indicate the opportunity for renewal.

## Internal Open Space Maintenance

Maintenance of the streetscape and the entire public viewshed is extremely important. Trash must be removed and streets and buildings must be kept in sound structural repair. A well maintained environment instills a sense of community spirit, pride of place, in its residents. In turn, this pride creates further desire in the inhabitants for continued community participation.

Internal parks and parkways must be kept clean and well maintained. A routine maintenance program must be implemented. Seasonal adjustments must be instituted. Seasonal flowers, leaf removal, painting of any storage or public structures, and holiday decorations must be part of the long term maintenance program.

Local private organizations can and should be used. Local schools, garden clubs, and senior clubs can contribute to the beautification and maintenance.

A maintenance program must include the following:
- a program of litter and trash pickup.
- the street must be swept, proper street cleaning equipment is required
- painting and maintaining street furniture like benches, light fixtures, street signs, etc.
- street trees require maintenance guarantees at time of planting
- leaf pick-up and composting
- tree and hedge pruning
- installing seasonal decorations
- snow plowing and removal

All these tasks must be completed, funded and staffed. Equipment must be purchased and storage facilities must be provided. Recycling will also be part of the maintenance cycle requiring space and facilities.

## Property Maintenance Codes

Property maintenance is critical. Of most serious concern is visible deterioration on multi-family and commercial structures. Structures which are boarded up are the most negative and destructive of a sense of community. I recommend that a property maintenance code be established for all commercial and multi-family units; single-family owner-occupied houses are seldom a problem.

When properties are not well maintained, it is analogous to cancer. Once it starts, it requires serious medicine to cure it or the patient dies. Too many times the deteriorated condition starts simply with the lack of painting or repairing a broken window. Once this happens, it is likely to spread. Too many municipal officials do not put sufficient resources into property maintenance. Deterioration cannot be allowed to start. If it is present, it should be corrected immediately. Maintenance programs should include several steps:

1. inspection
2. warning with time to repair or maintain
3. signing off on completed work or if not completed in a timely manner pressing legal action
4. having repairs or maintenance completed by outside contractor
5. assessing or preparing liens against property owner

6. assuring or withholding occupancy permits (Withholding a building permit is one of the most serious incentives to have a building brought up to code.)

Lack of maintenance is like cancer, once it is started it must be treated.

## Historic Preservation

Preservation and maintenance of existing historic buildings, features, and landscapes can enhance the design quality of a new or retrofitted small community. Historic hamlets, villages, and neighborhoods must be preserved and enhanced. Features which characterize a regional vernacular can be incorporated into the design vocabulary. If a site contains an existing historic structure or place, a preservation incentive can be given through an increase in density. Historic structures and places should be those listed on the local inventory of historic places.

Preservation ordinances have protected the historic structures and streetscapes.

New home buyers look for low maintenance exteriors and landscapes.

People on the street and people looking onto the street provide a sense of security.

## Building with Low Maintenance Materials

In today's busy society, people want minimal maintenance building exteriors. It is important to first have a look at the materials that have best weathered on older buildings in your region. Masonry, including brick and stone, are the best. Sheathing, including copper and aluminum, typically weather well. Wood, particularly stained or painted cedar and oak also weather well. New materials that emulate older materials and patterns and require less painting and replacement should be used. The building industry is responding with new lines of plastic, fiberglass, and aluminum based materials. These should be expressed in the design vocabulary.

## Maintaining a Sense of Security

People must feel secure in their community. The greatest security is in knowing the people who live and work in your community. The design, layout, and community organizations must promote personal interaction and neighborliness, while assuring privacy. The plan must encourage meeting and chance encounters. The plan must attempt to not only create neighbors, but acquaintances and friends.

Community organizations must bring people together and allow them to share decisions about their community. People must know that they have a voice in the control of their community's maintenance, the recreation facilities, and the variances requested. They must be able to celebrate together, from local parades to neighborhood picnics.

There is a greater sense of security when people own their home as opposed to renting. To the extent possible, including the low and moderate income households, the largest possible number of units should be owner occupied.

There is greater security in the sharing of values, when there is pride of place, when there are support organizations to respond to needs like van and car pooling, day care, religious and social needs.

# PROCESS STEP VI
## ILLUSTRATING CODES

# REVISING YOUR ORDINANCE

## Writing and Illustrating Codes and Ordinances
## Revising Your Ordinance

**CHAPTER EIGHT**

Ordinances must be illustrated, as well as written. They must be understandable to average residents, not just to planners and attorneys.

In the presentations I have maked throughout the country, I have stressed the need to illustrate the zoning ordinance, thereby making it more understandable, usable, and predictable. It should contain photographs and illustrations. I refer to this as a " Dick and Jane Ordinance." People must understand what quality and intensity of urban form and open space they are getting with new of development. The following draft ordinance can be used to create a hamlet, village, or neighborhood as an alternative to conventional subdivisions. It is a complex ordinance which can be refined and modified as required for your municipality. Many of the illustrations and photographs should be substituted with local, vernacular images and sketches. I have indicated in the text where this should occur. Photographs are required. They should be taken in your region to illustrate the text. The best photographs are those which have been tested through a VPS $^{TM}$. They have withstood the legal test of public acceptability and appropriateness.

It is modeled after the ordinance adopted in June of 1992 by Manhiem Township, Lancaster County, Pennsylvania. The original Manhiem Ordinance is the product of the complete process as recommended in this book. This ordinance is meant as a guide to amend and supplement your current ordinance.

This ordinance applies to the creation of a new hamlet, village, or neighborhood, or the retrofitting of an existing subdivision or strip commercial zone into a small community. The ordinance is generic and can apply to many sites and base densities. It presumes a basic acceptance of the process and ten principles.

This ordinance can be significantly simplified if a regulatory plan has been approved as part of the master plan and capitol improvement plan for your municipality. A regulatory plan consist of road right-of-ways, with accompanying pavement widths, build-to lines, the location of public and semi-public open spaces and the location of public and institutional buildings. Conceptual building footprints that create a figure-ground plan can enhance the impact of the regulating plan.

## MODEL ORDINANCE

Name of Municipality

_____

ORDINANCE NO. _____

AN ORDINANCE TO AMEND THE ZONING ORDINANCE OF _____ TOWNSHIP, TO ADD A NEW ARTICLE ___, PLANNED SMALL COMMUNITY, PROVIDING REGULATIONS FOR PLANNED SMALL COMMUNITIES WITHIN THE TOWNSHIP.

     BE AND IT IS HEREBY ORDAINED AND ENACTED by the governing committee, of _____ Township, _____ County, State of _____, as follows:

Section  The Zoning Ordinance of _____ Township - 19___ Article ___, shall be amended to add a new subsection which shall provide as follows:

## SECTION 1.  LEGISLATIVE INTENT

Each of the following goals and statements of intent should be illustrated using high and low rated images generated from the results of the Visual Preference Survey ™ competed by the community or other in which the board agrees.  Slides can be easily transformed into half tones for use.

The intent of the council in enacting this article is to:

1.  Encourage innovative, neo-traditional residential mixed- and multiple-use developments so that the growing demand for housing may be met by greater variety in type, design, and layout of dwellings and by the conservation and more efficient use of open space ancillary to said dwellings.

2.  Extend greater opportunities for traditional community living, working, housing, and recreation to all citizens and residents of this township.

3.  Encourage a more efficient use of land and public services and to reflect changes in technology of land development and by directing new development in a traditional pattern of mixed- and multiple-use and varied housing types.

4.  Provide a procedure which can relate the type, design, and layout of residential development to the particular site, the particular demand for housing existing at the time of development, and to the township's goal of encouraging neo-traditional residential/mixed-use development in a manner consistent with the preservation or enhancement of property values within existing residential areas.

5.  Insure that the increased flexibility and design specificity of regulations over land development authorized herein is carried out under such administrative standards and procedures as shall encourage the disposition of proposals for land development without undue delay.

6.  Preserve the remaining rural, historic, and agricultural character of the community by directing new development to appropriate locations and minimizing the visual impact of development upon the viewsheds from the public roadway.

## Illustration 1

**Provide photograph of rural, historic, and/or agricultural character**

7. Promote alternative land development practices which will otherwise promote the public health, safety, and welfare. Neo-traditional neighborhoods and developments, including new hamlets and villages, are the desired alternative to conventional, modern, use-segregated developments, such as large lot suburban subdivisions and strip commercial developments.

8. Reduce the excessive sprawl of development and the segregation of land uses that results in the inefficient use of irreplaceable natural energy sources due to the almost total dependence upon private vehicles for transportation. Refer to Illustrations 2 and 3.

Illustration 2

Provide a photograph of
vehicular traffic

Illustration 3

Provide a photograph of
vehicular traffic

*Provide a minimum of two photographs with captions of vehicular congestion.*

9. Reduce the excessive sprawl of development and the segregation of land uses that cause unnecessary traffic congestion. Discourage the development of drive-through and drive-to facilities which encourage the use of private automobiles contributing to traffic congestion. Refer to Illustrations 4 and 5.

Illustration 4

Provide a photograph of segregated land
use which contribute to sprawled development

Illustration 5

Provide a photograph of segregated land
use which contribute to sprawled development

*Provide a minimum of two photographs here with captions.*

10. Discourage generic, modern suburban development that bears no relation to the historic development pattern of _____ County. Refer to Illustrations 6 through 9.

## Illustration 6

Provide a photograph which illustrates negatively rated new development which violates historic development patterns

## Illustration 7

Provide a photograph which illustrates negatively rated new development which violates historic development patterns.

## Illustration 8

Provide a photograph which illustrates negatively rated new development which violates the historic development patterns

## Illustration 9

Provide a photograph which illustrates negatively rated new development which violates the historic development patterns

*Provide a minimum of four photographs with captions*

11. Promote the creation of new neighborhoods and developments that exhibit the design features of traditional neighborhoods, hamlets, villages, and small towns in _____ County. Refer to Illustrations 10 and 11.

<table>
<tr>
<td>

### Illustration 10

Provide a photograph of traditional design features, streetscapes, etc.

</td>
<td>

### Illustration 11

Provide a photograph of traditional design features, streetscapes, etc.

</td>
</tr>
</table>

*Provide a minimum of two photographs here with captions*

12. Promote the creation of places which are oriented to the pedestrian, promote citizen security, and social interaction. Refer to Illustration 12.

### Illustration 12

Provide a photograph
of pedestrian friendly places.

*Provide one or more photographs with captions*

13. Promote developments with a mix of residential dwelling types, a range of lot sizes, and mixed-use structures with offices and/or apartments above ground level retail uses that surrounde a community green with related community facilities.

Illustration 13

Provide a photograph of those development types which rate positively in the Visual Preference Survey ™.

*Provide at least one photograph with caption here*

14. Promote developments with the desired visual and spatial characteristics expressed in highly positive responses in the Township's Visual Preference Survey ™. Refer to Illustrations 10 through 14.

Illustration 14

Provide a photograph here.

*Provide a minimum of one photograph here.*

15. Promote developments which will create a strong sense of community identity as expressed in the township's Visual Preference Survey ™. Refer to Illustrations 10 through 14.

| | |
|---|---|
| **Illustration 15**<br><br>Provide a minimum of two photographs with captions that illustrate the most positive image of community identity. | **Illustration 16**<br><br>Provide a minimum of two photographs with captions that illustrate the most positive image of community identity. |

*Provide a minimum of two photographs with captions*

16. Promote developments where the physical, visual, and spatial characteristics are established and reinforced through the consistent use of compatible urban design and architectural design elements. Such elements shall relate the design characteristics of an individual structure or development to other existing and planned structures or developments in a harmonious manner, resulting in a coherent overall development pattern and streetscape.

17. Promote the creation of developments that are identifiable in the landscape, surrounded by open space, and help preserve sensitive natural features.

18. Discourage commercial or industrial uses that create objectionable noise, glare, or odors.

## SECTION 2. APPLICABILITY OF ARTICLE

The provisions of this Article are a furtherance of the land use and development controls of land in the township. This article shall not affect any of the provisions of the township subdivision and land development ordinance or this zoning ordinance as they apply to the township as a whole. After a development plan is duly filed, approved, and recorded under the provisions of this article, the land area included in the development plan shall be governed entirely by the provisions of this article with the exception that provisions of the township subdivision and land development ordinance and this zoning ordinance specifically referenced within this article shall also apply.

## SECTION 3. BASIS FOR CONSIDERATION

Consideration for approval or disapproval of a planned small community shall be based on and interpreted in light of the effect of the development on the comprehensive plan of the township, and in light of the effect of the development on the use of the property adjacent to and in the areas close to the planned small community.

This article shall not be construed to mean the developer of a hamlet, village, or neighborhood can by right merely meet the standards set herein. These standards and requirements are minimums only. The board may require more stringent standards, based on the specific and unique nature of the site and the surrounding areas, in order to protect the health, safety, and welfare of the citizens of the township. In cases where additional standards are necessary for a specific site, this zoning ordinance and the township subdivision and land development ordinance shall apply towards the site until the proposed development plan has been filed, approved, and recorded having met these additional standards.

## SECTION 4. MODIFICATIONS

The board may, by conditional use approval, permit the modification of the provisions of this article, including but not limited to provisions relating to the percentage of types of dwelling units and the amount of commercial development, in order to encourage planned small community. Any conditional use to permit a modification of the requirements of this article shall be subject to the following standards:

1. The design and improvement of the planned small community shall be in harmony with the purpose and intent of this article.

2. The design and improvement of the planned small community shall generally enhance the development plan, or in any case not have an adverse impact on its physical, visual, or spatial characteristics.

3. The design and improvement of the planned small community shall generally enhance the streetscape and neighborhood, or in any case not have an adverse impact on the streetscape and neighborhood.

4. The modification shall not result in configurations of lots or street systems which shall be impractical or detract from the appearance of the proposed planned small community.

5. The proposed modification shall not result in any danger to the public health, safety, or welfare by making access to the dwellings by emergency vehicles more difficult, by depriving adjoining properties of adequate light and air, or by violating the other purposes for which zoning ordinances are to be enacted.

6. Landscaping and other methods shall be used to insure compliance with the design standards and guidelines of this article.

7. The minimum lot size of any lot to be created shall not be reduced below the requirements of this article.

8. The landowner shall demonstrate that the proposed modification will allow for equal or better results and represents the minimum modification necessary.

If the board determines that the landowner has met his burden, it may grant a modification of the requirements of this article. In granting modifications, the board may impose such conditions as will, in its judgment, secure the objectives and purposes of this article.

## SECTION 5.  APPLICABILITY OF DEVELOPMENT STANDARDS AND GUIDELINES

1.  The development standards and guidelines contained in this article are derived from the Visual Preference Survey ™ and shall be used by any applicant in preparing a development plan and by the board in reviewing the same.  In the exercise of its powers of review, the board may approve, deny, conditionally approve, or request modifications to a development plan that is deemed to be inconsistent with the development standards and guidelines or the purposes of this article in accordance with the provisions of Section 4 herein.

2.  This article contains both development standards, which are normative and set forth specific requirements, and development guidelines, which define a framework and are only indicative.  However, both standards and guidelines shall be interpreted with flexibility.  The board shall view such standards and guidelines as tools, since exceptional situations, requiring unique interpretations, can be expected.  When applying such standards and guidelines, the board shall carefully weigh the specific circumstances surrounding each application, and strive for development solutions that best promote the spirit, intent, and purposes of this article.

3.  The development standards and guidelines contained in this article shall be used as the township's minimum requirements for evaluating planned small community.  However, such standards and guidelines are not intended to restrict creativity, and an applicant may request a modification or exception from any development standard or guideline.  Modifications to the design guidelines and standards contained in this Section shall be approved by the board in accordance with Section 4 herein.

4.  The development standards and guidelines contained in this article are both written and illustrated.  Every effort has been taken to assure that illustration and text are complementary.  However, in the event of inconsistencies between the two, the text shall be interpreted in conjunction with the overall intent and character established by all of the illustrations contained herein.

## SECTION 6.  DEFINITIONS

Unless otherwise stated, the following words shall, for the purpose of this article, have the meaning herein indicated.  Any word used in this Article which is not defined herein and which is defined in article 5 of this zoning ordinance or the township subdivision and land development ordinance shall, for the purpose of this article, have the meaning defined therein.

Accessory Dwelling.  A year-round housing unit not exceeding 900 square feet, with cooking facilities, sanitary facilities, and an independent means of access, either attached to a single-family unit or located on the same lot as a single-family unit.

Bay.  A regularly repeated unit on a building elevation defined by columns, pilasters, or other vertical elements, or defined by a given number of windows or openings.

Belt Course (also string course or horizontal course).  A projecting horizontal band on an exterior wall marking the separation between floors or levels.

Blank Wall.  An exterior building wall with no openings and generally constructed of a single material, uniform texture, and on a single plane.

Boulevard.  A major road with a planted median in the center of two cartways, with parkways on both outside edges.

Buffer.  An area within a property or site, generally adjacent to and parallel with the property line, either consisting of existing natural vegetation or created by the use of trees, shrubs, berms, and/or fences, and designed to limit views and sounds from the development tract to adjacent properties and vice versa.

**Build-to Line.** An alignment which dictates the front yard setback from a street or public right-of-way, to be followed by buildings or structures fronting thereon. The build-to line does not apply to building projections or recesses.

**Build-up Line.** An alignment which dictates an average height to the cornice line or to the roof edge line on a street or space.

**Building Scale.** The relationship between the mass of a building and its surroundings, including the width of street, open space, and mass of surrounding buildings.

**Caliper.** The diameter of a tree trunk measured in inches, six inches above ground level for trees up to four inches in diameter and measured twelve inches above ground level for trees over four inches in diameter.

**Column.** A vertical pillar or shaft, usually structural.

**Common Open Space.** A parcel, or parcels, of land, an area of water, or a combination of land and water, including floodplain and wetland areas within a development site designed and intended for the use and enjoyment of residents of the development and, where designated, the community at large. The area of parking facilities serving the activities in the common open space may be included in the required area computations. Common open space shall not include:

1. The land area of lots allocated for single family detached dwellings, single family semi-detached dwellings, and duplex dwellings, front yards, side yards, and rear yards, whether or not the dwellings are sold or rented.

2. The land area of lots allocated for apartment and townhouse dwelling construction, including front yards, side yards, rear yards, interior yards, and off street parking facilities whether or not the dwellings are sold or rented.

3. The land area of lots allocated for total commercial use, including front yards, side yards, rear yards, and parking facilities whether or not the commercial facilities are sold or rented.

4. The land area of lots allocated for public and semi-public uses, community clubs and community facilities, including open space for playgrounds and athletic fields which are a part of the principal use; and front yards, side yards, rear yards, and other open space around the buildings; and parking facilities whether or not the schools and churches are sold or rented.

5. Street rights-of-way, parkways, driveways, off street parking, and service areas, except the landscaped central median of boulevards.

**Context.** The character of the buildings, streetscape, and neighborhood which surround a given building or site.

**Cornice.** The top part of an entablature, usually molded and projecting.

**Cupola.** A small roof tower, usually rising from the roof ridge.

**Curtain Wall.** A light, non-structural outer wall of a building in the form of a metal grid with infill panels of glass and other materials.

**Directional Emphasis.** The combination of building height and width, together with the placement of fenestration, structural elements, and architectural details may convey a predominantly horizontal or a predominantly vertical directional emphasis to a building's facade.

Elderly Day Care Center. A building or space in a building and grounds used for the day care of senior citizens. However, it does not provide daily heath-related care or services of any kind.

Elevation. An exterior facade of a structure, or its head-on view, or representation drawn with no vanishing point, and used primarily for construction.

Environmental Constraints. Features, natural resources, or land characteristics that are sensitive to improvements and may require conservation measures or the application of creative development techniques to prevent degradation of the environment, or may require limited development, or in certain instances may preclude development.

Facade. A building face or wall.

Fenestration. Window and other openings on a building facade.

Fascia. A projecting flat horizontal member or molding, also part of a classical entablature.

Figure-Ground Plan. A drawing which shows the footprint of a building(s) and building appurtenances which touch or cover the ground, the outline of which is rendered in solid (figure) and the openings, spaces or non-built areas surrounding these buildings shown in void or non-rendered spaces (ground).

Focal Point. (See Visual Termination).

Gable. The part of the end wall of a building between the eaves and a pitched or gambrel roof.

Gateway. A principal point of entrance into a district or neighborhood.

Gateway Building. A building located at a gateway and which dramatically marks this entrance or transition through massing, extended height, use of arches or colonnades, or other distinguishing features.

Horizontal Course. (See Belt Course).

Human Scale. The relationship between the dimensions of a building, structure, street, open space, or streetscape element and the average dimensions of the human body.

Internal Open Space. A component of common open space, comprising one or more parcels with a minimum area of 500 square feet, of a distinct geometric shape, and bounded by streets with curb side parking on a minimum of 50 percent of their perimeter.

Lane. A private street or easement located through the interior of blocks and providing vehicular and service access to the side or rear of properties.

Linkage. A line of communication, such as a pathway, arcade, bridge, lane, etc., linking two areas or neighborhoods which are either distinct or separated by a physical feature (e.g. a railroad line, major arterial) or a natural feature (e.g. a river, stream).

Lintel. A horizontal beam over an opening in a masonry wall, either structural or decorative.

Main Street (Commercial Area)  A street containing a mix of uses, including the planned small community greatest concentration of commercial development.  If included within a planned small community, the Main Street commercial area, together with the community green, shall form the focus of the neo-traditional neighborhood.

Masonry.  Wall building material, such as brick or stone, which is laid up in small units.

Massing.  The three-dimensional bulk of a structure: height, width, and depth.

Modified Grid Street Pattern.  An interconnected system of streets which is primarily a rectilinear grid in pattern, however, modified in street layout and block shape as to avoid a monotonous repetition of the basic street/ block grid pattern.  Streets are limited to a length from 200 to 1,000 feet in length.

Neighborhood Motor Vehicle Service Station or Garage.  A motor vehicle service station or garage that is limited in the intensity of use to serve primarily the immediately surrounding neighborhood.  Such facilities shall be limited to two fuel dispensers serving no greater than four motor vehicles at any one time and/or two indoor service bays servicing no greater than two motor vehicles at any one time.

Neo-traditional Neighborhood.  A pedestrian-oriented neighborhood, with variable lot width and sizes, a mix of dwelling unit types, on-street parking, and non-residential uses generally located along a Main Street commercial area or fronting on a community green.  The size of the neighborhood is a five minute walk from the core.

Net Residential Density.  The number of dwelling units in relation to the total land area proposed to be used for residential purposes, not including rights-of-way, interior parking areas, access drives, private streets, sidewalks, common open space, and public or semi-public parks and playgrounds.  This can also apply to the specific lot on which a building(s) is sited. It can be measured in dwelling units per acre (DU/A) or in Floor Area Ratios (FAR).

Open Space, Internal.  (See Internal Open Space).

Parkway.  A planting area located within the public right-of-way, typically located between the curb and the sidewalk, and planted with ground cover and trees.

Pilaster.  A column partially embedded in a wall, usually non-structural.

Pitch.  The angle of slope of a roof or berm.

Portico.  An open sided structure attached to a building sheltering an entrance or serving as a semi-enclosed space.

Proportion.  The relationship or ratio between two dimensions, e.g. width of street to height of building wall, or width to height of window.

Public Viewshed.  That which is reasonably visible, under average conditions, to the average observer located on any public land or right-of-way, or on any semi-public or private space which is normally accessible to the general public.

Quoins.  Corner treatment for exterior walls, either in masonry or frame buildings.

Rhythm. The effect obtained through repetition of architectural elements such as building footprints, height, roof lines, or side yard setbacks; of streetscape elements, such as decorative lamp posts; or of natural elements, such as street trees.

Rhythm of Solids to Voids. The relationship between the solid portions of a building facade and the voids formed by doors, windows, other openings and recesses. May also refer to the relationship between building mass (solids) and side yard setbacks (voids) along a street.

Semi-Public Recreation Area. (See Recreation Area).

Public Sidewalk. A paved path provided for pedestrian use and usually located at the side of a road within a right-of-way. In residential areas it is separated from the cartway by a parkway.

Sidewalk Display. The outdoor display of merchandise for sale by a commercial establishment. The displayed merchandise must be similar to the merchandise sold within the establishment.

Sign, Graphic. (See Sign, Icon).

Sign, Icon. A sign that illustrates, by its shape and graphics, the nature of the business conducted within.

Sign Fascia. The vertical surface of a lintel over a storefront which is suitable for sign attachment.

Signable Area. The area or areas on a commercial building facade where signs may be placed without disrupting facade composition. The signable area will often include panels at the top of show windows, transoms over storefront doors and windows, sign boards on fascias, and areas between the top of the storefront and the sills of second story windows.

Street Furniture. Functional elements of the streetscape, including but not limited to benches, trash receptacles, planters, telephone booths, kiosks, sign posts, street lights, bollards, and removable enclosures.

Streetscape. The built and planted elements of a street which define its character.

String Course. (See Belt Course).

Texture. The exterior finish of a surface, ranging from smooth to coarse.

Viewshed. (See Public Viewshed).

Visual Preference Survey ™. (VPS ™) A process by which a community participates in evaluating its existing environment and in developing a common vision for its future.

Visual Termination. A point, surface, building, or structure terminating a vista or view, often at the end of a straight street or coinciding with a bend.

Visually Impervious. A buffering or screening device which partially or totally blocks the view to, or from, adjacent sites by a discernible factor ranging up to 100 percent.

## SECTION 7. PERMITTED PRINCIPAL USES

The following uses are permitted in a planned small community, subject to all the applicable development standards and requirements.

1. The following residential uses:

    A. single family detached dwellings

    B. single family semi-detached dwellings

    C. duplex dwellings

    D. townhouse dwellings

    E. apartment dwellings, containing less than 10 units

    F. accessory dwellings

2. Public and semi-public uses, including parks and playgrounds and structures typically constructed as part of this type of facility

3. Community clubs

4. Community facilities

5. Day care centers

6. Elderly day care center

7. Churches

8. The following commercial uses:

    A. banks and other financial institutions, including drive-through banking facilities provided such are located at the rear of a site

    B. offices

    C. retail sales of goods and services

    D. restaurants, except drive-through facilities

    E. neighborhood motor vehicle service station or garage

9. Golf courses

10. Agricultural uses, except agri-business structures

11. Public and semi-public recreational uses

12. Equestrian uses, limited to horses for the personal use of residents of the development

13. Cemeteries

14. Bed and Breakfast Establishments

## SECTION 8. PERMITTED ACCESSORY USES

The following uses are permitted in a planned small community, subject to all the applicable development standards and requirements

1. All residential accessory uses shall comply with the Residential Accessory Use Regulations of this Zoning Ordinance, except as modified in this article

2. Home-based offices, providing the following conditions apply:

A. The home-based office is located in a single family detached dwelling located on a Main Street or residential Type A roadway.

B. Medical, dental and real estate offices shall not be permitted as home offices.

C. In addition to the family occupying the dwelling containing the home office, there shall not be more than one outside employee in the home office.

D. The employee and clients shall park in on-street curbside parking spaces and shall not park on the lot containing the home office.

E. Permitted signage area is limited to one facade or free-standing sign not exceeding two square feet.

F. The home office shall not exceed 1,000 square feet or 30 percent of the total square footage of the dwelling or can be located in an accessory building not to exceed 500 square feet.

G. All exterior aspects of the home office operation shall not disrupt the residential character of the area.

3. Accessory uses, buildings, or structures for all other non-residential uses as approved by the board of commissioners.

## SECTION 9. MINIMUM AREA

The minimum contiguous gross acres of land shall be required on which at the current or revised density a landowner can have ten or more units to qualify for consideration as a planned small community.

## SECTION 10. UTILITY SERVICES

Individual septic and well are required for small communities of less than 35 units in municipalities without utility service. Small communities over 35 units are required to provide community sewer and water, although individual well may be used. Smaller communities located in municipalities which do not have sewer service are required to provide secondary treatment and filtration using underground filter beds or utilizing overground disposal of treated effluent. Each single family unit, duplex, mixed-use, or apartment building should be provided with individual septic tanks and the "gray water" piped to and treated in a community treatment plant before disposal of effluent. Small communities located in municipalities with existing treatment plants, should, to the extent possible, utilize the municipal or regional plant. Where a phased approach is required, the site should be engineered for standard sewer lines and the community treatment plant employed until such time that the municipal or regional facilities can accommodate the generated effluent. At such time the treatment plant can be converted to a pump station.

## SECTION 11.  COMMON OPEN SPACE

1.  Not less than 50% to 75% of the gross area of the hamlet, or 45% to 70% for a village, or 15 to 35% for a neighborhood shall be allocated to and shall remain in common open space in perpetuity.  Refer to Illustration 17.  Common open space shall be deed restricted to prohibit future subdivision or development, except for agricultural, recreational, golf course, equestrian, and cemetery uses which may be permitted with the approval of the board. Common open space shall be used for social, recreational, and/or natural environment preservation purposes.  The uses authorized must be appropriate to the character of the common open space, including its topography, size, and vegetation; as well as to the character of the development, including its size and density, the characteristics of the expected population, and the number and type of dwellings to be provided.  The common open space shall be provided in the form of internal open space and peripheral open space.

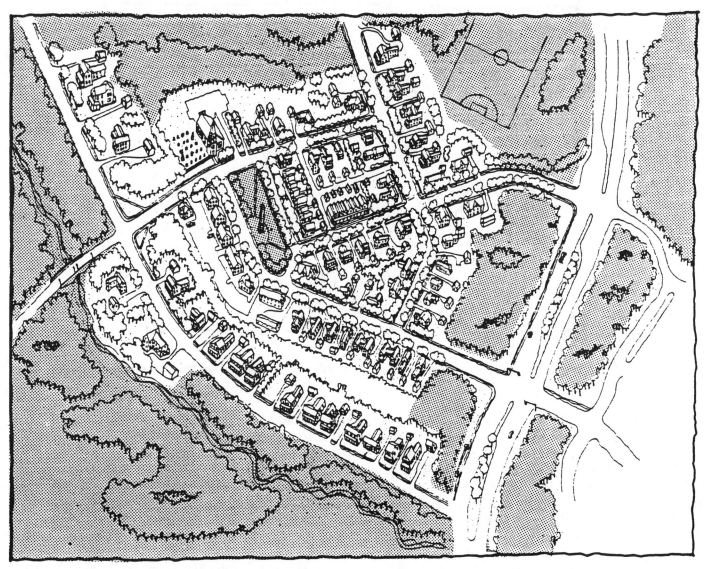

Illustration 17 *Neighborhood development focused on central internal open space (community green) and surrounded by peripheral open space.*

2. Internal open spaces shall contain a minimum area of 500 square feet and shall be of a distinct geometric shape, generally rectilinear or square, bounded by streets with curb side parking on a minimum of 50% of its perimeter. Refer to Illustration 18. Internal open spaces shall be spatially enclosed by the buildings that front on the area or front upon the streets bounding the area. The internal open spaces shall be landscaped such that a minimum of 75% of the area is covered with trees, shrubs, lawn, and groundcover. The type of trees and shrubs shall be such that vistas through the internal open space are largely unobstructed. Internal open spaces shall be landscaped using elements such as formal gardens, walkways, monuments, statues, gazebos, fountains, park benches, and pedestrian-scale lamp posts. Internal open spaces shall be designed as village commons, town squares, or urban park, and shall be designed as an active gathering place for all residents of the development in both day and evening, and shall include places for strolling, sitting, social interaction, and informal recreation.

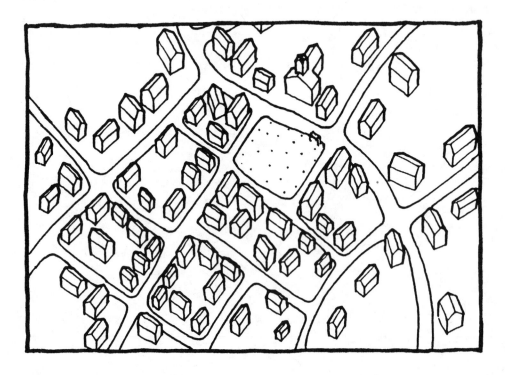

Illustration 18 *Every small community must have adequate internal open space to meet the civic and recreational needs of the residents.*

3. Each small community shall be designed to have one primary internal open space which shall be considered as part of the dedicated common open space requirement and shall be referred to as the community green. Refer to Illustration 19. The community green shall have a minimum area of 10,000 square feet and the size, shape, and design of the community green shall provide adequate space for concerts, outdoor exhibits, and community gatherings based on the number of residents expected in the development. Public restrooms, public telephones, and police/fire call boxes shall be provided in each community green. A bus stop shall be provided in or adjacent to the community green. The community green shall be surrounded by a concentration of high density development which may include commercial, residential, and public and semi-public uses, community clubs, and community facilities. If the development includes a Main Street commercial area, the community green shall either front upon a Main Street, Main Street shall terminate at the community green, or Main Street and the community green shall otherwise be incorporated into a combined community focus for the development. Nothing herein shall preclude a large tract from containing two separate developments with two separate community greens.

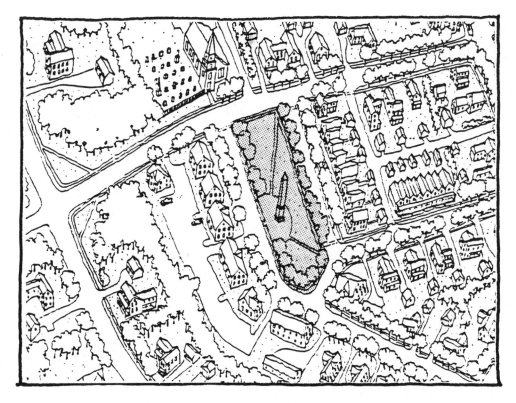

Illustration 19 *Every small community shall have a community green surrounded by neighborhood development.*

4. The community green shall be centrally located to be within 1,500 feet of 90 % of all dwelling units in the development. This is determined by a 1,500 foot radius from the outermost boundary of the community green. In developments where the community green is combined with a Main Street commercial area, the 1,500 foot radius shall also be measured from the outermost boundary of the lots fronting on the Main Street commercial area. Refer to Illustration 20.

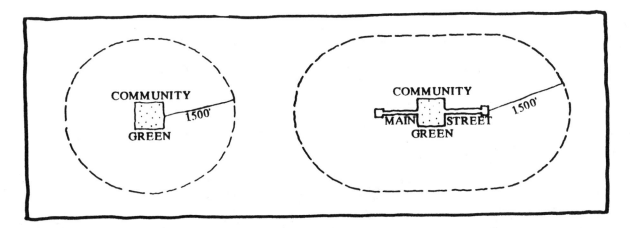

Illustration 20 *Diagrams of a 1,500 foot radius from the outermost boundary of the community green and 1,500 foot radius from the outermost boundary of a community green combined with a Main Street commercial area.*

5. Peripheral open space shall be required surrounding a hamlet or village where certain conditions exist adjacent to the tracts, as specified below:

A. A peripheral open space area of a minimum of 200 feet in width shall be provided where the tract abuts any roadway listed as an arterial or highway. Refer to Illustration 19. Refer to a photograph with caption of peripheral open space.

ILLUSTRATION 21

Provide photograph here peripheral open space abutting a roadway

B. A peripheral open space area of a minimum of 300 feet in width shall be provided where the tract abuts an existing tract of agricultural land, open space, public parkland, or an undeveloped tract.

C. Peripheral open space areas may be used for agricultural purposes, including wood lots, with the approval of the Board. Peripheral open space areas used for agricultural purposes shall be a minimum of 400 feet in width from the boundary of the developed area to the property line of the tract and shall provide for appropriate buffering adjacent to the developed area of the property. Refer to Illustration 22.

ILLUSTRATION 22

Provide photograph(s) of peripheral open space area used for agricultural purposes with high positive VPS ™ ratings

D. Unless peripheral open space areas abutting arterials and highways contain existing mature trees and vegetation, such areas shall be densely planted with a mixture of indigenous species trees to achieve a year round visually impervious screen within five years, provided no trees are planted so near an agricultural field that shadows from such trees may effect the growth of crops.

6. Common open space, particularly peripheral open space areas, containing existing attractive or unique natural features, such as streams, creeks, ponds, woodlands, specimen trees, and other areas of mature vegetation worthy of preservation may be left unimproved and in a natural state. As a general principle, the preservation of undeveloped open space in its natural state or existing farms is encouraged. A developer may make certain improvements such as the cutting of trails for walking or jogging, and the provision of picnic areas. In addition, the board may require a developer to make other improvements such as removal of dead or diseased trees, thinning of trees or other vegetation to encourage more desirable growth, and grading and seeding. To the greatest extent possible common open space shall include all environmentally sensitive areas, including areas with slopes greater than 20%, 100 year floodplains, wetlands, areas of seasonally high water, and other such critical areas as may be determined by the board. Existing man-made features, such as farmsteads and stone walls, may be preserved through incorporation in common open space.

7. Peripheral open space areas may be used for golf courses, and public and semi-public recreation purposes with the approval of the board. Recreational facilities shall be required to serve the anticipated needs of the residents of the development, taking into account the anticipated characteristics and demographic profile of the development's population, the recreational facilities available in neighboring developments, and the relevant provisions regarding recreational facilities contained in the comprehensive plan. Recreation facilities may include soccer, baseball, football, and other field sports that require open, unlit fields.

8. Cemeteries may be permitted in both internal and peripheral open space areas with the approval of the board.

9. The buildings, structures, and improvements permitted in the common open space shall be appropriate to the authorized uses and shall conserve and enhance the amenities of the common open space with regard to its topography and unimproved condition.

10. The construction schedule of the development shall coordinate the improvement of the common open space with the construction of residential dwellings. At no time in the development of various phases of the planned small community may the total area of common open space in the developed phases be less than 50% of the gross area of the developed lands unless additional areas to produce the required percentage are permanently reserved as common open space on the remaining land of the total development. The location or size of this reserved common open space on remaining land may be altered or changed upon the approval and recording of the development plan of an additional phase of development.

11. The method utilized for ownership, administration, and maintenance of common open space shall be approved by the board and council of the municipality.

A. The ownership, administration, and maintenance of common open space shall be arranged to be in accordance with one or more of the following:

(1) The township may accept dedication of common open spaces or any interest therein for public use and maintenance, for no consideration to be paid by the township. Unless waived by the board and council of the municipality at time of approval, the township shall have the option to accept all or any portion of the common open space at any time within ten years of the recording of the final subdivision plan for the development. The final plan shall contain a note, in language acceptable to the township solicitor, that the common open space are irrevocably

dedicated to the township for a period of ten years from the date of the recording of the final plan. Said note shall also state that the township shall have no duty to maintain or improve the dedicated common open space unless and until it has been accepted by formal action of the council.

(2) The landowner may establish an automatic-membership property owners' association made up of the owners of property in the planned small community, as a non-profit corporation for the purpose of owning, administering, and maintaining common open space; provided however, the association shall not be dissolved nor shall it dispose of the common open space by sale or otherwise (except to an organization conceived and established to own, administer and maintain common open space approved by the board and/or council) without first offering the common open space for dedication to the township. The property owners' association shall be empowered to levy and collect assessments from the property owners of the planned small community to cover replacements, working capital, operating expenses, insurance against casualty and liability, and contingencies.

(3) The landowner may establish a deed or deeds of trust, approved by the board and/or council, for the purpose of owning, administering and maintaining common open space, with the trustee empowered to levy and collect assessments from the property owners of the planned small community to cover replacements, working capital, operating expenses, insurance against casualty, liability, and contingencies.

(4) With permission of the township, and with appropriate deed restrictions in favor of the township and in language acceptable to the township solicitor, the developer may transfer the fee simple title in the common open space or a portion thereof to a private, non-profit organization among whose purposes is the conservation of open space land and/or natural resources; provided that:

> a. the organization is acceptable to the township and is a bona fide conservation organization with a perpetual existence
>
> b. the conveyance contains appropriate provisions for proper retransfer or reverter in the event that the organization becomes unable to continue to carry out its functions
>
> c. a maintenance agreement acceptable to the township is entered into by the developer, organization and township

(5) If a portion of the common open space is to be used for agricultural purposes, that portion of the common open space may be transferred to a person or other entity who will farm the land. Prior to the transfer of any common open space for agricultural purposes, a permanent conservation easement in favor of the township, in language acceptable to the township solicitor, shall be imposed against such land. The conveyance shall contain appropriate provisions for the retransfer or reverter to the township or any association or trustee holding the remainder of the common open space in the event the land ceases to be used for agricultural purposes.

(6) If a portion of the common open space is to be used for cemetery purposes, that portion of the common open space may be transferred to a religious organization, cemetery corporation, or other similar entity which will operate or maintain the cemetery. Prior to the transfer of any common open space for cemetery purposes, a permanent deed restriction in favor of the township, in language acceptable to the township solicitor, shall be imposed against such land. The conveyance shall contain appropriate provisions for the retransfer or reverter to the township or any association or trustee holding the remainder of the common open space in the event the land is not used for cemetery purposes.

B. In the event that the organization established to own and maintain common open space, or any successor organization, shall at any time after the establishment of the planned small community fail to maintain the common open space in reasonable order and condition in accordance with the development plan, the board and/or council may serve written notice upon such organization or upon the residents of the planned small community setting forth the manner in which the organization has failed to maintain the common open space in reasonable condition, and said notice shall include a demand that such deficiencies of maintenance be corrected within 30 days thereof, and shall state the date and place of a hearing thereon which shall be held within fourteen days of the notice. At such hearing the board and/or council may modify the terms of the original notice as to the deficiencies and may give an extension of time within which they shall be corrected. If the deficiencies set forth in the original notice or in the modifications thereof shall not be corrected within said 30 days or any extension thereof, the board of commissioners, in order to preserve the taxable values of the property within the planned small community and to prevent the common open space from becoming a public nuisance, may enter upon the common open space and maintain the same for a period of one year. Said maintenance by the township, as directed by the board and/or council, shall not constitute a taking of said common open space, nor vest in the public any rights to use the same. Before the expiration of said year, the board and/or council shall, upon its initiative or upon the request of the organization theretofore responsible for the maintenance of the common open space, call a public hearing upon notice to such organization, or to the residents of the planned small community, to be held by the board and/or council or its designated agency, at which hearing such organization or the residents of the planned small community shall show cause why such maintenance by the township, shall not, at the option of the township, continue for a succeeding year. If the board and/or council, or its designated agency, shall determine that such organization is ready and able to maintain the common open space in reasonable condition, the township shall cease to maintain said open space at the end of said year. If the board and/or council or its designated agency shall determine that such organization is not ready and able to maintain said common open space in a reasonable condition, the township may, in its discretion, continue to maintain said common open space during the next succeeding year and, subject to a similar hearing and determination, in each year thereafter. The decision of the board and/or council shall be subject to appeal to court in such manner, and within the same time limitation as is provided for zoning appeals by the State of _____ Municipalities Planning Code, as amended or supplemented. The cost of maintenance of such common open space by the township shall be assessed ratably against the properties within the planned small community that have a right of enjoyment of the common open space, and shall become a lien on said properties. The township, at the time of entering upon said common open space for the purpose of maintenance, shall file a notice of lien, in the office of _____, upon the properties affected by the lien within the planned small community.

## SECTION 12.  BLOCKS WITHIN PLANNED SMALL COMMUNITY

1.  BLOCK SIZE  The street shall be designed to create blocks that are generally rectilinear in shape, a modified rectilinear shape, or another distinct geometric shape.  Amorphously shaped blocks are generally discouraged, except where topographic or other conditions necessitate such a configuration. To the greatest extent possible, blocks shall be designed to have a maximum length of 480 feet.  Lanes shall be permitted to bisect blocks.  Refer to Illustration 23.

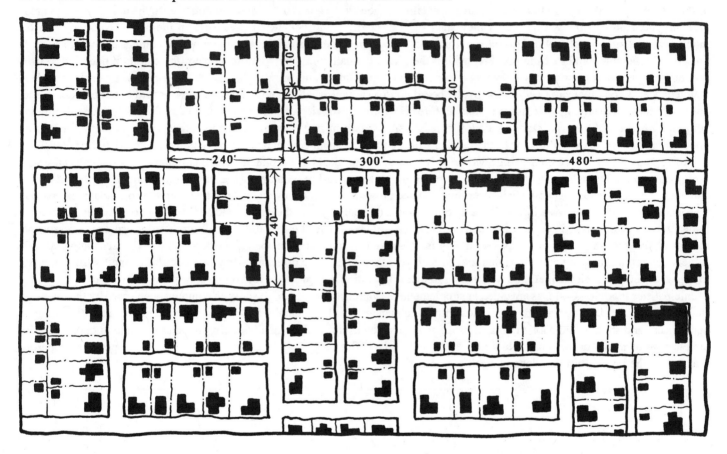

Illustration 23 *Diagram of a street defining geometrically shaped blocks a basic street block diagram must be prepared for each small community.*

2.  BUILD-TO LINE  Each block shall be designated with a build-to line which shall establish the front yard setback for the lots on the block.  The build-to line shall fall between the minimum and maximum front yard setbacks for the proposed uses (refer to Section 18, Area and Bulk Regulations).  A minimum of 80% of all buildings on the block shall conform to the build-to line, with the remaining 20% allowed to vary by being further setback no greater than 75% of the distance from the right-of-way to the build-to line for residential or no further than the maximum setback for commercial uses.  Buildings shall be allowed to come forward of the build-to line by no greater than 25% of the distance between the right-of way and the build-to line for residential structures.

3.  VARIATION OF LOT WIDTH AND AREA  Lot areas and lot widths shall vary at random to the greatest extent possible, in order to eliminate the appearance of a standardized subdivision. To the extent possible, no more than two lots in a row shall have the same width.  Lots shall vary by a minimum of five foot increments.

4.  A maximum of five percent of all lots for single family detached dwellings may be flag lots.  Refer to Illustration 24.

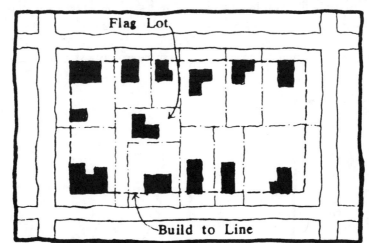

*Illustration 24  Diagram of varied lot sizes, including a flag lot.    Front yard setbacks must conform to a build -to line.*

## SECTION 13.  STREETS WITHIN PLANNED SMALL COMMUNITY

1.  The street layout shall be a modified grid street pattern adapted to the topography, unique natural features environmental constraints of the tract, and peripheral open space areas.  The street layout shall take into consideration the location of the community focus, other internal open space areas, gateways, and vistas.  Refer to Illustration 25.  A minimum of two interconnections with the existing public street system rated as an arterial or collector shall be provided where possible.  Linkages to adjacent developments and neighborhoods with pedestrian and bicycle paths are recommended where possible.

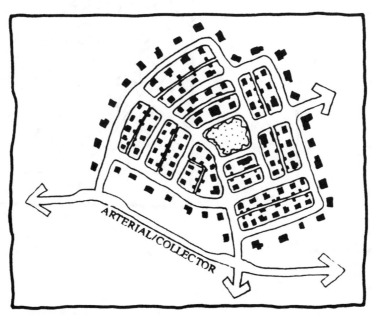

*Illustration 25  Diagram of a modified grid street pattern with three connections to the surrounding street system.  Each small community must have at least two peripheral attachments.*

2. The street layout shall form an interconnected system of streets primarily in a rectilinear grid pattern, however, modified to avoid a monotonous repetition of the basic street/block pattern. The use of cul-de-sacs and other roadways with a single point of access shall be minimized. To the greatest extent possible, streets shall be designed to have a maximum length of 600 feet, from intersection to intersection, and, to the greatest extent possible, shall either continue through an intersection, or terminate in a "T" intersection directly opposite the center of a building, an internal open space area, or a view into a peripheral open space area. Refer to Illustration 23.

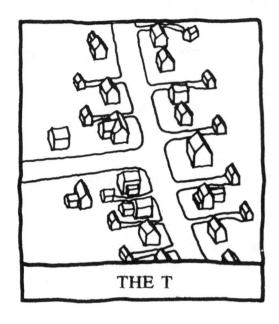

THE T

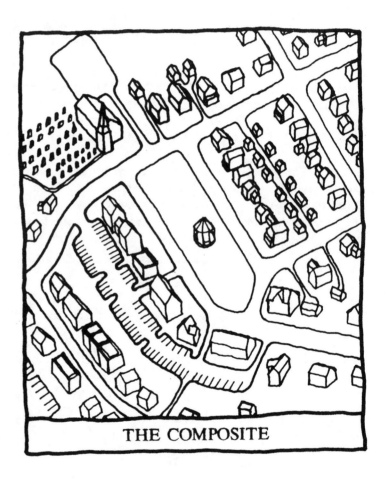

THE COMPOSITE

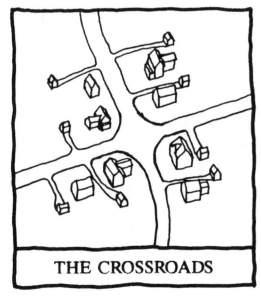

THE CROSSROADS

*Illustration 26 Diagrams of modified rectilinear street and intersection configurations which can be composed in a variety of ways.*

3.  The street layout shall incorporate a hierarchy of street types as specified.

Note: Use those street types as appropriate for the specific community.  Not all the street types as shown in the earlier text are appropriate for every small community.  A more complete list of street types and sections are found in Principle 6.

To illustrate, only five street configuration will be used

Hierarchy of Street Types

Type 1 Lane or alley

Type 3 Two-way residential street (parking on one side)

Type 4 Two-way residential street  (parking on two sides)

Type 5 Commercial mixed-use street (main street)

Type 9 Two lane arterial

The main street (Type 5) shall be used for the primary commercial and civic streets within the small community.  The residential street Type 4 is a collector street, while the residential streets Type 3 and Type 2  are local street; a combination of these residential street types shall be used for the residential streets.  Lanes or alleys (Type 1) are require for certain uses and may be used to provide service access; they shall be treated as private streets and any lot having access from a lane shall additionally front upon one of the other types of streets.  All streets shall generally conform to one of the following street categories.

Illustration 27 sets forth the relationship of the various street types as listed above.

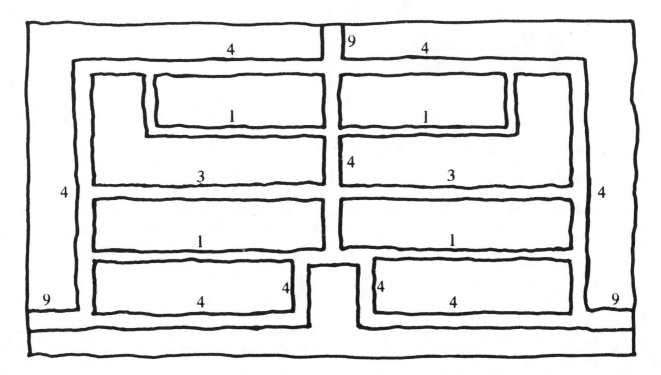

Illustration 27 *A diagram illustrating the relationship of various selected street types.  This type of graphic illustration must be prepared for each small community.*

**TYPE 1 Lane or Alley Type** Refer to Illustration 28 below.

**Adjacent Land Use**

Garages
Parking lots (Landscaped edges)
Accessory units above garage

Story height: 1 to 2 stories
Build-to line: 3 Feet
Finished ground floor level: On grade

Section

Figure Ground

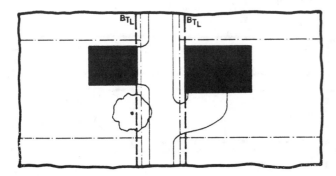

**Illustration 28** *Section and figure ground of alley*

A. A lane shall be a private street or easement and shall not be dedicated to the township. Such streets or easements may be dedicated to the property owners' association of the planned small community or may be dedicated as common easements across the rear portions of lots.

B. Minimum paved width: 12 feet

C. Width of easement: 20 feet

D. Buildings or fences set back a minimum of 3 feet

E. No parking permitted on either side of the cartway of a lane

F. Curbing shall not be required except at corners of intersections with other street types. At such corner locations, curbing shall be required for the entire corner radius and five feet preceding same. Such curbing shall not extend more than six inches above the finished pavement

G. Lane or alley lighting shall be provided on all garages or on poles adjacent to parking areas. Lighting fixtures and poles shall be of consistent architectural style and shall complement the predominant architectural theme

H. Design speed shall not exceed 10 m.p.h.

**TYPE 3  Two-Way Residential Street**  See Illustration 29 below

**Adjacent Land Uses**
Small and  medium single family lots
Duplex Units
Townhouses
Multi-family
Large lot single family with large setbacks

Build-to Line: 10 to 15 feet
Story Height: 2 - 3 stories
Finished ground floor level: 2 to 4 feet above sidewalk

Section

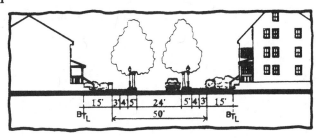

Figure Ground

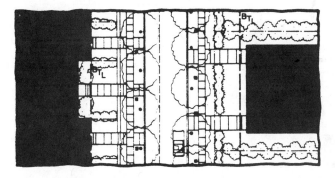

Illustration 29 *Section and figure ground of a narrow, two-way residential street.*

    A.  Right-of-way width:  50 feet
       Paved width:  24 feet
    B.  Curbside parking shall be permitted on one side of the road.
    C.  Sidewalks shall be provided on both sides of the road, a minimum of four feet in width.
    D.  Curbing shall be required.
    E.  Granite block curbing, or equivalent, is recommended.
    F.  Decorative street lamps, a maximum of twelve feet in height shall be provided on both sides of the street, at minimum spacing of 80 feet on-center, and at intersections.
    G.  Shade trees shall be planted in the  five foot  parkway  on both sides of the street at a minimum spacing of 24 feet on-center.
    H.  Design speed shall not exceed 25 m.p.h.
    I.  Average daily traffic limited to 4000.
    J.  Bicycles can use streets without a separate path.

**TYPE 4   Two-Way Residential Street**   See Illustration 30 below

**Adjacent Land Uses**
  Small, medium and large width single family lots
  Duplex Units
  Townhouses
  Multi-family
  Home offices

**Build-to Line:** 15 feet
**Story Height:** 2 - 3 stories
**Finished ground floor level:** 2 to 4 feet above sidewalk grade

Section

Figure Ground

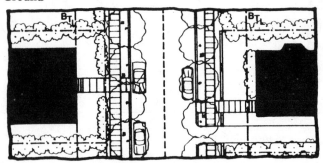

Illustration 30   Section and figure ground plan of a wide, two-way residential street

  A.   Right-of-way width: 60 feet
      Paved width: 34 feet
  B.   Curbside parking is permitted on both sides of the street, except within 25 feet of any intersection.
  C.   Sidewalks are required on both sides of the street, a minimum of five feet in width.
  D.   Curbing shall be required.
  E.   Granite block curbing, or equivalent, is recommended. Curb radii are not to exceed 8 feet.
  F.   Decorative street lamps, a maximum of twelve feet in height, shall be provided on both sides of the street and at intersections. They shall be at a minimum spacing of 80 feet on-center
  G.   Shade trees shall be planted in the parkways on both sides of the street at a minimum spacing of 24 feet on-center.
  H.   Design speed shall not exceed 25 m.p.h.
  I.   Average daily traffic limited to approximately 6000

**TYPE 5   Main Street - The Commercial Mixed-use Street**   Refer to Illustration 31 below

Section

**Adjacent Land Uses**
Community Commercial, Office or Retail
Mixed Use

Story Height: 2 - 3 stories
Build-to line: 15 feet
Finished Ground Floor Level: On grade with sidewalk
grade

Figure Ground

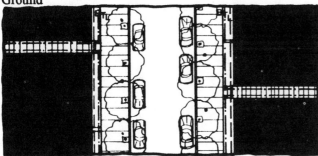

Illustration 31 *Section and figure ground of a mixed-use/commercial street.*

A. Right-of-way width:  64 feet
   Paved width:  34 feet
B. Parallel parking shall be provided on both sides of the street.  Diagonal head-in parking may be permitted along the front of commercial uses and/or the community green, in which case no parking shall be permitted on the other side of the street.  Curbside parking shall not be permitted within 25 feet of an intersection.
C. Planted parkways with a minimum width of five feet shall be provided, except where the road abuts the community green. The planting parkway abutting the community green shall be a minimum of nine feet in width.  Along commercial uses, brick pavers may be substituted for vegetative ground cover typically found in parkways of residential areas.  Sidewalks shall have a minimum width of six feet, except along commercial uses where the sidewalk shall be ten feet in width. At corners, handicapped ramps shall be provided and sidewalks shall be continued across street surfaces using paving materials to delineate crosswalks.
D. Curbing shall be required with a curb radius not to exceed 8 feet.
E. Granite block curbing, or equivalent, is recommended.
F. Decorative lighting shall be provided at a minimum interval of eighty (80) feet and at intersections.  Light poles shall form a 40 foot staggered pattern when measured using both sides of the street. See illustration 25 A.  Lighting fixtures and poles shall be no higher than twelve feet and constructed from steel, cast iron, or aluminum, with poles and fixtures complementing the architectural character of the small community.  Lighting fixtures and poles shall be of consistent architectural style throughout the zone and shall complement the predominant architectural theme.
G. Street trees, with a minimum of three inch caliper or twelve feet high at the time of planting shall be planted at a minimum of 24 foot intervals. Bottom branches shall be trimmed to a minimum of twelve feet from the ground to allow pedestrian passage in commercial areas.  Street trees shall be planted on both sides of the street, in the parkway between the curb and the sidewalk if such exists.  Existing  trees shall be used where possible.
H. Design speed shall not exceed 25 m.p.h.

**TYPE 9    Two Lane Arterial with optional Bike lane**    Refer to Illustration 32 below

**Adjacent Land Uses**
Agricultural
Openspace/environmentally sensitive
Large lot single family estates (6 to 25 acres)

Story Height: 2 - 3 stories
Build-to line: 150 to 250  feet
Finished ground floor level: not applicable

Section

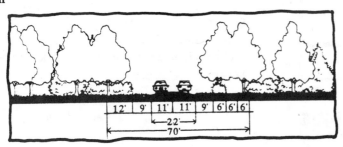

Figure Ground

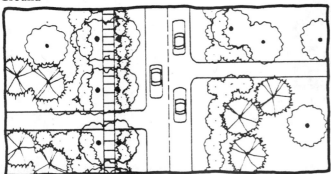

Illustration 32 *Section and figure ground of a two lane arterial.*

A. Right-of-way width:  70 feet
   Paved width:  22 feet (uncurbed)
   A nine foot graded shoulder shall be provided on both sides of the road.  Within 100 feet of an intersection of equal or higher status in the hierarchy of streets, the shoulders shall be paved to allow for turns.
B. A six foot wide bicycle path and/or a five foot wide sidewalk shall be located on a minimum of one side of the road, with a minimum setback of six feet from the cartway.
C. Two rows of shade trees shall be located in parkways along both sides of this roadway at a minimum staggered interval of 24 feet (a spacing of 48 feet on center for each individual row).  A four to five foot high split-rail or board-rail fence, or a stone wall may be substituted for the second, outermost row of trees on each side.  Existing vegetation shall be incorporated wherever possible.  The first, innermost row of trees shall be planted a minimum of three feet from the edge of the shoulder.
D. Only uses allowed in the peripheral open spaces shall front upon or have access from this road.
E. Curbside parking shall not be permitted.
F. Curbing shall be provided along all road slopes in excess of five percent or where accumulation of drainage in roadway swales exceeds a flow of five cubic feet per second (cfs) or a velocity of three feet per second (fps).
G. Design speed shall not exceed 45 m.p.h.
H. Decorative street lamps, not exceeding sixteen feet in height, shall be provided at intersections only.

## SECTION 14.  RESIDENTIAL DEVELOPMENT WITHIN A PLANNED SMALL COMMUNITY

1.  The maximum allowable number of units and corresponding non-residential uses shall be determined by a holding capacity analysis using a development suitability analysis of the land characteristics, septic, sewage and water availability overlaid on the current base zoning.  To the extent possible, the largest number of contiguous and adjacent parcels should be used to create a small community.  Adjacent site transfer techniques and bonuses should be employed.

A small community designed in the hamlet, village, or neighborhood form shall be required in where the existing or proposed density ranges are as follows:

Residential Zoning Densities (.25 DU per acre to 6 DU per acre)

A 25 percent increase in the number of units above the base holding capacity is allowed for the creation of small communities provided that a minimum of 10 percent of the total units are set aside for households of moderate and low income. To the extent possible, these units should be slated for ownership with the conditional provision of only the cost of living increment assigned upon selling to another low or moderate income family.  Half of the units shall be for low and half shall be for moderate income families.

2.  A range of residential dwelling types shall be provided in the small community.  Refer to Illustrations 33 through 35. The number of single family detached dwellings, including both large lot and small lot types, shall range from a minimum of 65 percent to a maximum of 90 percent.  Of the remaining number of dwellings other than single family detached dwellings, no more than 75percent shall be the same type of dwelling unit (e.g. semi-attached, duplexes, townhouses, apartments, or accessory dwellings).

Illustration 33 *A single family residential streetscape in the Kentlands that receives a positive VPS* TM *rating .*

Illustration 34 *A new, small lot single family unit in Corn Hill, Rochester, NY.*

Illustration 35 *New townhouses with a positive rating.*

3.   Residential net density shall generally decrease from the community green and/or center-core towards the periphery of the small community.   A mix of dwelling unit types shall be distributed throughout the development. Smaller lots and higher net density dwellings are generally located closer to the community green and main street commercial area, if such is provided. The segregation of different dwelling unit types is discouraged and different types of dwelling units may be mixed in any distribution within any single block, if desired.   A minimum of 90 percent of the dwelling units shall be located within a 1,500 foot radius of the outermost boundary of the community green, and main street or core commercial area.   Very large lot, single family detached dwellings, including accessory dwellings, shall be the only dwelling type permitted further than 1,500 feet from the community green.   Refer to Illustration 36.

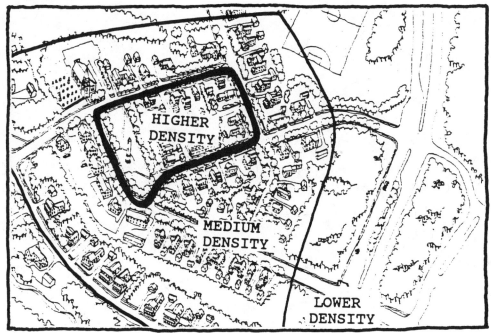

Illustration 36 *Residential density should generally decrease from the community green towards the periphery of the neighborhood.*

4.   Buildings containing dwelling units shall be designed in conformance to the selected design vocabulary. See Section 28 of this Ordinance. Building designs shall vary in terms of footprint, architectural elevations, fenestration, type of roof, height, front entrance, and porch locations.   Colors, materials, and architectural details should be limited in number, compatability, and repetition throughout the neighborhood.   Refer to Illustration 37

Illustration 37 *Buildings containing dwelling units should vary in appearance but share a common design vocabulary.*

5. Accessory dwellings include apartments intergrated within single family dwellings, or those located in detached accessory dwellings, such as carriage houses or agricultural-type outbuildings, located on the same lot as single family dwellings. Accessory dwellings shall be limited to 850 square feet in floor area and, for the purposes of calculating residential density, each accessory dwelling shall count as one-half dwelling unit. There shall not be more than one accessory dwelling located on a lot in addition to the single family dwelling. Refer to Illustration 38.

Illustration 38 *Accessory dwellings may take the form of detached outbuildings, such as carriage houses. This photo of a carriage house located at the rear of a lot in the village of Cranbury, NJ, received a positive VPS TM rating.*

6. Apartment dwellings located on upper floors above commercial uses shall be a minimum of 1,000 square feet in gross floor area, and, for the purposes of calculating residential density, each such apartment dwelling shall count as one-half dwelling unit. Refer to Illustration 39. No more than two units can share a common entrance stair from the ground floor. Elevator access shall be provided for eight or more interconnected units.

Illustration 39 *Apartments may be located on the upper floors of mixed-use buildings.*

7. All residential units shall be raised above the level of the adjacent sidewalk as specified for the various street types, Residential units shall be raised above ground level at the front of the building by a minimum of two feet. Refer to Illustration 40.

Illustration 40 *The ground floor level, preferably combined with a covered entry porch, should be raised at least two feet above sidewalk grade to provide security and privacy.*

8. A minimum of 50 percent of all dwelling units, excluding accessory dwellings and apartment dwellings located on upper floors, shall have a clearly defined front yard using landscaping, hedging, fencing, or a brick or stone wall, none of which shall exceed three feet in height. Front yards of attached duplexes or townhouses may be unified into one common yard treated as a single front yard for the entire building. Refer to Illustration 41.

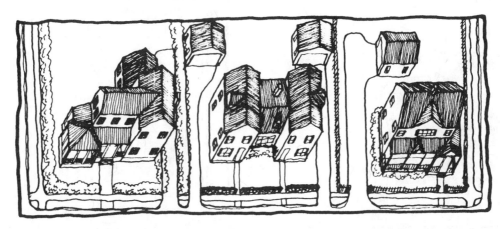

Illustration 41 *The front yard of 50 percent of all dwellings units should be clearly defined by landscaping, hedges, fencing, or a brick or stone wall at least three feet high.*

9.  A minimum of 50 percent of dwelling units, except apartments, shall have a front entrance articulated with a covered front entry porch. Front porches shall generally be located on the front of the dwelling facing the sidewalk, but may occasionally be located on the side wall of a dwelling. The size of front entry porches shall be a minimum of five feet deep from the front wall of the dwelling to the enclosing porch rail and ten feet long. Refer to Illustration 42.

 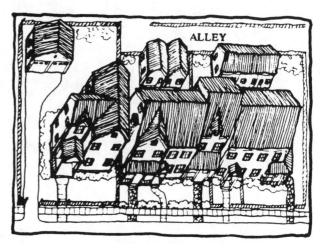

Illustration 42 *The front entrance of 50 percent of all dwelling units should have a covered front entry porch raised a minimum of two feet above ground level.*

10.  All dwelling units, except apartments located on upper floors, shall have a private yard or patio a minimum of 400 square feet in area and enclosed by a masonry wall, wooden fence, trellis or lattice, evergreen hedge, vines, or some combination thereof. The height of such yard or patio enclosure shall not exceed six feet and shall be suitable to provide privacy and screen views of neighboring uses. Each upper floor apartment dwelling shall be provided with a terrace consisting of a minimum of 64 square feet, recessed inside the exterior building wall of the dwelling or a balcony of 72 square feet projecting on the outside of the building wall. If a terrace or balcony is not provided for upper floor apartment, each dwelling shall be provided with access to a conveniently located common space, park, or green with an additional 100 square feet of area above the required internal open space. Such additional space shall be designed as outdoor rooms with hard surfaces and places for grills, movable chairs, and tables. Refer to Illustration 43.

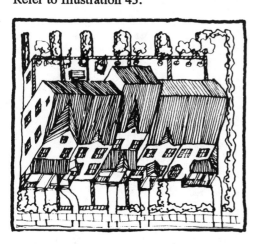 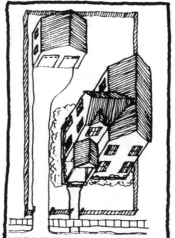

Illustration 43 *All dwelling units shall have a private yard, patio, or upper floor terrace.*

## SECTION 15.  COMMERCIAL DEVELOPMENT WITHIN A PLANNED SMALL COMMUNITY

1.  The commercial density of a planned small community shall range from a minimum of 125 square feet of commercial floor area per residential dwelling unit to a maximum of 300 square feet of commercial floor area per dwelling unit. This shall include the provision of jobs for retail and office/job generating uses. The local convenience retail component shall be 25 to 50 square feet per unit. The office and service component shall be a minimum of 100 square feet and a maximum of 250 square feet per unit.  The commercial component of a planned small community shall be mandatory and shall be constructed prior to the commencement of construction of the final 25 percent of the dwellings in the development. If build-out of a small community is phased, then the minimum the amount of commercial use shall be in proportion to the number of residential units constructed during that phase. For the purposes of calculating the commercial uses, accessory dwellings and apartment dwellings located on upper floors above a commercial use shall be counted as one dwelling unit each.

2.  At no time in the development of a small community may the commercial density in the developed sections be cumulatively greater than the above permitted density.

3.  The commercial component shall consist of a minimum of 50 percent commercial uses which are primarily oriented to serve both the residents of the small community and those of the immediately surrounding residential area, located within 1,500 feet of the core of the community.  The remaining commercial uses may consist of any permitted commercial uses, including other types of retail and service uses.

4. Commercial components shall front on the interior streets of the small community. Commercial uses can be mixed and integrated with dwelling units and public and semi-public uses, community clubs, and community facilities.  The greatest concentration of commercial development shall be located around a community green and/or within a main street commercial area. Refer to Illustration 44.

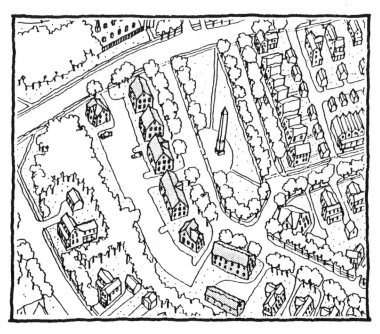

Illustration 44  *The greatest concentration of commercial development in a small community should be around a community green and/or within a main street commercial area.*

If the development includes a main street commercial area the community green shall either front upon main street, the Main Street shall terminate at the community green, or the main street and the community green shall be otherwise incorporated into a combined community focus for the development. Individual commercial uses may also be located in corner stores. Refer to Illustrations 45 through 47.

Illustration 45 *Commercial use situated on Main Street across from the community green in the village of Lititz, PA, with a very positive rating.*

Illustration 46 *Ground level offices with upper level apartments in New Holland , PA, with a positive VPS $^{TM}$ rating.*

Illustration 47 *High concentration of commercial/mixed use with a positive rating should be located on main street.*

5. Commercial uses shall be contained in multi-story, mixed-use structures with commercial/retail uses on the ground level and apartment dwellings or offices on the upper levels. Such buildings shall vary in terms of footprint and architectural elevations. The maximum ground level footprint of a commercial building shall be 5,000 square feet. In a three story building, the second floor may contain either apartment dwellings or commercial uses. Refer to Illustration 48.

Illustration 48 *Multi-story mixed-use structures may contain retail uses on the ground floor, offices uses on the second floor, and apartments on the second or third floor.*

6.  Corner stores may be located in residential areas of the small community away from the core, provided that it is located on Type 4 or 5 residential streets. Corner store buildings shall be designed to appear as a residential building and shall be limited to one ground level commercial use not to exceed 1,000 square feet in gross floor area with apartment dwellings on the upper level(s). The commercial use in a corner store shall be primarily oriented to serve the residents of the immediately surrounding neighborhood. Refer to Illustration 49. A corner store building shall be set back a maximum of ten feet from the right-of-way line.

Illustration 49 *Commercial uses may be located in corner stores within residential areas. These should be located approximately 1000 feet away from the core.*

7.  Restaurant shall be permitted to operate outdoor cafes on sidewalks, including areas within the public right-of-way and in courtyards, provided that pedestrian circulation and access to store entrances shall not be impaired. Refer to Illustration 50. The following standards and guidelines are applicable:

> A.  To allow for pedestrian circulation, a minimum of five feet of sidewalk along the curb and leading to the entrance to the establishment shall be maintained free of tables and other encumbrances.
>
> B.  Planters, posts with ropes, or other removable enclosures are encouraged and shall be used as a way of defining the area occupied by the cafe.
>
> C.  Extended awnings, canopies, or large umbrellas shall be permitted and located to provide shade. Colors shall complement building colors.
>
> D.  Outdoor cafes shall be required to provide additional outdoor trash receptacles.
>
> E.  Tables, chairs, planters, trash receptacles, and other elements of street furniture shall be compatible with the architectural character of the building where the establishment is located.
>
> F.  Outdoor cafes shall not be entitled to additional signage, over and beyond what is permitted for this type of establishment.

Illustration 50 *Restaurants may have outdoor cafes on sidewalks or in courtyards.*

G.  The operators of outdoor cafes shall be responsible for maintaining a clean, litter-free, and well-kept appearance within and immediately adjacent to the area of their activities.

8.  Commercial uses shall be permitted to have sidewalk displays of retail merchandise.  Refer to Illustration 49.  The following standards and guidelines are applicable:

A.  Sidewalk displays are permitted directly in front of an establishment, provided that at least five feet of clearance is maintained at the storefront entrance, for adequate and uncluttered pedestrian access, provided the display is located against the building wall and not more than three feet deep, and provided the display area does not exceed 75 percent of the length of the storefront.

B.  Display cases shall be permitted only during normal business hours and shall be removed at the end of the business day.  Cardboard boxes shall not be used for sidewalk displays.

C.  Sidewalk displays shall maintain a clean, litter-free, and well-kept appearance at all times and shall be compatible with the colors and character of the storefront from which the business operates.

Illustration 51 *Commercial uses may have sidewalk displays of retail merchandise.*

## SECTION 16.  PUBLIC AND SEMI-PUBLIC USES AND COMMUNITY FACILITIES WITHIN PLANNED SMALL COMMUNITIES

   1.  Not less than two percent of the gross tract or 450 square feet per dwelling shall be dedicated as sites for public and semi-public uses, community clubs, or community facilities.

   2.  Sites for such uses shall be located around the community green or within a main street commercial area.  Refer to Illustration 52.

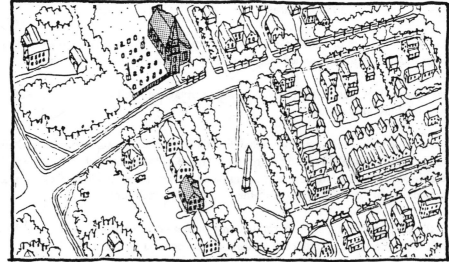

Illustration 52 *Sites for public or semi-public uses, community clubs, and commercial facilities should be pre-eminently located around a community green or within a main street commercial area.*

3. Sites for such uses shall be dedicated to appropriate users, as determined by the board. Such uses can include churches and religious institutions, day care, and other institutional uses.

4. Such uses shall occupy prominent buildings. Buildings that employ additional mass and height, civic architectural design, or other distinguishing features. Refer to Illustration 53.

Illustration 53 *Buildings for public and semi-public uses, community clubs, and community facilities should be prominent by virtue of their additional mass and height, civic architectural design, or other distinguishing features.*

5. Parking for such uses shall utilize on-street parking to the extent possible. If additional off-street parking is required, it shall be located in the rear of the building or structure and screened from the viewshed of the street.

## SECTION 17. SIDEWALKS AND BIKEWAYS

1. A sidewalk network shall be provided throughout the development that interconnects all dwelling units with other units, non-residential uses, and common open space. Sidewalks shall promote pedestrian activity within each site and throughout the development; they shall be separate and distinct from motor vehicle circulation to the greatest extent possible, provide a pleasant route for users, promote enjoyment of the development, and encourage incidental social interaction among pedestrians. Sidewalks shall be of barrier-free design to the greatest extent possible. The pedestrian circulation system shall include gathering/sitting areas and provide benches, landscaping, and other street furniture where appropriate.

2. Sidewalks shall be a minimum of four feet in width, expanding to five feet and six feet along major pedestrian routes; sidewalks in commercial areas shall be ten to fifteen feet in width. Sidewalks shall be constructed of brick, slate, colored/textured concrete pavers, concrete containing accents of brick, or some combination thereof that is compatible with the style, materials, colors, and details of the surrounding buildings. The functional, visual, and tactile properties of the paving materials shall be appropriate to the proposed functions of pedestrian circulation.

3. Walkways shall be raised and curbed along buildings and within parking lots, where suitable. Pedestrian street crossings shall be clearly delineated by a change in pavement color and/or texture. All sidewalks and other pedestrian walkways shall have appropriate lighting, using poles and fixtures consistent with the overall design theme for the development.

4. Bikeways shall be provided, where possible, to link internal open space areas with peripheral open space areas and continuing on routes through peripheral open space areas. Bikeways do not have to be marked on local residential streets with low average daily traffic. Bikeways are required on access and entry roads and on boulevards with high average dailly traffic. Bikeways shall be a minimum of six feet wide and may use asphalt paving. Bike racks shall be provided in internal open space areas and recreation areas in the peripheral open space.

## SECTION 18. AREA AND BULK REGULATIONS

1. Large lot single family detached dwellings  (Refer to illustration 54).
   A. Minimum lot area: 20,000 square feet
   B. Minimum lot width at front yard setback line: 65 feet
   C. Minimum lot depth: 120 feet
   D. Minimum yard dimensions
   > Build-to line: 25 feet **unless specified in the regulating plan** or street sections
   > Front yard: minimum of 20 feet with a maximum of 30 feet
   > Side yard (each side): 25 feet
   > Rear yard: 50 feet
   > E. Build-up line: Two and one half stories first finished floor level must be a minimum of two feet above sidewalk grade
   > maximum building height: 40
   F. maximum building coverage: 25 percent
   G. minimum non-impervious surface: 50 percent
   H. Rear or side yard garage required
   I. Bulk standards for accessory dwellings:  an accessory dwelling located on the same lot as a large lot single family dwelling, whether attached or detached to same, shall additionally comply with the bulk standards as specified above without modification, except that a detached accessory dwelling shall be limited to a maximum building height of 25 feet

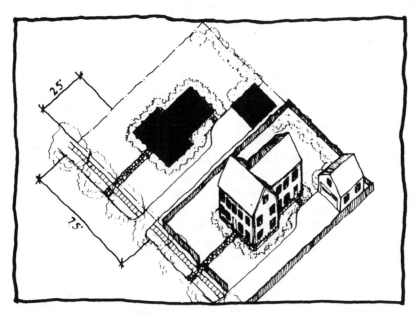

Illustration 54 *Figure ground and axonometric of large lot single family detached dwelling.*

J. Area and bulk standards for flag lots: flag lots shall comply with the above specified area and bulk standards, except that minimum lot width at the street line and minimum lot width at the front yard setback line shall be fifteen feet and minimum yard dimensions for all yards shall be 50 feet

2. Small lot single family detached dwellings ( Refer to illustration 55).

   A. Lot area: a minimum of 5,000 square feet and a maximum of 10,000 square feet
   B. Lot width
      At front yard setback line: minimum of 50 feet, maximum of sixty-five (65) feet
   C. Minimum lot depth: 100 feet
   D. Yard dimensions
      Build-to line fifteen feet unless specified in the regulating plan
      Front yard: minimum of ten feet; maximum of 25 feet
      Side yard (each side): minimum of six feet, maximum of 20 feet
      Rear yard: minimum of 25 feet
   E. Build-up line: Two stories, first finished floor level must be a minimum of two feet above sidewalk grade
      Maximum building height: 35 feet
   F. Maximum building coverage: 40 percent
   G. Minimum non-impervious area: 50 percent
   H. Rear yard parking required alley optional
   I. Additional standards for accessory dwellings: an accessory dwelling located on the same lot as a small lot, detached single family dwelling, whether attached or detached to same, shall additionally comply with the standards as specified above without modification, except that a detached accessory dwelling shall be limited to a maximum building height of 25 feet
   J. Area and bulk standards for flag lots: flag lots shall comply with the above specified area and bulk standards, except that minimum lot width at the street line and the minimum lot width at front yard setback line shall be fifteen feet and the minimum yard dimensions for all yards shall be 25 feet

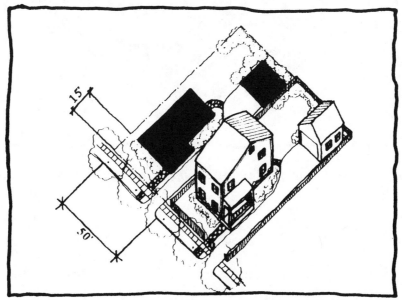

Illustration 55 *Figure ground and axonometric of a small lot, detached single family dwelling.*

3. Single family semi-detached dwellings  (Refer to illustration 36).
  A. Lot area: minimum of 3,000 square feet per dwelling unit or attached office commercial, maximum of 6,000 square feet per dwelling unit/office commercial
  B. Lot width
     At front yard setback line: minimum of 40 feet, maximum of 80 feet per dwelling unit
  C. Minimum lot depth: 100 feet
  D. Yard dimensions
     Build-to line: 15 feet unless specified in the regulating plan
     Front yard: minimum of 10 feet, maximum of 25 feet
     Side yard (one side): minimum of six feet, maximum of 20 feet
     Rear yard: minimum of 25 feet
  E. Build-up line: two stories, first finished floor level must be a minimum of two feet above sidewalk grade
     Maximum building height: 35 feet
  F. Maximum building coverage: 40 percent
  G. Minimum non-impervious surface: 50 percent
  H. Rear yard or side yard parking required, alley access optional
  I. Attached structure shall be subordinate to the main structure characterized at minimum by a lower ridge line

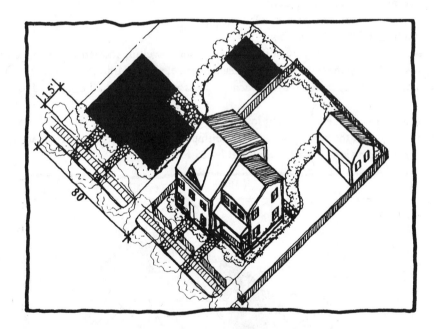

Illustration 56 *Figure ground and axonometric of semi-detached dwellings.  Second unit could be a small office or residential rental unit.*

4. Duplex Dwellings  (Refer to illustration 57).

    A. Lot area: minimum of 3,000 square feet per dwelling unit and a maximum of 5,000 square feet per dwelling unit

    B.  Lot width

       At front yard setback line: minimum of 30 feet per dwelling unit, maximum of 50 feet per dwelling unit

    C. Minimum lot depth: 100 feet

    D. Yard dimensions

          Build-to line: fifteen feet or as specified in the regulating plan

          Front yard: minimum of ten feet and a maximum of 20 feet

          Side yard (one side): minimum of four feet and a maximum of 10 feet

          Rear yard: minimum of twenty-five feet

    E. Build-up line: two stories, first finished floor level must be a minimum of two feet above sidewalk grade

          Maximum building height: 35 feet

    F. Maximum building coverage: 50 percent

    G. Minimum open area: 40 percent

    H. Rear yard parking and alley required

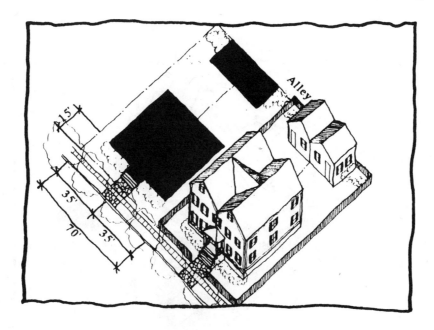

Illustration 57 *Figure ground and axonometric of duplex dwelling.*

5. Townhouse (rowhouse) Dwellings  (Refer to illustration 58).
    A. Lot area: minimum of 1,800 square feet per dwelling unit and a maximum of 4,500 square feet per dwelling unit
    B. Lot width
       At front yard setback line: a minimum of 20 feet per dwelling unit and a maximum of 30 feet per dwelling unit
    C. Minimum lot depth: 100 feet
    D. Yard dimensions
       Build-to line: 10 feet or as specified in the regulating plan
       Front yard: a minimum of five feet and a maximum of 20 feet
       Side yard (each end of row): minimum of eight feet, maximum of twelve feet
       Rear yard: a minimum of 25 feet
    E. Build-up line: two and a half stories,  first finished floor level must be a minimum of two feet above sidewalk grade
       Maximum building height: 35 feet
    F. Maximum building coverage: 60 percent
    G. Minimum non-impervious surface: 30 percent
    H. Maximum building size: Four dwelling units in a row and 100 feet in length
    I. Minimum interior yards (open space between buildings on the same lot): 30 feet
    J. Rear yard garage and alley required

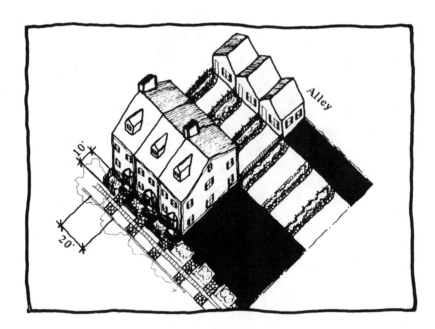

Illustration 58 *Figure ground and axonometric of town house dwelling.*

6. Apartment Dwellings  (Refer to illustration 59).
   A.   Minimum lot area -  8,800 square feet
   B    Lot width: a minimum of 80 feet and a maximum of 115 feet
   C.   Minimum lot depth: a maximum of 110 feet and a minimum of 150 feet
   D.   Yard dimensions
         Build-to line: fifteen feet or as specified in the regulating plan
         Front yard: minimum of ten feet and a maximum of twenty feet
         Side yard (each side): minimum of ten feet
         Rear yard: minimum of 55 feet
   E.   Build-up line: three stories,  first finished floor level must be a minimum of two feet above sidewalk grade
         Maximum building height: 42 feet
   F.   Maximum building coverage: 60 percent
   G.   Minimum non-impervious area: 30 percent
   H.   Maximum building size: eight dwelling units in a building and 95 feet in length
   I.   Minimum interior yards (open space between buildings on the same lot): 20 feet
   J.   Rear yard parking and alley access are required

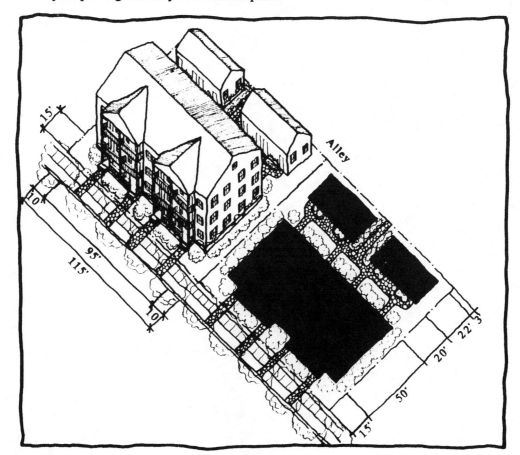

Illustration 59 *Figure ground and axonometric of an apartment building on 110 foot deep lot. The building contains 9 units. There are garage spaces for one car per unit.*

7. Commercial Uses and Mixed-Use Buildings (Refer to illustration 60).
  A. Lot area: minimum of 2,500 square feet and a maximum of 16,000 square feet.
  B. Lot width
     At front yard setback line: minimum of 25 feet and a maximum of 80 feet
  C. Minimum lot depth: 100 feet
  D. Yard dimensions
         Build-to line
         Commercial/retail: 0 feet
         Mixed-use, retail/office: four feet
         Mixed-use, retail/residential: four feet
         Front yard: a minimum of zero feet, maximum of ten feet
         Side yard (each side): a minimum of zero feet, if attached to an adjacent building or a minimum of five feet if
         not attached to an adjacent building; maximum of 20 feet
         Rear yard: a minimum of 55 feet (one row of parking)
  E. Build-up line: three stories, finished first floor must be level with sidewalk
         Maximum building height: 45 feet
  F. Maximum building coverage: 70 percent
  G. Minimum Non-impervious area: 10 percent
  H. Maximum building size: 100 feet in length, including adjacent buildings on adjacent lots if attached thereto
  I. Minimum interior yards (open space between buildings on the same lot): fifteen feet
  J. All off-street parking must be in rear yards. Alleys are recommended.

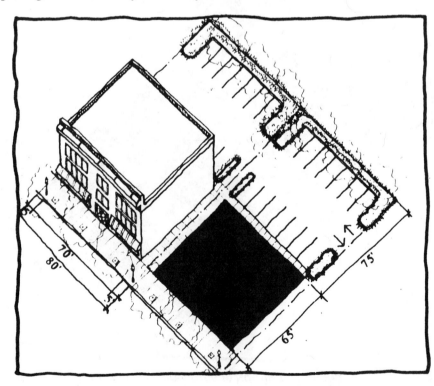

Illustration 60 *Figure ground and axonometric of commercial mixed use buildings.*

8. Community Facilities and Institutional and Religious Buildings  (Refer to illustration 61).
   A. Lot area: a minimum of 10,000 square feet and a maximum of 40,000 square feet
   B. Lot width
      At front yard setback line: a minimum of 80 feet and a maximum of 150 feet
   C. Minimum lot depth: 110 feet
   D. Yard dimensions
      Build-to line
      Community facilities: fifteen feet
      Religious: twenty-five feet
      Institutional: twenty feet
      Side yard (each side): minimum of fifteen feet and a maximum of 30 feet
      Rear yard: a minimum of 75 feet
   E. Build-up line: three stories
      Maximum building height: 45 feet
      Steeples or decorative towers: 75 feet
   F. Maximum building coverage: 70 percent
   G. Minimum non-impervious area: 20 percent
   H. Maximum building size: 100 feet in length, including adjacent buildings on adjacent lots if attached thereto
   I. Minimum interior yards (open space between buildings on the same lot): fifteen feet
   J. All off-street parking must be in the rear yards.  Alleys are recommended.

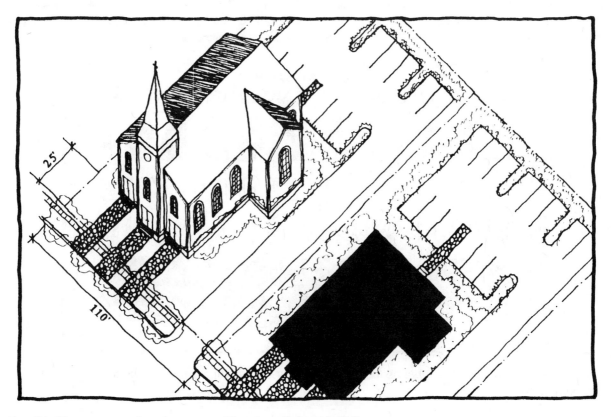

Illustration 61 *Figure ground and axonometric of a religious building.*

## SECTION 19.  REQUIRED OFF-STREET AND ON-STREET PARKING

1.  Off-street parking shall be provided according to minimum requirements as specified below:

| USE | REQUIRED PARKING |
|-----|------------------|
| Large lot single family | Two garage spaces per unit |
| Townhouse and duplex | One space per first bedroom, plus half of a space per each additional bedroom |
| Apartment dwellings | One space per bedroom |
| Accessory dwellings | One space per bedroom |
| Retail* | One space for the first 1,000 sq. ft.and one space for each additional 750 square feet |
| Office uses * | One space for each 500 square feet of gross floor area |
| Institutional/Churches | One space for each six seats |

*Additional spaces needed for such uses will be provided by on-street parking.  Total on-street and off-street paring for retail and offices shall not exceed one car per 450 square feet for retail and one space per 300 square feet for  offices.

2.  Off-street parking for commercial uses shall be sufficient to provide parking for the employees of all proposed uses as well as long-term customer parking.  Spaces reserved for employees shall be designated as such by means of striping and signage. Off-street parking lots shall be prohibited in any front yard setback area, shall be located at the rear of buildings on the interior of lots and shall be accessed by means of common driveways, preferably from side streets or lanes.  Such lots shall be small-sized (less than 25 parking spaces), where possible, and interconnected with commercial parking lots on adjacent properties. Cross-access easements for adjacent lots with interconnected parking lots shall be required, in language acceptable to the township solicitor. Common, shared parking facilities are encouraged, where possible.  Refer to Illustration 62.

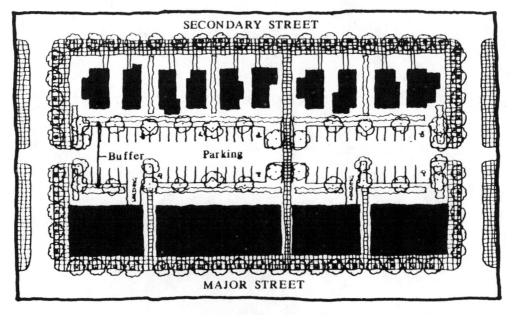

Illustration 62 *Off-street parking areas must be located to the rear of buildings and appropriately landscaped, buffered, and screened.*

3. In addition to the off-street parking requirements specified above, on-street parking shall be provided to serve customers of commercial uses. The minimum requirement for on-street parking shall be one curbside space for each 500 square feet of gross floor area of commercial uses. Where the minimum on-street parking requirement can not be completely complied with, the deficient number of spaces shall be provided in off-street parking lots. Commercial on-street parking shall be provided as curbside, parallel, or angle parking located along both sides of the streets on all blocks upon which commercial uses front.

4. Parking for all dwelling units shall be prohibited in front yard setback areas. With the exception of detached single family dwellings, semi-detached single family dwellings, and duplexes, driveways shall be prohibited in any front yard area. For other dwelling types driveway access shall be provided from lanes. Driveways and parking areas shall be setback a minimum of three feet from the side of dwelling units and 20 feet from the rear of dwelling units. Driveways shall be setback a minimum of three feet from any side property line, unless such driveway is shared by dwellings on two adjacent lots in which case the driveway may be located with the driveway center line on the common side lot line. Parking for townhouses shall be provided in a common off-street parking area or in garages or parking spaces with access from a rear lane. Private driveways for townhouses shall connect to lanes only and not to street. However, a common driveway serving a minimum of eight units and not exceeding eighteen feet in width may be permitted from a street. Parking for apartments may be located in common parking lots located on a lot other than that containing the apartment building, but within 400 feet of the apartment building entrances. If access to a garage is provided from a street, the front entrance of such a garage shall be setback fifteen feet further than the front wall of the dwelling unit. The location of a garage shall be setback a minimum of five feet from side or rear property line.

5. Parking Lot Landscaping, Buffering, and Screening.

A. Lots for apartment and non-residential uses shall balance the functional requirements of parking with the provision of pedestrian amenities. Transition areas between parking and civic, commercial, or residential uses shall be designed with textured paving, landscaping, and street furniture.

B. Parking lot layout, landscaping, buffering, and screening shall prevent direct views of parked vehicles from streets and sidewalks, avoid spill-over light, glare, noise, or exhaust fumes onto adjacent properties, in particular residential properties, and provide the parking area with a reasonable measure of shade, when trees reach maturity. In order to achieve these objectives, parking lots exposed to view shall be surrounded by a minimum of a five foot high, year-round visually impervious screen, hedge, or wall. The height of any required screen, hedge, or wall shall decrease where driveways approach sidewalks or walkways, in order to provide adequate visibility of pedestrians from motor vehicles, and shall not interfere with clear sight triangle requirements.

C. The interior of all parking lots shall be landscaped to provide shade and visual relief. This is best achieved by protected planting islands or peninsulas within the perimeter of the parking lot. Parking lots with ten or less spaces may not require interior landscaping if the planning board determines that there is adequate perimeter landscaping. If this perimeter landscaping is found to be inadequate, and in parking lots with eleven or more spaces, a minimum of one deciduous shade tree shall be planted for every six parking spaces. A six foot planting diamond or equivalent planter is required. Choice of plant materials, buffer width, type of screening, location, and frequency of tree planting shall be flexible, provided these objectives are substantially satisfied.

D. Parking lot layout shall take into consideration pedestrian circulation--pedestrian crosswalks shall be provided, where necessary and appropriate, shall be distinguished by textured paving, and shall be integrated into the wider network of pedestrian walkways. Pavement textures shall be required on pedestrian accessways, and strongly encouraged elsewhere in the parking lot, as surfacing materials, or when used as accents.

## SECTION 20.  REQUIRED LOADING AND SERVICE AREAS

1.  When required, loading docks, solid waste facilities, recycling facilities, and other service areas shall be placed to the rear or side of buildings in visually unobtrusive locations.

2.  Screening and landscaping shall prevent direct views of the loading areas and their driveways from adjacent properties or from the public right-of-way.  Screening and landscaping shall also prevent spill-over glare, noise, or exhaust fumes.  Screening and buffering shall be achieved through walls, fences, and landscaping, shall be a minimum of five feet tall, and shall be visually impervious.  Recesses in the building, or depressed access ramps may be used.

## SECTION 21.  FLOODPLAIN CONTROL
All floodplain areas shall comply with the requirements of the Department of Environmental Protection and Energy. Floodplain areas may be utilized in meeting open space requirements.

## SECTION 22.  SIGNS
All signs located within a small community shall comply with the sign regulations.

1.  Exempt signs

A.  Temporary civic, cultural, and public service window posters, when posted inside commercial establishments, provided they do not, individually or combined, occupy more than 25 percent of the total area of said window or five square feet, whichever is less.  Temporary window signs are permitted on ground floor windows only

B.  Temporary promotional or special sales signs when erected in conjunction with a commercial establishment provided they do not, individually or combined with other window signs, exceed 25 percent of the total area of the display window or sixteen square feet, whichever is less.  Temporary signs advertising a business opening or change in ownership shall not exceed an area of sixteen square feet, and shall require a temporary zoning permit, specifying the date of removal.  All temporary signs shall have the date of removal printed clearly on the lower right hand corner, as viewed from the exterior, and shall be permitted for a period not to exceed 30 days.  Temporary promotional signs are permitted on ground floor windows only

2.  Prohibited signs

A.  Signs employing mercury vapor, low pressure and high pressure sodium, and metal halide lighting; plastic panel rear-lighted signs
B.  Signs on roofs, dormers, and balconies
C.  Billboards
D.  Signs painted or mounted upon the exterior side or rear walls of any principal or accessory building or structure, except as otherwise permitted hereunder

3. Permitted signs

A.  Wall-mounted or painted signs, provided the following standards are met:
(1)  The sign shall be affixed to the front facade of the building, and shall project outward from the wall to which it is attached no more than six inches.

(2) The area of the signboard shall not exceed five percent of the ground floor building facade area or 24 square feet, whichever is less.

(3) The maximum permitted height is fifteen feet above the front sidewalk elevation, and shall not extend above the base of the second floor window sill, parapet, eave, or building facade.

(4) The height of the lettering, numbers, or graphics shall not exceed eight inches.

(5) The sign shall be granted to commercial uses occupying buildings facing on public streets only and shall not be allocable to other uses.

(6) Limited to one sign per business.

B. One wall-mounted sign, not exceeding six square feet in area, shall be permitted on any side or rear entrance open to the public. Such wall signs may only be lighted during the operating hours of the business.

C. Wall-mounted building directory signs identifying the occupants of a commercial building, including upper story business uses, provided the following standards are met:

(1) The sign is located next to the entrance.

(2) The sign shall project outward from the wall to which it is attached no more than six inches.

(3) The sign shall not extend above the parapet, eave, or building facade.

(4) The area of the signboard shall not exceed three square feet, with each tenant limited to one square foot.

(5) The height of the lettering, numbers, or graphics shall not exceed four inches.

D. Applied letters may substitute for wall-mounted signs, if constructed of painted wood, painted cast metal, bronze, brass, or black anodized aluminum. Applied plastic letters shall not be permitted. The height of applied letters shall not exceed eight inches.

E. Projecting signs, including graphic or icon signs, mounted perpendicular to the building wall, provided the following standards are met:

(1) The signboard shall not exceed an area of six square feet.

(2) The distance from the ground to the lower edge of the signboard shall be ten feet or greater.

(3) The height of the top edge of the signboard shall not exceed the height of the wall from which the sign projects, if attached to a single story building, or the height of the sill or bottom of any second story window, if attached to a multi-story building.

(4) The distance from the building wall to the signboard shall not exceed six inches.

(5) The width of the signboard shall not exceed three feet.

(6) The height of the lettering, numbers, or graphics shall not exceed eight inches.

(7) Limited to one sign per business. Projecting signs are not permitted in conjunction with wall-mounted, free-standing, or applied letter signs.

F. Painted window or door signs, provided that the following standards are met:

(1) The sign shall not exceed ten percent of the window or door area or four square feet, whichever is less.

(2) The sign shall be silk screened or hand painted.

(3) The height of the lettering, numbers, or graphics shall not exceed four inches.

(4) Limited to one sign per business, painted on either the window or the door, but not on both.

(5) May be in addition to only one of the following: a wall-mounted sign, a free-standing sign, an applied letter sign, a projecting sign or a valance awning sign.

G. Awning signs, for ground floor uses only, provided that the following standards are met:

(1) If acting as the main business sign, it shall not exceed ten square feet in area, and the height of the lettering, numbers, or graphics shall not exceed eight inches.
(2) If acting as an auxiliary business sign, it shall be located on the valance only, shall not exceed four square feet in area, and the height of the lettering, numbers, or graphics shall not exceed four inches.
(3) Limited to two such signs per business, on either awning or valance, but not on both.
(4) If acting as the main business sign, it shall not be in addition to a wall-mounted sign.

H. One free-standing sign, provided that the following standards are met:
(1) The building, where the business to which the sign refers is located, shall be set back a minimum of five feet from the street line.
(2) The area of the signboard shall not exceed three square feet.
(3) The height of the lettering, numbers, or graphics shall not exceed four inches.
(4) The height of the top of the signboard, or of any posts, brackets, or other supporting elements shall not exceed six feet from the ground.
(5) The signboard shall be constructed of wood, with wood or cast iron brackets, and shall be architecturally compatible with the style, composition, materials, colors, and details of the building.
(6) The signboard shall not be illuminated after 10:00 P.M.
(7) The sign shall be located within four feet of the main entrance to the business and its location shall not interfere with pedestrian or vehicular circulation.
(8) Limited to one sign per building and shall not be in addition to wall-mounted applied letters or projecting signs.

I. Businesses located in corner buildings are permitted one sign for each street frontage.

J. Businesses with service entrances may identify these with one sign not exceeding two square feet.

K. One directional sign, facing a rear parking lot. This sign may be either wall-mounted or free standing on the rear facade, but shall be limited to three square feet in area.

L. In addition to other signage, restaurants and cafes shall be permitted the following, limited to one sign per business:

(1) A wall-mounted display featuring the actual menu as used at the dining table, to be contained within a shallow wood or metal case, and clearly visible through a glass front. The display case shall be attached to the building wall, next to the main entrance, at a height of approximately five feet, shall not exceed a total area of two square feet, and may be lighted.
(2) A sandwich board sign, as follows:

(a) The area of the signboard, single-sided, shall not exceed five square feet.

(b) The signboard shall be constructed of wood, chalkboard, and/or finished metal.

(c) Letters can be painted or handwritten.

(d) The sign shall be located within four feet of the main entrance to the business and its location shall not interfere with pedestrian or vehicular circulation.

(e) The information displayed shall be limited to daily specials and hours of operation.

(f) The sign shall be removed at the end of the business day.

(g) The following schedule summarizes, in matrix form, how different types of signs can be associated.

M. Each business shall identify the number of its address within the signboard with a minimum of one sign facing each street or parking lot.

Illustration 63 *Signs scaled to the pedestrian and to vehicles can be small and function appropriately when correct point sizes are used.*

## Sign Matrix

| | Wall-Mounted | Wall-Mounted (side and rear entrances) | Applied Letters | Projecting | Painted Window/ Door |
|---|---|---|---|---|---|
| Wall-mounted | NA | Y | N | N(6) | Y |
| Wall-mounted (side and rear entrances) | Y | NA | Y | Y | Y |
| Applied Letters | N | Y | NA | N | Y |
| Projecting | N | Y | N | NA | Y |
| Painted Window/ Door | Y | Y | Y | Y | NA |
| Awning (1) | N(4) | Y | N(4) | Y | Y(5) |
| Directory (2) | Y | Y | Y | N | Y |
| Menu (3) | Y | Y | Y | Y | Y |
| Sandwich Board (3) | Y | Y | Y | Y | Y |
| Service Entrances | Y | N | Y | Y | Y |
| Free-standing | N | Y | N | N | Y |
| Directional | Y | N | Y | Y | Y |

(1) ground floor uses only

(2) upper floor uses only

(3) cafes and restaurants only

(4) if awning is acting as main business sign

(5) valance awning sign only

(6) directional only

Y - indicates a use is permitted to display the two signs in conjunction

N - indicates a use is not permitted to display the two signs in conjunction

Sign Matrix (cont)

| | Awning (1) | Directory (2) | Menu (3) | Sandwich Board (3) | Service Entrances | Free-standing | Directional |
|---|---|---|---|---|---|---|---|
| Wall-mounted | N(4) | Y | Y | Y | Y | N(6) | Y |
| Wall-mounted (side and rear entrances) | Y | Y | Y | Y | N | Y | N |
| Applied Letters | N(4) | Y | Y | Y | Y | N | Y |
| Projecting | Y | N | Y | Y | Y | N | Y |
| Painted Window/Door | Y(5) | Y | Y | Y | Y | Y | Y |
| Awning (1) | NA | N | Y | Y | Y | Y | Y |
| Directory (2) | N | NA | Y | Y | Y | Y | Y |
| Menu (3) | Y | Y | NA | Y | Y | Y | Y |
| Sandwich Board (3) | Y | Y | Y | NA | Y | Y | Y |
| Service Entrances | Y | Y | Y | Y | NA | Y | Y |
| Free-standing | Y | Y | Y | Y | Y | NA | Y |
| Directional | Y | Y | Y | Y | Y | Y | NA |

(1) ground floor uses only
(2) upper floor uses only
(3) cafes and restaurants only
(4) if awning is acting as main business sign
(5) valance awning sign only
(6) directional only

Y - indicates a use is permitted to display the two signs in conjunction
N - indicates a use is not permitted to display the two signs in conjunction

## 4. Design Standards for Signs

   A.  Signs affixed to the exterior of a building shall be architecturally compatible with the style, composition, materials, colors, and details of the building, as well as with other signs used on the building or its vicinity.  Refer to Illustration 64.

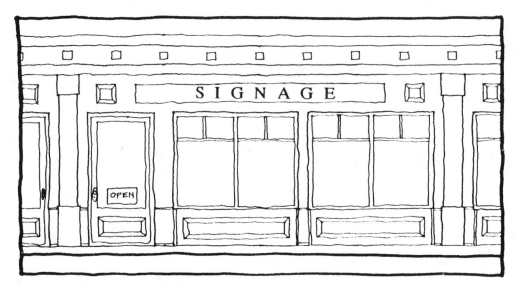

Illustration 64 *Signs should be architecturally compatible with a building's facade.*

   B.  Signs shall fit within the existing facade features, shall be confined to signable areas, and shall not interfere with door and window openings, conceal architectural details or obscure the composition of the facade where they are located.  Signs shall be placed on a facade only in a manner historically appropriate to the style of the building.

   C.  Whenever possible, signs located on buildings within the same blockface shall be placed at the same height, in order to create a unified sign band.

   D.  Wood and painted metal are the preferred materials for signs.  Flat signs should be framed with raised edges.  Wood signs shall use only high-quality exterior grade wood with suitable grade finishes.

   E.  Sign colors should be compatible with the colors of the building facade.  A dull or matte finish is recommended, for it reduces glare and enhances legibility.

   F.  Signs shall be either spot-lighted or back-lighted with a diffused light source.  Spot-lighting shall require complete shielding of all light sources; light shall be contained within the sign frame and shall not significantly spill over to other portions of the building, or site.  Back-lighting shall illuminate the letters, characters, or graphics on the sign but not its background.  Warm fluorescent bulbs may be used to illuminate the interior of display cases.  Neon signs placed inside the display case shall insure low intensity colors.

   G.  Signs shall be mounted so that the method of installation is concealed.  Signs applied to masonry surfaces should be mechanically fastened to mortar joints only, and not directly into brick or stone.  Drilling to provide electrical service should also follow the same rule.

## SECTION 23. NEIGHBORHOOD DESIGN STANDARDS AND GUIDELINES

1.  Buildings located at gateways entering the planned residential development shall mark the transition into and out of the neighborhood in a distinct fashion using massing, additional height, contrasting materials, and/or architectural embellishments to obtain this effect. Buildings located at gateways to a community green area or a Main Street commercial area shall mark the transition to such areas in a distinct fashion using massing, additional height, contrasting materials, and/or architectural embellishments to obtain this effect. Refer to Illustration 65

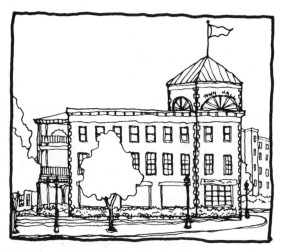

Illustration 65 *Gateway buildings should mark transition areas.*

2.  Focal points, or points of visual termination, shall generally be occupied by more prominent, monumental buildings and structures that employ enhanced height, massing, distinctive architectural treatments, or other distinguishing features. Refer to Illustration 66.

Illustration 66 *Focal points should terminate views down streets.*

3. Buildings shall define the streetscape through the use of uniform setbacks along the build-to line for each block. The build-to line shall be generally continued across side yard setback areas between buildings by using landscaping. The streetscape shall also be reinforced by lines of closely planted shade trees, and may be further reinforced by walls, hedges, or fences which define front yards. Refer to Illustration 67.

Illustration 67 *Buildings should define the streetscape through setbacks formed by the build-to line.*

4. Exterior public and semi-public spaces, such as courtyards or plazas, shall be designed to function, to enhance surrounding buildings, and to provide amenities for users, in the form of textured paving, landscaping, lighting, street trees, benches, trash receptacles, and other items of street furniture, as appropriate. Courtyards shall have recognizable edges defined on at least three sides by buildings, walls, elements of landscaping, and elements of street furniture, in order to create a strong sense of enclosure. Refer to Illustration 68.

Illustration 68 *Courtyards and plazas should be designed to enhance surrounding buildings.*

5. Buildings shall be considered in terms of their relationship to the height and massing of adjacent buildings, as well as in relation to the human scale. Refer to Illustration 69.

Illustration 69 *Buildings should relate to the scale of adjacent buildings.*

6. Buildings shall be located to front towards and relate to public streets, both functionally and visually, to the greatest extent possible. Buildings shall not be oriented to front toward a parking lot. Refer to Illustration 70.

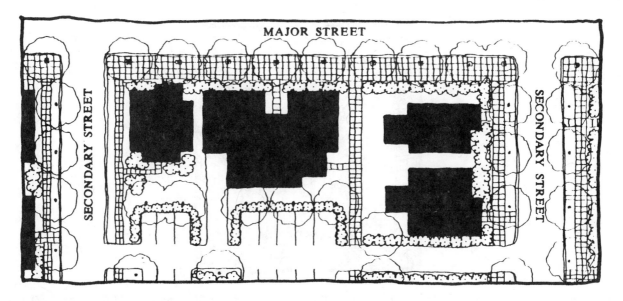

Illustration 70 *Buildings must be located to front upon the street.*

7.  Spatial relationships between buildings and other structures shall be geometrically logical and/or architecturally formal.  On a lot with multiple buildings, those located on the interior of the site shall front towards and relate to one another, both functionally and visually.  A lot with multiple buildings may be organized around features such as courtyards, greens, or quadrangles which encourage pedestrian activity and incidental social interaction among users.  Smaller, individualized groupings of buildings are encouraged.  Buildings shall be located to allow for adequate fire and emergency access.  Refer to Illustration 71.

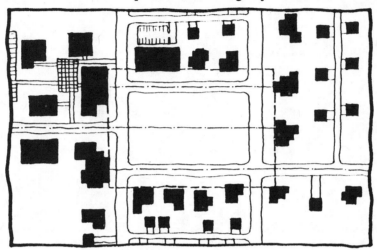

**Illustration 71** *Spaces framed by buildings should be geometrically logical and/or architecturally formal.*

8.  The acoustic, thermal, visual, and tactile properties of the proposed paving materials shall be appropriate to the proposed functions of pedestrian circulation.  Modular masonry materials, such as brick, slate, and concrete pavers, or gridded cast-in-place materials, such as exposed aggregate concrete slabs shall be used, whenever possible, on sidewalks, pedestrian walkways and pathways, and public or semi-public plazas, courtyards, or open spaces.  Asphalt, and non-aggregate exposed concrete slabs should be avoided.  Refer to Illustration 72.

**Illustration 72** *Textured paving materials should be used on sidewalks, plaza, courtyards, and urban open spaces.*

9. Walls and fences shall be architecturally compatible with the style, materials, and colors of the principal building on the same lot. Stone walls or brick walls with a stone or cast stone cap are encouraged. Wood fences, decorative metal, or cast iron fences, masonry or stucco walls, and stone piers shall be encouraged. Solid wooden fences are permitted in rear and side yards only. Highway-style guard rail, stockade, or contemporary security fencing such as barbed wire or razor wire are prohibited. Refer to Illustration 73.

Illustration 73 *Walls and fences should be architecturally compatible with buildings.*

## SECTION 24.  LANDSCAPING

1. Extensive landscaping shall be required in accordance with a landscape plan conceived for the planned small community as a whole. All areas of a site not occupied by buildings, parking lots, other improvements or textured paving shall be intensively planted with trees, shrubs, hedges, ground covers, and/or grasses, unless such area consists of attractive existing vegetation to be retained. Perennials and annuals are encouraged.

2. Landscaping shall be integrated with other functional and ornamental site design elements, where appropriate, such as recreational facilities, ground paving materials, paths and walkways, fountains or other water features, trellises, pergolas, gazebos, fences, walls, street furniture, art, and sculpture.

3. Plant suitability, maintenance, and compatibility with site and construction features are critical factors which shall be considered. Plantings shall be designed with repetition, structured patterns, and complimentary textures and colors, and shall reinforce the overall character of the area.

4. Landscaping plans shall be prepared by a certified professional in the field of landscape architecture.

5. Removal of debris. All stumps and other tree parts, litter, brush, weeds, excess or scrap building materials, or other debris shall be removed from the area of the site to be constructed and disposed of in accordance with the law. No tree stumps, portions of tree trunks, or limbs shall be buried anywhere in the development. All dead or dying trees, standing or fallen, shall be removed from the site. If trees and limbs are reduced to chips, they may, subject to approval of the municipal engineer, be used as mulch in landscaped areas. Areas which are to remain as open space and undeveloped, shall be cleaned of all debris and shall remain in their natural state.

6. Protection of existing plantings. Maximum effort should be made in the areas in which the village or hamlet will be constructed to save fine or mature specimens because of size or relative rarity. These should be protected and preserved. No material or temporary soil deposits shall be placed within four feet of shrubs or within two feet of the drip line of trees designated to be retained. Protective barriers or tree wells shall be installed around each plant and/or group of plants at the drip line, that are to be retained. Barriers shall not be supported by the plants they are protecting, but shall be self-supporting. Barriers, such as snow fences, shall be a minimum of four feet high and constructed of a durable material that will last until construction is completed.

7. Slope plantings. Landscaping of the area of all cuts, fills, and/or terraces shall be sufficient to prevent erosion, and all roadway slopes steeper than one foot vertically to three horizontally shall be planted with ground covers appropriate for the purpose, soil conditions, water availability, and environment.

8. Additional landscaping. In addition to the required screening and street trees, additional plantings or landscaping elements shall be required throughout the village or hamlet, where necessary, for climate control, privacy, or for aesthetic reasons.

9. Planting specifications. Deciduous trees shall have at least a three-inch caliper at the time of planting. Evergreen trees shall be a minimum of five to six feet high at the time of planting. Shrubs shall be two feet in height at the time of planting. Only nursery-grown plant materials shall be acceptable; and all trees, shrubs, and ground covers shall be planted according to accepted horticultural standards.

10. Within two years from the time of planting, all dead or dying plants, installed new, transplanted, or designated as existing trees to be retained on the plan, shall be replaced by the developer. With required maintenance and watering, it shall be as appropriate for the plant type. Trees of other vegetation which dies after the second year shall be replaced and maintained by the property owners association.

11. Plant species. The plant species selected should be hardy for the particular climatic zone in which the development is located and appropriate in terms of function and size. Street trees can be selected by referring to the background section of the Model Subdivision and Site Plan Ordinance. Shrubs and other plantings may be selected from those recommended in a standard reference book, such as *Shrubs and Vines for American Gardens* by Donald Wyman (New York, Macmillan, 1969). Final selection shall be reviewed by the shade tree commission and the landscape plan shall be submitted to the commission for its review and recommendations.

Trees shall have a caliper of three inches, shall be nursery grown, shall be of substantially uniform size and shape, and shall have straight trunks. Trees shall be properly planted and staked and provision made by the applicant for regular watering and maintenance until they are established. Dead or dying trees shall be replaced by the applicant during the next planting season.

12. Other Landscape Improvements. Landscaping and site treatment plans shall consider seasonal flowers in planters, planting beds and hanging baskets.

13. Garbage and Recycling. Garbage collection, recycling areas, and other utility areas shall be screened around their perimeter by wood enclosures with a roof or by brick walls, with a minimum height of seven feet, and shall extend on three sides of such an area, with a gate or door on the third side. Such a wall shall be capped on the top. A landscaped planting strip a minimum of three feet wide shall be located on three sides of such a facility. Planting material shall be separated from the parking lots by Belgian block curbing, but shall have ramp access to such facility for vehicles and carts. A mixture of hardy flowering and/or decorative evergreen and deciduous trees may be planted; the area between trees shall be planted with shrubs, ground cover, or covered with mulch.

14. Energy Conservation.  To conserve energy, landscaping shall include the planting of evergreen windbreaks to block northwest winds in the winter, thereby reducing heating energy costs in the winter.  Deciduous shade trees shall be planted near the southern facades of buildings to block summer sun, thereby reducing solar heat gain during the summer months.

## SECTION 25. DETENTION BASINS

Detention basins, headwalls, outlet structures, concrete flow channels, rip rap channels, and other drainage improvements shall be screened with plant material and/or berms.  Such drainage structures, as appropriate, shall be situated in the least visible location or, if visible, incorporated in to the natural curves of the land.  Detention basin embankments and the basin itself shall be extensively landscaped with wet site tolerant plant materials with the intention of re-creating a seasonal and high water wet eco-structure. The detention facility shall be sized to accommodate the future growth of vegetation planted in the basin.

In lieu of peripheral fencing, detention basins edges shall be contoured and shaped to form low angles at primary water line thereby insuring greater pedestrian safety.

Illustration 74 *Detention basins should be designed to complement the landscape.*

## SECTION 26. SHADE TREES

1. Shade trees shall be provided along each side of all streets, public or private, existing or proposed. Shade trees shall also be massed at critical points, such as at focal points along a curve in the roadway. In locations where healthy and mature shade trees currently exist, the requirements for new trees may be waived or modified. Refer to Illustration 75.

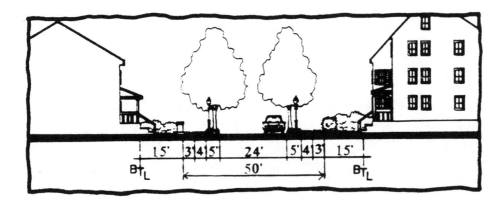

Illustration 75 *Shade trees must be provided along both sides of all streets.*

2. Shade trees shall have a minimum caliper of three- to three-and-a-half inches and/or a minimum height of twelve feet at time of planting, and a maximum spacing of 30 feet on center, with exact spacing to be evaluated on a site-specific basis.

3. The particular species of shade trees shall be determined upon specific locational requirements, soil types, geology, climate, and indigenous species. The following urban tolerant street trees are recommended for streets and elsewhere in a planned small community:

        Village Green Zelkova
        Littleleaf Linden
        Thornless Honeylocust
        Green Ash
        Regent Scholar Tree
        London Plane
        Hackberry
        Bradford Callery Pear
        Redspire Pear
        Red Maple
        October Glory Red Maple

## SECTION 27.  LIGHTING

1. Street lights shall be decorative and blend with the architectural style of the small community.  (See Design Vocabulary)

2.  Streets and sites shall provide adequate lighting, while minimizing adverse impacts, such as glare and overhead sky glow, on adjacent properties and the public right-of-way.  House side shields shall be provided where abutting a residential use.

3.  Along all commercial or mixed use streets, parking areas, sidewalks, walkways, courtyards, community greens, and interior open spaces in a planned small community, twelve foot high decorative lamp posts shall be provided at regular intervals.  Posts shall be spaced at no greater than 80 feet on center on both sides of a commercial or main street. Lighting on residential streets should be confined to the intersections and corners.   Lighting standards shall be consistent throughout the small community.  Refer to Illustration 76.

Illustration 76 *Decorative lamp posts should be used along all streets, parking areas, sidewalks, walkways, courtyards, community greens, and internal open spaces.*

4.   In parking lots, post heights may be extended to a maximum of sixteen feet.

5.  Use of minimum wattage metal halide or color corrected sodium light sources is encouraged.  Non-color corrected low pressure sodium and mercury vapor light sources are prohibited.

6. Porch light and yard post lighting shall be incorporated into the street lighting design.

## SECTION 28. ARCHITECTURAL DESIGN STANDARDS AND GUIDELINES

1. Buildings shall generally relate in scale and design features to the surrounding buildings, showing respect for the local context. As a general rule, buildings shall reflect a continuity of treatment obtained by maintaining the building scale or by subtly graduating changes; by maintaining front yard setbacks at the build-to line; by maintaining base courses; by continuous use of front porches on residential buildings; by maintaining cornice lines in buildings of the same height; by extending horizontal lines of fenestration; and by echoing architectural styles and details, design themes, building materials, and colors used in surrounding buildings. Refer to Illustration 77.

Illustration 77 *Buildings should respect the local context and relate in scale and design to the surrounding buildings, if they are rated as positive and appropriate.*

2. Buildings on corner lots shall be considered significant structures, since they have at least two front facades visibly exposed to the street. If deemed appropriate by the board of commissioners, such buildings may be designed with additional height and architectural embellishments, such as corner towers, to emphasize their location. Refer to Illustration 78.

Illustration 78 *Corner buildings should be designed as more dramatic structures to emphasize their prominent location.*

3.  Buildings shall avoid long, monotonous, uninterrupted walls or roof planes.  Building wall offsets, including projections, recesses, and changes in floor level shall be used in order to add architectural interest and variety, and to relieve the visual effect of a simple, long wall.  Similarly, roof-line offsets shall be provided, in order to provide architectural interest and variety to the massing of a building and to relieve the effect of a single, long roof.  The exterior of townhouses or apartments may be designed to appear as a single building, such as a large single-family detached dwelling.  Refer to Illustration 79 & 80.

Illustration 79 *The buick building represents an ideal way to modulate a large building.  It acts a landmark and form giver to the streetscape.*

Illustration 80 *Long building walls and roof lines should be offset to provide interest and variety.*

4.  The brick buildings, facing a public street or internal open space, shall be architecturally emphasized through fenestration, entrance treatment, and details.  Buildings with more than one facade facing a public street or internal open space shall be required to provide several front facade treatments.  Refer to Illustration 81.

Illustration 81 *Front facades should be architecturally emphasized, although all  visible facades must be compatible.*

5. The architectural treatment of the front facade shall be continued, in its major features, around all visibly exposed sides of a building. All sides of a building shall be architecturally designed to be consistent with regard to style, materials, colors, and details. Blank wall or service area treatment of side and/or rear elevations visible from the public viewshed is discouraged. Refer to Illustration 82.

Illustration 82 *All sides of a building should be architecturally consistent with the front facade.*

6. All visibly exposed sides of a building shall have an articulated base course and cornice. The base course shall align with either the kickplate or sill level of the first story. The cornice shall terminate or cap the top of a building wall, may project horizontally from the vertical building wall plane, and may be ornamented with moldings, brackets, and other details. The middle section of a building may be horizontally divided at the floor, lintel, or sill levels with belt or string courses. Refer to Illustration 82.

Illustration 83 *Buildings should be designed with a base course and cornice.*

7. Gable roofs with a minimum pitch of 9/12 should be used to the greatest extent possible. Where hipped roofs are used, it is recommended that the minimum pitch be 6/12. Both gable and hipped roofs should provide overhanging eaves on all sides, that extend a minimum of one foot beyond the building wall. Flat roofs should be avoided on one story buildings and are recommended on buildings with a minimum of two stories, provided that all visibly exposed walls have an articulated cornice that projects horizontally from the vertical building wall plane. Other roof types should be appropriate to the building's architecture. Mansard roofs are generally discouraged, particularly on buildings less then three stories in height. Architectural embellishments that add visual interest to roofs, such as dormers, belvederes, masonry chimneys, cupolas, clock towers, and other similar elements are encouraged. Refer to Illustration 84.

Illustration 84 *Gable roofs with a minimum 9/12 pitch should be used to the greatest extent possible. Other types of roofs should be appropriate to the architectural style of the building.*

8. Fenestration shall be architecturally compatible with the style, materials, colors, and details of the building. Windows shall be vertically proportioned wherever possible. To the extent possible, upper story windows shall be vertically aligned with the location of windows and doors on the ground level, including storefront or display windows. Refer to Illustration 85.

Illustration 85 *Type and location of windows should be appropriate to a building's architectural style.*

9. Blank, windowless walls are discouraged. Where the construction of a blank wall is necessitated by local building codes, the wall should be articulated by the provision of blank window openings trimmed with frames, sills, and lintels, or, if the building is occupied by a commercial use, by using recessed or projecting display window cases. Intensive landscaping may also be appropriate in certain cases. Refer to Illustration 86.

Illustration 86 *Blank windowless walls should be articulated in order to reduce the negative appearance.*

10. All entrances to a building shall be defined and articulated by architectural elements such as lintels, pediments, pilasters, columns, porticoes, porches, overhangs, railings, balustrades, and others, where appropriate. Any such element utilized shall be architecturally compatible with the style, materials, colors, and details of the building as a whole, as shall the doors. Refer to Illustration 87.

Illustration 87 *Entrances to buildings should be architecturally defined and articulated.*

11. In mixed-use buildings, the difference between ground floor commercial uses and entrances for upper level commercial or apartment uses shall be reflected by differences in facade treatment. Storefronts and other ground floor entrances shall be accentuated through cornice lines. Further differentiation can be achieved through distinct but compatible exterior materials, signs, awnings, and exterior lighting. Refer to Illustration 88.

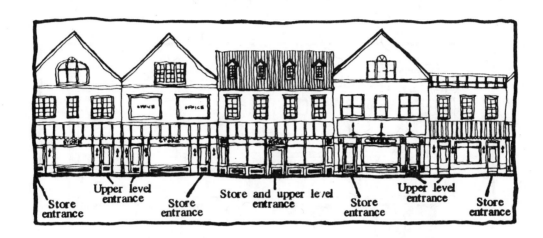

Illustration 88 *Ground floor commercial uses should be differentiated by the facade treatment.*

12. Storefronts are an integral part of a building and shall be integrally designed with the upper floors to be compatible with the overall facade character. Ground floor retail, service, and restaurant uses shall have large pane display windows. Such windows shall be framed by the surrounding wall and shall not exceed 75 percent of the total ground level facade area. Buildings with multiple storefronts shall be unified through the use of architecturally compatible materials, colors, details, awnings, signage, and lighting fixtures. Refer to Illustration 89.

Illustration 89 *Storefronts should be integrally designed as part of the entire facade. Buildings with multiple storefronts should be architecturally compatible.*

13. Fixed or retractable awnings are permitted at ground floor level, and on upper levels where appropriate, if they complement a building's architectural style, materials, colors, and details; do not conceal architectural features, such as cornices, columns, pilasters, or decorative details; do not impair facade composition; and are designed as an integral part of the facade. Canvas is the preferred material, although other water-proofed fabrics may be used; metal or aluminum awnings are prohibited. In buildings with multiple storefronts, compatible awnings should be used as a means of unifying the structure. Refer to Illustration 90.

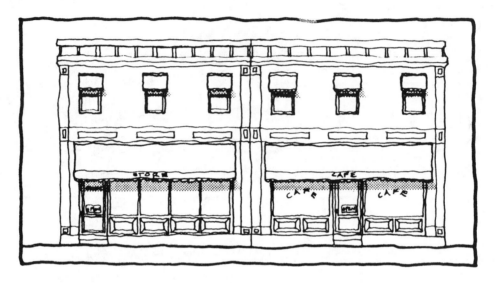

Illustration 90 *Awnings may be used to complement a buildings's architectural style.*

14. Light fixtures attached to the exterior of a building shall be architecturally compatible with the style, materials, colors, and details of the building and shall comply with local building codes. The type of light source used on the exterior of buildings, signs, parking areas, pedestrian walkways, and other areas of a site, and the light quality produced, shall be the same or compatible. Facades shall be lit from the exterior, and, as a general rule, lights should be concealed through shielding or recessed behind architectural features. The use of low pressure sodium, fluorescent, or mercury vapor lighting either attached to buildings or to light the exterior of buildings shall be prohibited. Mounting brackets and associated hardware should be inconspicuous. Refer to Illustration 91.

Illustration 91 *Lighting fixtures attached to a building should be architecturally compatible with the facade.*

15. All air conditioning units, HVAC systems, exhaust pipes or stacks, elevator housing, and satellite dishes and other telecommunications receiving devices shall be thoroughly screened from view from the public right-of-way and from adjacent properties by using walls, fencing, roof elements, penthouse-type screening devices, or landscaping.

16. Fire escapes shall not be permitted on a building's front facade. In buildings requiring a second means of egress pursuant to the local building codes, internal stairs or other routes of egress shall be used.

17. Solid metal security gates or solid roll-down metal windows shall not be permitted. Link or grill type security devices shall be permitted only if installed from the inside, within the window or door frames. If installed on the outside, the coil box shall be recessed and concealed behind the building wall. Security grilles shall be recessed and concealed during normal business hours. Models which provide a sense of transparency, in light colors, are encouraged. Other types of security devices fastened to the exterior walls are not permitted.

18. All materials, colors, and architectural details used on the exterior of a building shall be compatible with the building's style, and with each other. A building designed of an architectural style that normally includes certain integral materials, colors, and/or details shall incorporate such into its design. Where appropriate to the architectural style of a building, shutters shall be provided on all windows fronting a street or visible from the public right-of-way. Shutters shall be proportioned to cover one-half the width of the window.

## SECTION 29. DESIGN VOCABULARY

A design vocabulary shall be established for each hamlet, village, or neighborhood and shall include the general design qualities as well as the specific architectural standards to be used. The design vocabulary shall respond to the general and specific design standards as specified in this ordinance and relate to the proposed development plan. These must be presented at concept, preliminary, and final plan phases. There must be a style or styles selected and used throughout the small community. A variation on the existing historical vernacular architectural style in the region or the township is recommended. Images and styles that have been tested through the VPS ™ to generate a negative image of place are to be avoided. The use of materials, colors, and massing incompatible with the selected design vocabulary shall be avoided.

A listing of significant compatible features that will be incorporated into the design of the buildings and streetscape of a small community shall be prepared in matrix form. Photographic colored images, drawings, or a combination can be used. The horizontal axis of the matrix shall include all the categories of residential, commercial, parks and open space, and industrial if used. The vertical axis of the matrix shall include the following:

1. Building Mass and Style - which includes the volume of the selected building types and the style selected

2. Roofs and Roof Materials - the various types and pitches of roofs

3. Facade Treatment and Facade Materials - the types of materials textures and colors

4. Entry and Doors - door openings and the area immediately surrounding

5. Windows - window types with detailing

6. Eaves, Porches, and Arcades

Decorative building elements - like pergolas, cupolas, shutters, etc.

7. Trim.

Details of these features in elevation and section that reflect the architectural styles selected both vertical and horizontal .

8. Towers

9. Cross Gables and Dormers

10. Gutters

11. Chimneys

12. Walls, Fences, and Hedges (frontyard)

13. Walls, Fences, and Hedges (side yards)

14. Colors

15. Driveway

16. Pavement Materials and Textures

17. Curb Treatment

18. Streetlights

19. Street Signs

20. Street Furniture

Under each category specific written instructions can be included.  See illustration below.

**Design Vocabulary**

| | | |
|---|---|---|
| **1. Building Massing & Style**<br>75% of buildings shall be two and one half (2 ) stories high in residential styles as shown with up to 25% one (1) and one and one half (1 ) stories which shall emulate the ground level of the buildings shown.<br><br>50% of the principle ridge line shall be parallel to the principle street on which it fronts. | | |
| **2. Roofs**<br>Roof types shall be gable or salt box. Roof pitches shall be a minimum of 6 over 12<br><br>**Roof Materials**<br>Cedar Wood Shingles<br>Dimensioned Asphalt<br>Standing Seam<br>(on porch and bay windows only) | | |
| **3. Facade Treatment**<br>Neo-colonial as shown.<br><br>**Facade Materials**<br>Wood Clapboard (4" showing)<br>Simulated Clapboard (4" showing)*<br>Board and batton verticle<br>Indigenous Stone<br>Brick with corner quoining | | |

*This can be vinyl, provided that no butt joints are used.

## SECTION 30.  STREET FURNITURE

Elements of street furniture, such as benches, waste containers, planters, phone booths, bus shelters, bicycle racks, and bollards should be carefully selected to ensure compatibility with the architecture of surrounding buildings, the character of the area, and with other elements of street furniture.  Consistency in the selection and location of the various elements of street furniture is critical for maximum effect and functional usage.

## DESIGN VOCABULARY MATRIX  (Each rectangle needs to be infilled with a sketch,

### Residential Building Types

| | | | | | | | | | |
|---|---|---|---|---|---|---|---|---|---|
| 1. Building Massing and Style | | | | | | | | | |
| 2. Roof Types & Materials | | | | | | | | | |
| 3. Facade Treatment & Materials | | | | | | | | | |
| 4. Entry and Doors | | | | | | | | | |
| 5. Windows | See pages 346 and 347 | | | | | | | | |
| 6. Eaves, Porches, & Arcades | for specific illustrations | | | | | | | | |
| 7. Trim | | | | | | | | | |
| 8. Towers | | | | | | | | | |
| 9. Cross Gables and Dormers | | | | | | | | | |
| 10. Gutters | | | | | | | | | |
| 11. Chimneys | | | | | | | | | |
| 12. Walls, Fences, and Hedges Front Yard | | | | | | | | | |
| 13. Walls, Fences, and Hedges (Side and Rear Yards) | | | | | | | | | |
| 14. Colors | | | | | | | | | |
| 15. Driveway | | | | | | | | | |
| 16. Pavement Materials and Textures | | | | | | | | | |
| 17. Curb Treatment | | | | | | | | | |
| 18. Streetlights | | | | | | | | | |
| 19. Street signs | | | | | | | | | |
| 20. Street furniture | | | | | | | | | |

a photograph of existing buildings, or from manufacturer catalogues).

**Commercial Building Types**          **Civic Building Types**          **Out Building Types**

Example of partially completed Design Vocabulary Matrix | **RESIDENTIAL TYPES**

| | | | | |
|---|---|---|---|---|
| **BUILDING MASSING AND STYLE** | | | | |
| **ROOF TYPES & MATERIALS** | | | | |
| **FACADE TREATMWENT & MATERIALS** | | | | |
| **ENTRY & DOORS** | | | | |
| **WINDOWS** | | | | |
| **EAVES, PORCHES, & ARCADES** | | | | |

Illustrative Portion of Matrix

| | | | | |
|---|---|---|---|---|
| **TRIM** | | | | |
| **TOWERS** | | | | |
| **CROSS GABLES & DORMERS** | | | | |
| **GUTTERS** | | | | |
| **CHIMNEYS** | | | | |
| **WALLS, FENCES (FRONTYARDS)** | | | | |

# PROCESS STEP VII
## SUBMISSION AND REVIEW PROCESS

THE APPLICATION AND APPROVAL PROCESS

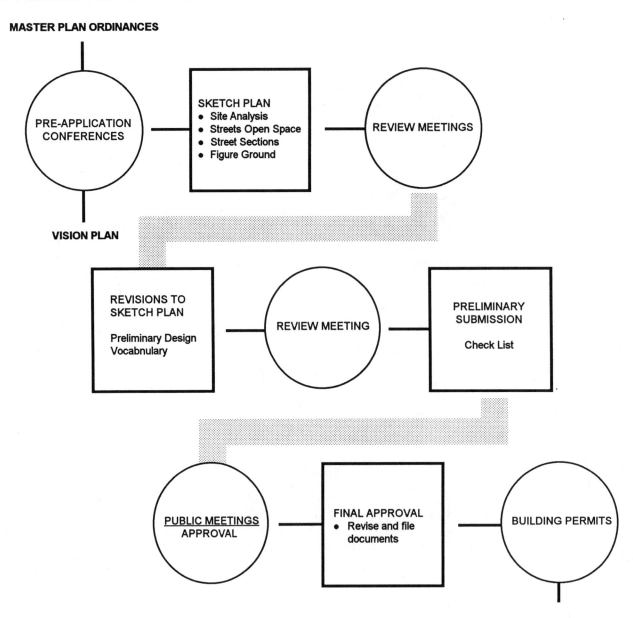

**MASTER PLAN ORDINANCES**

PRE-APPLICATION CONFERENCES

**VISION PLAN**

SKETCH PLAN
- Site Analysis
- Streets Open Space
- Street Sections
- Figure Ground

REVIEW MEETINGS

REVISIONS TO SKETCH PLAN

Preliminary Design Vocabnulary

REVIEW MEETING

PRELIMINARY SUBMISSION

Check List

PUBLIC MEETINGS APPROVAL

FINAL APPROVAL
- Revise and file documents

BUILDING PERMITS

BUILD

# THE APPROVAL PROCESS AND SUBMISSION DOCUMENTS

A Hamlet, Village, or Neighborhood Design which meets the standards set forth in this book should not have to endure a long an protracted approval process.

The approval process on most larger projects is long and difficult. The national average is seven years between acquisition and preliminary approval. Much of this delay is due, I believe, to the unacceptable character and quality of the development proposal. Many people simply do not want more of the same suburban sprawl with its accompanying negative impacts. They want an alternative vision to the proposal development. They want to be involved in the process and to have new development conform to the new American dream. Unfortunately, many developers have invested significant amounts into development plans and preliminary engineering based on an unacceptable vision only to be stonewalled by the municipality and residents who live adjacent to the project area. If the developers or the municipality has gone through the Visioning Planning process and accepted, at least in concept, the principles advocated in this book, the approval process should be quick and easy.

The fundamental desire is to get new small communities built as quickly as possible so that people can begin to live and enjoy them. To facilitate the preliminary and final approvals the follow meeting schedule should be set up to include:

A. The pre-application conference with the board
B. Series of informal meeting with planning staff as the sketch plan material is being
developed.
C. Sketch plan meeting(s) with the board or technical review committee
D. Submission of sketch plan for review
E. Revision reviewed by planning staff and/or technical review committee
F. Submission of preliminary application
G. Review by planning board and preliminary approval

The following is a recommendation for the submission process and documents. Use this to supplement what is already in your ordinance, or use it to delete sections which are unnecessary.

## THE APPROVAL PROCESS AND SUBMISSION DOCUMENTS

The following submission sequence and submission documents shall be required for sketch and preliminary approval. Final approval shall conform to local stationary requirements and shall incorporate into the final filed drawings all changes and amendments required for preliminary approval.

### SECTION 1. PRE-APPLICATION CONFERENCE.

A. This conference shall inform the board of the intention to construct a small community, the location, lots, owners, and expected holding capacity of the site; preliminary land suitability analysis using generalized soils or township GIS data; the locations of road and street access and interconnections the internal and peripheral open space, and expected means of sewage disposal and potable water. The general style and architectural character of the proposed small community should be discussed.

The pre-application conferences should be an evolving dialogue with continued refinements to the regulating plan, street sections, and design vocabulary.

B. Evolution of the Sketch Plan. A series of informal meetings should be set up with the planner as the sketch plan is generated. Meetings should be set up as each portion of the sketch/preliminary application, documents, plans, and sketches are prepared. These drawing can be loosely drawn at scale in freehand. The intention is to develop an acceptable regulating plan as early in the process as possible.

### SECTION 2. SKETCH PLAN

A. The landowner(s) shall submit a sketch plan for preliminary discussion of intent.

B. The planning board shall review the sketch plan in conference with the landowner and, by mutual agreement, determine a sketch plan which conforms with the intent of this article. The landowner may then proceed with the preparation of the development plan for preliminary plan submittal.

C. The submission of a sketch plan shall not be deemed the beginning of the time period for review as prescribed by law, and the review of the sketch plan by the planning board shall not bind the township to approve the Application for Tentative or final approval.

D. The sketch plan shall include the following:

1. The sketch plan may be an approximate drawing but should generally be drawn to a scale of either 50 or one 100 feet to the inch.
The approximate tract boundary, north point, names of adjoining property owners, name and location of all abutting streets and utilities, and the location of any significant topographical and physical features.

2. The sketch plan need not be illustrated in final graphic form, should be informal, and should contain at least the following information:
      a. topography at two foot contours
      b. soils
      c. floodways
      d. wetlands
      e. mature trees
      f. preliminary development suitability

3. The sketch plan shall contain a conceptual holding capacity analysis which indicates the following:
    a. the number of units allowed
    b. the square footage of non-residential uses
    c. the land area to be devoted to civic or public uses
    d. the amount of land to be preserved as common openspace, and the form of organization proposed to own and maintain the common open space, if the intent is not to dedicate

4. A conceptual figure ground plan showing approximate locations of all roads, streets, buildings and building uses, parking, and open spaces.

5. The general location and size of the common open space and the form of organization proposed to own and maintain the common open space, if the intent is not to dedicate. This can be included on the figure-ground plan.

6. A sketch regulating plan which shows build-to and build-up lines. (This can be an overlay on the figure-ground plan.

7. Street sections which illustrate the height and bulk of buildings and other structures, the proportion of the streets, and the streetscape features.

8. A conceptual sketch as an overlay on the figure-ground plan of the infrastructure including:
    a. sewer system, method, and location of treatment
    b. provision of water
    c. drainage and detention
    d. electric, gas, telephone, and cable

9. A written statement from a qualified professional concerning the feasibility of proposals for sewerage, water supply, and stormwater management, but not to include drawings.

10. The substance of protective covenants, grants, or easements, or other restrictions intended to be imposed upon the land, or the use of the land, buildings and other structures including proposed easements or grants for public utilities.

11. The required modifications in the township regulations which would otherwise be applicable to the subject property.

12. Urban design concept diagrams which graphically depict the planning principles expressed in the ordinance as such have been applied in the development plan. The diagrams may be prepared at any appropriate scale and should illustrate the planning relationships of the community green and commercial uses to residential areas, sites for public and semi-public uses, community clubs and facilities, internal and peripheral open spaces, vistas and focal points, walking distances, interconnections with the existing street system and sidewalk network, buffers areas, and similar features of the plan.

13. A preliminary design vocabulary.

14. Axonometric drawings of building types, larger axonometric drawings, and/or a model of the core area and typical residential neighborhoods.

## SECTION 3.  APPLICATION FOR PRELIMINARY APPROVAL

**A.**  Sufficient copies of an application for preliminary approval for a planned small community shall be submitted by the landowner to the township. The landowner shall also submit a filing fee to the township in an amount specified on the fee schedule adopted from time to time by resolution of the board. No plan shall be considered as properly filed until such time as the filing fee is submitted to the township.

**B.**  Each copy of the application for preliminary approval shall include the following four (4) parts:

    1.  application form

    2.  site maps, profiles, cross-sections, and architectural drawings

    3.  declaration of covenants, grants of easements, conditions, and restrictions

    4.  supporting information report

**C.**  The following information, maps and graphics are to be provided:

1. Application Form.  The application for approval of a planned small community, supplied by the township, shall be completed by the landowner or his agent.

2. Site Maps, Profiles, Cross-Sections, and Architectural Drawings.  Each map, plan, and drawing shall be prepared by a planner, professional engineer, surveyor, landscape architect, or architect, who shall place his or her seal and signature on all applicable plans, maps, and drawings.

3.  Site plans shall be drawn on sheets having a minimum sheet size of 18 inches by 22 inches and a maximum sheet size of 34 inches by 44 inches and shall be at a scale of 10 feet, 20 feet, 30 feet, 40 feet, 50 feet, 60 feet, or 100 feet to the inch. The applicant should utilize the scale and plan format which presents the most readable plans. Site plans may consist of multiple sheets if a key map showing the relationship of each sheet to the overall site plan is placed on all of the multiple sheets. Site plans shall show:

    a.  the project name or identifying title

    b.  the name and address of the landowner of the tract, the developer, and the firm that prepared the plans

    c.  the file or project number assigned by the firm that prepared the plan, the plan date, and the dates of all plan revisions

    d.  a north arrow, a graphic scale, and a written scale

    e.  the entire tract boundary with bearings, distances, and identification of all corner markers

    f.  a location map, for the purpose of locating the site to be subdivided or developed, at a minimum scale of 2,000 feet to the inch, showing the relation of the tract to adjoining property and to all streets, municipal boundaries, and streams existing within 1,000 feet of any part of the property proposed to be developed

g. the plotting of all existing adjacent land uses and lot lines within 200 feet of the proposed development including the location of all public and private streets, drives, alleys, railroads, power lines, gas lines, towers, easements, embankments, walls, streams and watercourses, buildings and other structures, fences, walls, all residential and non-residential land uses, sewer mains, water mains, fire hydrants, storm drainage structures, historic sites, and other significant natural or man-made features

h. the names of all immediately adjacent landowners and the names and plan book numbers of all previously recorded plans for adjacent projects

i. contours at vertical intervals of two feet for land with average natural slope of twelve percent or less, and at vertical intervals of five feet for more steeply sloping land, location of bench mark, and datum used

j. delineation of the 100 year floodplain

k. the delineation of all soil types as indicated by the U.S.D.A. Soil Conservation Service Soil Survey

l. an environmental analysis map(s) showing and identifying the location of unique land forms or natural features (such as hills, berms, knolls, mounds, swales, bowls, depressions, rock outcroppings, or scenic views), areas exceeding twelve percent slope, type of bedrock and associated environmental characteristics affecting the tract type of soils and associated environmental characteristics (such as depth to seasonal high water table, depth to bedrock, erodibility, and permeability), water courses or bodies of water, floodplain, wetlands or other hydrologic conditions affecting the tract (proof of the non-existence of such conditions shall be provided by the applicant), and any other environmentally sensitive features

m. the plotting of all existing landmarks within the proposed development including the location of all existing streets, buildings, easements, rights-of-way, sanitary sewers, water mains, storm drainage structures, and watercourses

n. the location of all existing vegetation, including all agricultural fields, lawn areas, shrubs, wooded areas, and trees over four inches db (diameter at breast height), dominant tree and plant species

o. a final development suitability map which includes:
   i. field delineated areas of wetlands
   ii. areas of severe development constraints
      - areas of 0 to 1.5 foot seasonal high water
      - areas of 0 to 3 foot non-rippable bedrock
      - areas of within floor hazard areas
      - areas of open water
      - areas of wetlands
      - areas over 25 percent slope
      - areas under or over electrical, gas or oil transmission lines

   iii. areas of moderate development constraints
      - areas of 1.6 to 3.0 foot seasonal high water
      - wetlands buffer areas
      - areas between 12 to 25 percent slope
      - areas of aquifer recharge
      - areas of mature-climax vegetation
      - areas adjacent to major highways or railroads

      iv.  areas of few or no development constraints

p.  a list of site data including but not limited to the following:
     i.     total acreage of the tract
     ii.    zoning district
     iii.   proposed use of the land
     iv.   proposed gross area of the development
     v.    proposed gross residential density
     vi.   proposed number of dwelling units and building type
     vii.  proposed number of lots
     viii. acreage of all street rights of way proposed for dedication
     ix.   acreage and percentage of common open space
     x.    acreage to be sold to individual owners
     xi.   acreage to be retained by landowner
     xii.  square footage and acreage of any commercial, public, or semi-public use areas
     xiii. proposed number of parking spaces

q.  the proposed location and dimensions of all streets, access drives, parking compounds, sidewalks, bikeways, and curbing

r.  the proposed location of all lot lines with approximate dimensions

s.  the approximate radius and arc dimensions for all lot line and street line curves

t.  the approximate size of all lots in square feet and acreage

u. a figure-ground plan which includes the proposed location and configuration of all buildings, single family detached and semi-detached dwelling units may be schematic in configuration, reference as to whether each existing structures are to be retained or removed

v. the identification of all lots and buildings by consecutive block and lot or building number, identification of building type with number of dwelling units in each multi-unit building

w.  the proposed location of build-to and build-up lines from all streets, and the distances between buildings and adjacent tract boundaries and lot lines

x.  the proposed location, size, and use of all common open space areas, structures, and recreation facilities

y.  clear sight triangles of 100 feet at all street intersections

z.  the proposed areas to be dedicated to the township with acreage of all areas and widths of all rights-of-way

aa.  proposed street names

bb.  the proposed location of all iron pins and concrete monuments cc.  the proposed size and location of all sanitary sewers, water mains, fire hydrants and laterals, storm drainage facilities, gas mains, and electric utilities, materials of all pipes, invert and top elevations of facilities, gradient of all pipes for sanitary sewers and storm drainage facilities

dd.  the proposed location, width, and purpose of all easements

ee.  a grading plan of the development, except for single family detached and semi-detached lots to be sold to individual owners

ff.  a clearing and vegetation protection plan showing and identifying the location of all areas to be cleared, all areas of soil disturbance, all areas of topsoil stockpiling during the period of development, all existing vegetation to be retained, and details for the methods of vegetation protection during the period of development

gg.  a sediment and erosion control plan for the development, or for each section to be developed separately

hh.  a lighting plan with the location and size of all street, parking compound, recreational, and open space lighting fixtures whether free-standing or affixed to buildings, including the delineation of isolux lighting lines at increments of 0.2, 0.5 and 1.0 footcandles for each fixture, as applicable, and construction details, manufacturers specifications, elevations, materials, and colors for each type of proposed fixture

ii. a planting plan for the development, except for single family detached and semi-detached lots to be sold to individual owners, the identification and location of the following information:

i. all pertinent information regarding the general site layout, existing man-made and natural features, proposed grading, existing vegetation to be retained, and other conditions affecting proposed landscaping

ii. proposed planting, including shade trees, designated by symbols appropriately scaled to represent the sizes of such at time of planting, planting beds shown by a clearly delineated border outline, identification of all proposed planting numerically quantified and keyed to the planting schedule by the first letters of each plants botanical name

iii. planting schedule for all proposed planting, including both botanical and common plant names, identification key, total quantity, size (height, width, and caliper) at time of planting based on American Association of Nurserymen increments and minimum size of maintenance after a three year growth period

iv. details and specifications for all proposed planting, topsoiling, seeding, and mulching, including notes regarding special maintenance requirements the period of establishment, or permanently, and the limits of any such special maintenance areas

v. proposed buffering, screening, walls, and fences, including construction details, cross sections, elevations, manufacturers specifications, materials, and colors

vi. proposed courtyards, plazas, alleys, walkways, paths, common open space, recreation areas and facilities, street or site furniture, ponds, fountains, trellises, pergolas, gazebos, accessory structures, art and sculpture, common mail boxes, solid waste and recycling storage facilities, HVAC equipment, and utility service box, to be located at or above grade, and construction details, cross sections, elevations, manufacturers specifications, materials, and colors for all of the above items, where applicable jj. a signage plan for the development, including construction details, elevations, signage message or content, materials, and colors for each type of proposed sign

kk. detailed prototypical yard and patio plans, except for single family detached and semi-detached lots to be sold to individual owners, including detailed plans for the proposed treatment of patios and private or semi-private yard areas, including screening, landscaping, ground material treatment, lighting, and access, for each residential dwelling

ll. a proposed phasing plan of the development

mm. profile drawings for all streets, storm sewers, and sanitary sewer mains at a scale of 50 feet to the inch horizontally and ten feet to the inch vertically, showing existing and proposed grades

nn. cross-sections, details, and specifications for all improvements including streets, parking lots, curbs, sidewalks, bikeways, recreation facilities, play equipment, lighting, planting, sanitary sewer facilities, and sediment and erosion control facilities

oo. design vocabulary matrix

pp. architectural drawings of each proposed structure type in the planned residential development, including but not be limited to, the following information:

i. exterior side elevations of all existing and proposed buildings and structures exposed to view, showing the proposed building treatment in terms of architectural style, materials, colors, and details, to be drawn at a scale not larger than one inch equals eight feet

ii. floor plans of all proposed buildings and structures, to be drawn at a scale not larger than one inch equals eight feet

iii. details of all fire walls

iv. a minimum of two ground level perspective drawings, one showing the community green and the surrounding buildings and one of a typical residential street as seen from the public right-of-way, including buildings fronting on the street

v. a minimum of one axonometric or isometric projection of the proposed development in its surrounding context, including adjacent buildings and properties as such exist, to be drawn at the same scale as the site plan

vi. accurately colored architectural renderings of all prototypical buildings, structures, and signs

qq. urban design concept diagrams, at any scale, which graphically depict the planning principles expressed in this ordinance as such have been applied in the development plan and illustrate the planning relationships of the community green and commercial uses to residential areas, sites for public and semi-public uses, community clubs and facilities, internal and peripheral open space, vistas and focal points, walking distances, interconnections with the existing street and sidewalk system, buffers areas, and similar features of the plan

rr. axonometric drawings of building types as well as larger axonometric drawings and/or model of the core area and typical residential neighborhoods

**D.    Declaration of Covenants, Grants of Easements, Conditions, and Restrictions**

1. All deeds for conveyance of property within the planned small community shall bind the purchasers to the declaration of covenants, grants of easement, conditions, and restrictions and shall state the requirement of mandatory membership for all residents in the development in the residents association, if such an association is to be created for the ownership, administration and maintenance of the common open space.

2. The Declaration of Covenants shall include but shall not be limited to the following:

    a. parties to the declaration

    b. effective date of declaration

    c. definition of terms used in declaration

    d. establishment of a residents association (if applicable)

    e. property rights of landowner and of individual owners of property in any and all lands included within the limits of the development

    f. title to common open space

    g. covenants and restrictions on common open spaces preventing future development

    h. membership and voting rights of developer and of residents in residents association (if applicable)

    i. rights of tenants or lessees

    j. covenant for maintenance agreement of all common open spaces and other improvements throughout the development

    k. responsibility of owners of property concerning maintenance of the individual property

    l. assessments for maintenance and special assessments

    m. collection of maintenance and special assessments

    n. exemptions from assessment

    o. architectural control

    p. party wall agreements where applicable

q. exterior maintenance including necessary enforcement of maintenance provisions

r. stage developments, including rights of all owners of property in all developed areas

s. number of occupants in an apartment unit based on number of bedrooms in the apartment

3.  Copies of proposed articles, certificates and by-laws of the residents association shall be submitted, when applicable, for approval. The by-laws of the residents association shall include but shall not be limited to the following:

    a. name of association

    b. organizational outline of association

    c. date, time and place for association meetings

    d. means of notification of meetings

    e. constitution of quorum for a meeting

    f. method of election and terms of office of officers

    g. board of directors of association

    h. powers, duties, and responsibilities of officers and of board of directors of association

    i. date, time, and place of meetings of board of directors

    j. records of association and of board of directors

    k. levying and collecting of assessments called for in declaration of covenants, conditions, and restrictions

    l. membership and voting rights of developer and residents in residents association

4.  Copies of any other restrictions which will run with the land and will become covenants in the deeds of the lots shall be submitted.

E. The Supporting Information Report. This report shall contain the following information:

1.  A statement explaining why the proposed planned small community would be in the public interest and would be consistent with the township comprehensive plan, and what modifications are necessary to the township land use regulations which would otherwise be applicable to the subject property.

2. Present zoning of the tract and adjacent properties.

3. A statement describing the natural features of the tract including, but not limited to, an analysis of the hydrology, geology, soils, topography, and vegetation.

4. A statement summarizing the probable impact of such a development on the immediate environment and adjacent neighborhood, and on the community as a whole, especially public facilities and services, utilities, the roadway system and traffic, and schools.

5. A comparison of the cost to the municipality versus the revenues to the municipality produced by the development as well as market analysis data estimating potential market demand for various types of housing.

6. A listing of all proposed dwelling unit types, number of bedrooms, and all non-residential structures with square footage figures.

7. A description of any phased development schemes with figures for gross residential density and approximate development cost for each phase, percent figures for common open space for each phase with the limit of improvement to each, an approximate construction schedule to updated annually until the development is completed and all public improvements are accepted by the township.

8. A description of the use and improvement of common open space throughout the tract, and the means by which the landowner will guarantee its continuity and maintenance.

9. The ratio of parking spaces to dwelling units and nonresidential uses proposed.

10. A statement of proposed lighting, sewerage, water, electric, gas, telephone, cable television, and refuse removal.

11. Signed and certified approvals from the appropriate utilities, authorities, and agencies that include the following:

   a. sewer authority: detailed approval of sanitary sewer plan

   b. water authority or company: general approval

   c. state Department of Transportation: highway occupancy permits

   d. county Soil and Water Conservation District: approval of site and improvement plans pertaining to possible flooding, soil erosion, and sediment control

   e. Department of Environmental Protection and Energy: sewer, water approval, erosion, and sediment control approval (earth moving)

   f. local electric company: lighting plan and location of all electric power lines and easements approval

   g. local gas company: locations gas line and easement approval

   h. utility and transmission companies: approval for development surrounding any right-of-way and easement

    i. railroad company: approval of any proposed grade crossings, utility crossings, rail extensions, or alterations

    j. local postmaster: approval of street names

12. Calculations for the design and location of storm drainage facilities.

13. An estimate of the construction cost for all required improvements. The township may submit the estimates to the township engineer for review and recommendation. The final amount of the security for each phase shall be determined by the township.

14. Within 45 days after the township receives both an application for preliminary approval of a planned small community and the required filing fee, a public hearing(s) shall be held by the board, which shall be advertised, conducted, and made a record in the manner prescribed by law.

15. The board, within 30 days following the conclusion of the public hearings, shall, by official written communication to the landowner, either:

    a. grant preliminary approval of the small community as submitted

    b. grant preliminary approval subject to specified conditions not included in the development plan as submitted

    c. deny tentative approval of the development plan

    Failure to so act within said period shall be deemed to be a grant of preliminary approval of the development plan as submitted.

16. The grant or denial of tentative approval by official written communication shall include not only conclusions but also findings of fact related to the specific proposal and shall set forth the reasons for the grant, with or without conditions, or for the denial. The written communication shall set forth with particularity in what respects the development plan would or would not be in the public interest including, but not limited to, findings of fact and conclusions based on the following:

    a. the extent to which the development plan departs from this zoning ordinance and the subdivision and land development ordinance, including, but not limited to density, bulk, use, and the reasons why such departures are, or are not deemed to be in the public interest

    b. the extent to which the development plan is or is not, consistent with the comprehensive plan for the development of the township, or with the objectives of this article

    c. the purpose, location, and amount of the common open space, the reliability of the proposals for ownership, administration, maintenance, and conservation of common open space, and the adequacy or inadequacy of the amount and purpose of the common open space as related to the proposed density and type of residential development

d.  the physical design of the development plan and the manner in which the design does, or does not, make adequate provisions for public services, provide adequate control over vehicular traffic, and further the amenities of light and air, recreation, and visual enjoyment

e.  the relationship, beneficial or adverse, of the proposed planned small community to the neighborhood in which it is proposed to be established

f.  in the case of a development plan which proposes development over a period of years, the sufficiency of the terms and conditions intended to protect the interests of the public and of the residents of the planned residential development in the integrity of the development plan

g.  the extent to which the original intent of the development plan is made clear for the benefit of future township officials and future residents of the planned small community, in the protective covenants which shall be imposed for the preservation of the integrity of the development plan over the years and through various stages of development where such are contemplated

17.  In the event a development plan is granted preliminary approval with or without conditions, the board may set forth in the official written communication the time within which an application for final approval of the development plan shall be filed, or, in the case of a development plan which provides for development over a period of years, the periods of time within which applications for final approval of each part thereof shall be filed. Except upon the consent of the landowner, the time so established between grant of tentative approval and application for final approval shall not be less than three months and in the case of developments over a period of years, the time between applications for final approval of each part of the plan shall not be less than twelve months.

18.  The official written communication shall be certified by the township clerk and shall be filed in his or her office, and a certified copy shall be mailed to the landowner. Where tentative approval has been granted, it shall be deemed an amendment to the zoning map, effective upon final approval, and shall be noted on the zoning map.

19.  In the event the planned small community is granted preliminary approval subject to conditions, the landowner may, within 30 days after receiving a copy of the official written communication from the board notify the board of his refusal to accept all required conditions, in which case the board shall be deemed to have denied tentative approval of the development plan. In the event the landowner does not, within 30 days, notify the board of commissioners of his refusal to accept all said conditions, tentative approval of the development plan along with any conditions shall stand as granted.

20.  Preliminary approval of a development plan shall not qualify a plan of the planned pmall community for recording nor authorize construction or the issuance of any zoning and/or building permits. A development plan which has been given tentative approval as submitted, or which has been given tentative approval with conditions which have been accepted by the landowner (provided the landowner has not defaulted or violated any of the conditions of the tentative

approval), shall not be modified or revoked or otherwise impaired by action of the township pending application for final approval, without the consent of the landowner, provided an application or applications for final approval is filed or, in the case of development over a period of years, provided applications are filed, within the periods of time specified in the official written communication granting tentative approval.

21. In the event a development plan is given tentative approval and thereafter, but prior to final approval, the landowner shall elect to abandon the development plan and shall so notify the board in writing, or in the event the landowner shall fail to file application or applications for final approval within the required period of time or times, as the case may be, the tentative approval shall be deemed to be revoked and all that portion of the area included in the development plan for which final approval has not been given shall be subject to those ordinances otherwise applicable thereto as they may be amended from time to time, and the same shall be noted on the zoning map and in the records of the township secretary.

*A whopping 84 percent said that if they had to do it over again, they would choose to live in a (new) traditional neighborhood development rather than a conventional development. What they liked most, they said, was the neighborliness - the sense of community.*
**Builder magazine, August 1993.  Survey conducted by John Schleimer of four active traditional neighborhood developments**

The key to attracting highly skilled professionals is to offer an environment with a high quality of living.  Innovation-based companies typically settle and remain in an environment that bright, creative people find attractive.
**Planning News. Creating Successful Communities: Paraphrased from David Birch, "Job Creation in America."**

*Eighty percent of everything ever built in America has been built in the last fifty years and most of it is depressing, brutal, ugly, unhealthy, and spiritually degrading:  the jive plastic commuter tract home wastelands, the Potemkin village shopping plazas with their vast parking lagoons, the Lego - block hotel complexes, the 'gourmet mansardic' junk food joints, the Orwellian office 'parks' featuring buildings sheathed in the same reflective glass as the sunglasses worn by chain gang guards, the particle board garden apartments rising up in every meadow and cornfield, the freeway loops around every big and little city with their clusters of discount merchandise marts, the whole destructive, wasteful, toxic, agoraphobia inducing spectacle that politicians proudly call 'growth'*
**James Howard Kunstler, The Geography of Nowhere: The Rise and Decline of America's Man - Made Landscape**

# AN OPTIMISTIC FUTURE

Our country has been promoting a pattern of sprawl land use in exurban areas to middle and upper income families since 1939. There has been an incredible evolution in the pattern of development dependent upon location, auto access, cheap land, ratable speculation, marketing gimmicks, and political connections. Many promote this sprawl pattern because it is good business and good politics. This is America where anything can happen, we are just building the American Dream. However, isn't this American Dream a little out of date for our generation and for future generations? Can we as a country and as individuals sustain it? Must we plan for more sprawl when we have a surplus of approved, though unbuilt, low density developments, and when a large supply of inner urban vacant and underutilized lands exist?

The economic and planning policies of sprawl have created a land use pattern which is extremely costly for individuals to use and to maintain. They have created large areas of low density sprawl which are incapable of achieving a sense of community, effective transit, or even basic walking connections. Meanwhile, we have neglected our cities and towns with high concentrations of poor and lower middle class residents, inadequate educational facilities, high drug use, and crime. We have created ghettos of economic, educational, and social wanting by promoting and marketing a quality of life of such grandeur and power that is unachievable for too many. This fustration, perhaps, leads to unprecedented levels of stress. Marketing experts sell the idea that only in suburbia or on that open road do we find happiness. Consequently, developers have created thousands of Fair-view subdivisions, malls, and office parks. The automobile interests have sold billions of private automobiles, trillions of gallons of gas, and built thousands of miles of roads and highways. Collectively they have created an extraordinary economy, where Wall-mart, the quintessential modern icon of sprawl, is honored as the ultimate American enterprise.

Many suburbanites and urban dwellers know that something is desperately wrong. The quality of life is not really improving as promised. We seem to be paying an outrageous amount in taxes, costs keep increasing, and there seems to be fewer services and benefits from the government. We work more though less money is available at the end of each paycheck. We are told that we have one of the highest standards of living in the world, though many of the places we live in do not meet the visual metaphors promoted by advertising agencies. How many time have you been on a road with no traffic? When is the last time you saw someone actually smiling while driving their car? Achieving the current American Dream will be harder for the new generations. It is out of date.

Exciting alternatives are available. The State of Oregon's Growth Management Plan, the Communities of Place Centers Concept of the New Jersey State Development and Redevelopment Plan, the small communities concept promoted in this book, traditional neighborhood development and transit oriented development provide alternative models which can be applied to both continued growth in low density areas and to retro-fitting the development of the past fifty years. All of these policies share one fundamental concept--a return to the basic, interlinked, mixed, and multiple-use community.

Other policies such as sustainable growth, growth boundaries, ISTEA, municipal fiscal balance, traffic calming, household fiscal management, urban retrofitting, and environmental protection mandate a new pattern. Large numbers of citizen groups who have organized against development or road widening, or who are pro-environmental lobby for a new pattern of development and redevelopment. This new pattern must be more positive and responsive to the user and the environment, while meeting the continued need to generate consumer markets at affordable prices. It is a pattern of neighborhoods and community, of safety and security, and stewardship of the land, water, and air.

This vision returns to the basic, small community concepts ignored since the 1930s and reestablished in this book. This vision consists of moderately dense, multiple-use communities with more efficient land-use, infrastructure, and human potentials. It can become the new American Dream. It is the logical evolution of place as we continue though the spiral of growth, optimization, deterioration, redevelopment, and growth based on technology, sociology, and finances. We have looked at the past; we want a better future. The future can result in a higher quality of living and affordability for those smart enough to want it. It can return handsome profits for those who build it. While it may be slightly more expensive and complex to build within traditional suburban growth area than on rural farmland, the saving in operating costs for individual households can be significant. As the country continues to subsidize the creation and maintenance of the inefficient sprawl pattern, more resources will be required. The creation of small communities in designated growth areas will make economic sense so that a new generation of Americans can reap the benefits rather than pay the costs. The money saved by living in a small community can be put to better uses like purchasing a house, education, or more quality family time.

We can prove to people that planning can be effective and responsible to all users. We must consider the potential alternatives which can enhance both the quality of life and the ability to manage and afford it. It cannot be sprawl and urban deterioration cannot continue as usual, with the constant exploitation of the lower and middle class. People with a range of income and backgrounds can become residents of small communities where all can lead happy and productive lives.

New Jersey is at the spiral vanguard of urban evolution. It is the most densely populated state in the country. It was one of the first states to have liberalized corporation charters, to build a major freeway, and to have a public participation process to develop a State Plan. It is quintessential sprawled growth with large amounts of remaining open land. Most of the major cities are desperately struggling for a comeback. Subdivisions in the sprawl pattern are still being built. Tens of thousands of subdivided units and millions of square feet of commercial have been approved and not yet built. Too many major corporations are still considering spreading into exurban areas. Highways and interchanges are still the major determinates of growth. Few regions of the country better represent the evolution of the sprawl pattern, and the political, bureaucratic, and entrepreneurial spirit that created it. It has been characterized as the essence of the 1930's American Dream. The area along the New Jersey Turnpike has been immortalize in song, "all gone to look for America." New Jersey is sprawled, polluted, growing, and struggling with its future pattern. Some are fearful of change because there is only a vague and sometimes conflicting vision of the future. Providing clarity to that vision for the new American Dream is the reason for this book. We must recognize the inevitable course of the built-form evolutionary spiral and plan for a new vision. After optimization of the existing pattern it will go through periods of decline, renewal, and growth into the next millennium.

Because New Jersey is at the forefront of suburban evolution, it is one of the most innovative concerning land use regulations, environmental protection, and affordable housing. Over 25 percent of the state, the Pinelands, has been set aside for preservation and protection. The State Planning Commission adopted, after six years of public debate, a general state plan which is aimed at strategic growth in the suburbs, preservation and protection of agricultural and environmentally sensitive lands, and redevelopment of older urban areas. The State Plan calls for future development to be primarily in centers. The State must now amend the requirements of the Municipal Land Use Law to require centers as part of the six year master plan, and needs a public relations effort to show people that the future can be far superior than today.

For those of you whose economic future is tied up in the continuation of sprawl, for you the good news is that a large amount of sprawled development has been approved and not yet built. Most of it is simple waiting until the inevitable upturn in the economy to begin construction. Plans which have been approved in suburban and rural locations are based on the old pattern and planning policies. Conservative banking power and auto, advertising, and farming lobbies will be pushing to maintain the sprawl status quo. The major land holders do not want to litigate for alternatives to sprawl. Those who moved from the city to a mansion between one and three acres in order to achieve the old American Dream see themselves as the quintessential promoters and guardians of sprawl. It is a status symbol of the 1980s. This attitude will take time to change, but change it will. It is unfortunate that the state legislature has allowed current unbuilt approvals to be extended without having to return to planning board for extensions. If we interpret what people have been telling us, planning boards should no longer allow strip commercial development or small office parks, except if they are located in a small community center. Visualize the positive quality that could be achieved if all of these approved though not yet built commercial builders were redesigned into centers of small communities or retro-fitted into older downtowns. Visualize what could be built if unbuilt subdivisions were redesigned to become small communities. Large lots for the rich and isolated research facilities could still be provided in the large amount of open space on the periphery of small communities.

Despite the pressures to maintain the status quo, you can see how I remain optimistic about small communities. They will happen because of social and economic pressures. They will happen because there is a fundamental intuitively, negative response to sprawl. They will happen as new traditional communities come on-line. As the success of small communities grows, bankers, developers, and politicians will begin to see the advantages. It will happen because a growing sprawl pattern cannot be sustained over a long period of time unless there is an infusion of enormous amounts of time and money. Neither of those are available. They will happen because of greater negative reactions as more sprawl projects get built out. They will happen because developers will be able to make money on these products. It will happen because of the historic evolutionary pattern of decline, rehabilitation, and growth will come around again.

For those of you who are searching for an alternative now, there are a sufficient number of individuals to make more than a niche market, who want to reaffirm a sense of place, to live in a neighborhood, to have a sense of community, and to feel in balance with nature and themselves. They are searching for alternatives to what is available in the tract developments. There are developers and financiers who understand this market and will meet it. They will provide the living testimony to the principles in this book. Existing communities, both new and historic, which exhibit the principles that have been rated very positively and provide living testimony to their livability. Why live in a sprawled development, shop at a strip mall, own two or more cars when you can live in and have all the economic and social benefits of a small community.

I have been able to present the history, process, and principles contained within this book at a large number of conferences and seminars throughout the United States and Canada. The continued application of the VPS™ and the Hands-on Model workshops reinforce the principles and the desire to develop and redevelop places into more humane, and ecologically and economically sensitive places. If you believe in these principles here are several recommendations:

- amend your master plan or general plan to allow an overlay district which will give the development community the option to build alternatives to the standard subdivision, office park, office building, or strip mall adjacent to highway interchanges
- indicate areas where new or retro-fitted small communities can be located, employ the circle technique
- small communities can be located over existing subdivisions and commercial and industrial areas
- eliminate the opportunity for additional cookie cutter subdivisions
- remove opportunities for strip commercial buildings or office parks, this square footage should be located in small community centers
- create a capital improvement plan which shows the location of all future roads, open spaces, parks, and public and semi-public buildings, these of small community components can be shown in a regulating plan
- use the ordinance in this book to craft an illustrated ordinance suited to your specific community

Let us gain a sense of respect for ourselves, our community, and our government by allowing a new American Dream of well designed small communities, linked to all other communities, where everyone can feel safe, know and respect their neighbors, and effectively use our wealth of technology to expand the quality of our lives.

The neighborhood in an urban setting and the hamlet or village in a low density environment are the basic genetic structures of small community; the basic DNA of planning. When we reaffirm the basic small community as the critical component of our planning policies we will activate the **vision.**

# R E F E R E N C E S

Adams, Thomas. *The Design of Residential Areas.* New York: Arno Press, 1974. Reprint of edition published by Harvard University Press (Cambridge, MA), issued as Harvard City Planning Studies, Vol, VI.

Aldus,Tony. *Urban Villages.* A concept for creating mixed-use urban developments on a sustainable scale. The Urban Villages Group, London: BAS Printers Ltd., 1991.

Alexander, Christopher. *A Pattern Language. Towns, Buildings, Construction.* London: Oxford Press, 1986.

American Association of State Highway Officials. *Geometric Design Guide for Local Roads and Streets.* Washington, DC: AASHTO, 1971.

American Automobile Association. *New Sensible Transportation Options for People, Traffic Calming.* Tag and Oregon, 1993.

Beacher, Edward H. *Growing Pains in the Suburbs.* The Pittsburgh Press, 1951.

Bookout, Lloyd W. *Neo-traditional Town Planning, Bucking Conventional Codes and Standards.* Urban Lands, April 1992.

Brambilla, Roberto and Gianni Longo. *For Pedestrians Only: Planning, design and management of traffic-free zones .*

Bucks County Planning Commision. *Performance Streets. A Concept and Model Standards for Residential Streets.* Doylestown, PA., 1980.

Bucks County Planning Commission. *Village Planning Handbook.* Doylestown, PA, 1989.

Calthrope, Peter. *The Next American Metropolis. Ecology, Community and the American Dream.* New York: Princeton Architectural Press. 1993.

City of Saint Paul, *Street Capacity, Function and Operations.* Saint Paul Planning Commission, 1992.

Corwin, M. A. *Parking Lot Landscaping.* Planning Advisory Service Report No. 335. Chicago, American Planning Association, 1978.

Cullen, Gordon. *Concise Townscape.* New York: Van Nostrand Reinhold, 1961.

Davidson, Dale James and William Cord Ress. *The Great Reckoning.* 1992.

DeChaiara, Joseph, and Lee E. Koppelman. *Urban Planning and Design Criteria.* Englewood Cliffs, NJ: Prentice - Hall, 1975.

DeChaiara, Joseph, and Lee E. Koppelman. *Time - Saver Standards for Site Planning.* NY: McGraw - Hill, 1984.

DeChaiara, Joseph, and Lee E. Koppelman. *Manual of Housing. Urban Planning and Design Criteria.* 3rd ed. New York: Van Nordstrand Reinhold, 1982.

Design Council and Royal Town Planning Institute. *Streets Ahead.* The Whitney Library of Design, 1979.

Duany, Andres and Elizabeth Plater-Zyberk. *Towns and Town Making Principles.* New York: Rizzoli Press, 1991.

Feldman, William. *Bicycle Compatible Roadways.* Trenton: New Jersey Department of Transprotation, December 1982.

Fleming, Ronald Lee and Laurie Halderman. *On Common Ground: Caring for Shared Land from Town Common to Urban Park.* The Harvard Common Press, 1982.

Glassford, Peggy. *Appearance Codes for Small Communities.* Planning Advisory Service report No. 379. Chicago: American Planning Association, 1983.

Howard, Edenezer. *Garden City of Tomorrow*: Ed. F. J. Osborn. Cambridge, MA: The MIT Press, 1976.

Hedman, Richard and Andrew Jaszewski. *Fundamentals of Urban Design* Washington, DC: American Planning Association, 1984.

Hegeman, Werner. *The American Vitruvious: an Architects Handbook of Civic Art.* New York: Princeton Architectural Press. 1988.

Institute of Traffic Engineers. *Trip Generation Manual.* 1990.

Institute of Transportation Engineers. *Recommended Guidelines for Subdivision Streets.* Washington, DC: ITE, 1984.

Kelbaugh, Doug. *The Pedestrian Pocket Book. A New Suburban Design Strategy.* New York: Princeton University Press, 1989.

Kendig, Lane. "Pipe Dreams", *Planning.* pp 16 - 19, June 1989.

Kulash, Walter. *Traditional Neighborhood Development, Will Traffic Work.* American Society of Civil Engineers, Successful land Development: Quality are profits Conference. March, 1990.

Kunstler, James Howard. *The Geography of Nowhere. The Rise and Decline of America's Man - Made Landscape.* New York: Simon and Schuster, 1993.

Land Design Research, Inc. *Cost-Effective Site Planning: Single-Family Development.* Washington, DC: National Association of Home Builders, 1976.

Lang, Christopher J. *Building with Nantucket in Mind.* Nantucket Historic District Commission , 1978.

Lears, Jackson. *No Place of Grace: Anti Modernism and the Transformation of American Culture.* New York: Pantheon Books, 1963.

Listoken, David, and Carol W. Baker. *Model Subdivision and Site Plan Ordinance.* New Jersey: Center for Urban Policy Research, 1990.

Londos, Skip. "Where Have All the Sidewalks Gone?", *The Urban Ecologist.* Summer, 1991.

Lynch, Kevin, and Gary Hack, *Site Planning.* 3rd ed. Cambridge, MA: The MIT Press, 1984.

Massachusetts Department of Environmental Management. *Dealing with Change in the Connecticut Valley. A Design Manual for Conservation and Development.* Lincoln Institute of Land Policy and the Environmental Law Foundation, Fourth Printing, 1990.

McAlester, Virginia and Lee. *A Field Guide to American Houses.* New York: Alfred A. Knopf, 1984.

McHarg, Ian L. *Design With Nature.* Garden City, NY: The Natural History Press. 1969.

McKeever, Ross (ed.). *The Community Builders Handbook.* Washington, DC: The Urban Land Institute, 1968.

Middlesex, Somerset, Mercer Regional Study Council *Traffic Study*, 1991.

Monmouth County Planning Board. *Not for Cars Only. A guide to innovative Parking Lot Design.* Freehold, NJ, 1992.

Moskowitz, Harvey S., and Carl G. Lindbloom. *The Illustrated Book of Development Definitions.* New Jersey: Center for Urban Policy Research, 1981.

Mumford, Lewis. *The City in History.* New York: Harcourt Brace Jovanovich, 1961.

National Association of Home Builders. *Subdivision Regulation Handbook,* NAHB Land Development Series. Washington, DC: 1978.

National Association of Home Builders Land Development. *Planning the Livable Community. A Humanistic Approach to 21st Century Development.*

National Association of Home Builders. "Are TND's Working." *Builder's Magazine.* May-August, 1993.

National Trust for Historic Preservation. *With Her Image So Rich.* The Preservation Press, 1983.

Nelson, Arthur and Kenneth Dueker. "Exurban Living Using Improved Waste and Wastewater Technology," *Journal of Urban Planning and Development.* December 1989.

New Jersey Department of Environmental Protection and Energy, Association of New Jersey Environmental Commission. *Keeping our Garden State Green: A Local Government Guide for Greenways and Open Space Planning.* 1987.

New Jersey Federation of Planning Officials. *Preserving Rural Character.* Information Report, Volume XXIII, Number 3, 1990.

New Jersey State Planning Commission. *Communities of Place, The New Jersey State Development and Redevelopment Plan,* 1992.

New Jersey State Soil Survey Conservation Committee. *Standards for Soil Erosion and Sediment Control in New Jersey.* Trenton: The Committee, 1972.

Newman, Oscar. *Architectural Design for Crime Prevention.* Washington, DC: US Government Printing Office, 1971.

Newman, Oscar. *Defensible Space.* New York: MacMillan, 1972.

Perso, Jeffery. *Building Utopias.* Shepherd Express: 1993.

Pinelands Commission. *Comprehensive Management Plan for the Pinelands Natural Reserve.* New Lisbon, NJ: 1980.

Propst, Luther and David Church. *Creating Successful Communities. Intergrating Local Strategies for Conservation and Economic Development.* New York: Planning News, 1993.

Real Estate Research Corporation. *The Costs of Sprawl. Environmental and Economic Costs of Alternative Residential Development Patterns at the Urban Fringe.* Washington DC: US Government Printing Office, 1974.

Sears, Stephen W. *Hometown, USA.* New York: American Heritage Publishing Co. Inc., 1975.

School of Planning and Public Policy. *Planning and Design for Communities of Place. Applying the Concept of Centers.* Rutgers University, Urban Design Studio, 1992.

Sharp, Thomas. *The Anatomy of a Village.* Middlesex: Penguin Books, 1946.

State of New Jersey, Scenic Roads Program. *A Manual for the Nomination: Designation and Conservation of Scenic Road Corridors.* Green Acre Program, July 1991.

Sutro, Suzanne. *Reinventing the Village.* American Planning Association, Planning Advisory Service, Report Number 430, 1992.

Trancik, Roger. *Hamlets: Development Strategies.* New York State Council on the Arts, 1985.

Untermann, Richard and Robert Small. *Site Planning for Cluster Housing.* New York: Van Nostrand Reinhold, 1977.

Unwin, Sir Raymond. *Town Planning in Practice: An Introduction to the Art of Designing Cities and Suburbs.* New York: Benjamin Blom, Inc. 1971.

US Department of Housing and Urban Development. Office of Policy Development and Research. *Affordable Residential Land Development: A Guide for Local Government and Developers.* 1987.

Wyscoki, Charles. *American Celebration.* New York: Greenwich Press Ltd. Workman Publishing, 1985.